The Missouri Review

EDITOR
Speer Morgan

MANAGING EDITOR
Greg Michalson

ASSOCIATE EDITOR
Evelyn Somers

OFFICE MANAGER
Dedra Earl

OFFICE ASSISTANTS
Jeff Gittel, Funmi Okunbolade, Andrew Rittgers

SENIOR ADVISORS
Marta Boswell, Mary Davis, Tina Hall,
Hoa Ngo, Kris Somerville

ADVISORS
Sara Berrey, Reagan Bowyer, Jean Braithwaite, Arkadia Delay,
Jake Magnuson, Polly Van Amburg, John Tait

INTERNS
Seth Fletcher, Jeff Langmead, Lynn Schenkman

Web Page at http://www.missourireview.org

Cartoons in this issue by Charles Barsotti
Cover design by Laurie Dolphin Designs

The selection of letters by Djuna Barnes ©The Authors League Fund, as literary executor of the Estate of Djuna Barnes. Used by arrangement with the McKeldin Library at the University of Maryland at College Park.

The letters of Emily Holmes Coleman ©Estate of Emily Holmes Coleman. Used by arrangment with University of Delaware Library, Newark, Delaware.

The Missouri Review is published by the College of Arts & Science of the University of Missouri-Columbia, with private contributions and assistance from the Missouri Arts Council and the National Endowment for the Arts.

The editors invite submissions of poetry, fiction and essays of a general literary interest with a distinctly contemporary orientation. Manuscripts will not be returned unless accompanied by a stamped, self-addressed envelope. Please address all correspondence to The Editors, *The Missouri Review*, 1507 Hillcrest Hall, University of Missouri, Columbia, Missouri, 65211.

SUBSCRIPTIONS
1 year (3 issues), $19.00
2 years (6 issues), $35.00
3 years (9 issues), $45.00

Copyright © 1999 by The Curators of the University of Missouri
ISSN 0191 1961   **ISBN** 1-879758-27-X
Printed by Thomson-Shore   Distributed by Ingram Periodicals
Indexed in the American Humanities Index.

The *Missouri* *Review*

CONTENTS

1999

Foreword

We sometimes assume that the world is our oyster, that we can take our cell phones and credit cards and go anywhere, anytime, and find plenty of people dying to pamper us in the accustomed ways. Or possibly we imagine that all it takes is respect for another culture to freely inhabit it. People are just people, after all. The young American in Julie Rold's thought-provoking story, "In Faculty Block Number 5," a seemingly caring and culturally literate woman working in a province of central China, is about to learn that sometimes distant places really can be quite foreign. Sharon Balentine's story "The Chair" is a wonderful jeu d'esprit concerning the same subject—culture clash between an American living abroad and the provincial town that she so wants to like.

Much of this issue of *TMR*, in fact, is concerned with different sorts of exile, primarily of the self-chosen, modern sort. Until fairly recently in human history, going far away, or being sent away and cut off from home, was thought to be a terrifying fate. The Greeks punished people for homicide by exiling them. The Romans developed different levels of *excilius*, considering it to be so disagreeable that a person could avoid trial for capital crimes by exiling himself.

In Jewish myth and history, mass exiles have been definitive events— the Egyptian and Babylonian exiles, World War II—each followed by a founding or reintegration of the Jewish nation. American history, too, is full of the stories of exile, both self-chosen and forced: fugitives from religious persecution and poverty risking the transatlantic voyage to found the Plymouth and Massachusetts Bay Colonies; Native Americans forced from their homelands; and the exile of constant wandering that has characterized the experience of so many on this restless continent.

Or Missourians fleeing the border wars with Kansas during the American Civil War, as Daniel Woodrell discusses in this issue's interview. Woodrell's first published story, "Woe to Live On," which originally appeared in *TMR*, centers on this subject. It became a novel of the same title before being made into the current motion picture *Ride with the Devil*, directed by Ang Lee. Something of a literary exile himself, choosing to live and write in the Missouri Ozarks, Woodrell talks about his literary and family roots and the role his fascination with history and place have played in his writing.

Writers, of course, are famous for self-exile, whether, like Thomas Mann or Nabokov, they are escaping political conflagration or, like Djuna Barnes and others in the 1920s, they are taking an extended leave from their culture of origin. American authors have often chosen to live abroad. One of our earliest important writers, Washington Irving, originator of the short story, did his literary inventing in England while studying German mythology. American expatriate artists became news in the 1920s in part because they represented the horde of Americans then traveling in Europe. Mass travel to Europe was perfected during the Great War, when over a million men of the American Expeditionary Force were sent to France. Prices were low in Europe, and there was an appreciation there for Americans.

Djuna Barnes and her friend Emily Coleman were acquainted with the whole lineup of fellow artists visiting Europe: Isadora Duncan; Scott Fitzgerald; Jane Heap and Margaret Anderson (publishers of the then Paris-based *Little Review,* which originally published *Ulysses*); Charlie Chaplin; Alfred Krembourg; Sylvia Beach, owner of Shakespeare and Company; Antonia White, fiction writer and translator of Colette; Peggy Guggenheim and Natalie Barney, celebrated arts patrons. These and hundreds more traveled or lived in Europe, where they felt a sense of freedom and receptivity to experiment. Some were there to escape the cloying American materialism and hypocrisy written about by realist authors such as Sherwood Anderson and Theodore Dreiser.

Philip Gould's story "The End of Those Things" is an atmospheric mystery about a troubled former schoolteacher's flight to North Africa. Todd Pierce's "Love" has quite a different tone; its young narrator experiences a never-to-be-forgotten romance as a result of his mother's deliberate self-exile. Beth Goldner's "Tour Europa" is a quirky tale about a woman who is driven to invest everything in what she does, and who covers a lot of ground doing it.

In her essay "Kicker," Kathrin Perutz describes being the gawky daughter of a glamorous exile in a relationship that was literally bound up in smoke. Bill Roorbach is a New Englander displaced to the Midwest, and his "Scioto Blues" is the droll portrayal of his dogs and him walking along a river observing the polluted state of their new home. Floyd Skloot lives in the moment partly out of necessity, owing to brain damage from a virus that left him clinically demented, but his "Wild in the Woods" describes the choice that he makes to relish each of those moments as much as he can.

Poems by Jeff Worley and Laura Kasischke are not about exile but about the small pleasures and wonders of life, played against a barely hidden darkness, as with Worley's father, "harboring a secret loneliness . . . (while) making his small corner of the world right." Kasischke savors the little joys even if they cost many sorrows. In "this open field between malignant / and benign," she writes, "God / is up there watching someone crucified." Poems by Eric Pankey and Charles Simic concern the attempt of the poet to hide behind words. "In the end I will be voiceless," Pankey's speaker says, describing the emotional exile of the narrator who hides through language. "What I do with a word or two: avoid scrutiny . . . avoid measuring . . . the weight of my own heart." In his playful but covertly dark way, Simic describes the same sort of thing: "We played an elaborate game / Of hide and seek with words / And our hearts while feigning / To find clues of divine presence / On streets steeped in shadow."

SM

CBurroott

" WRITER'S BLOCK? THAT'S A TOUGH
ONE, YOU MAY HAVE TO THROW IN
YOUR KIDS' SOULS AS WELL."

"OH SURE, I'M ASKED TO CHURN OUT THE OCCASIONAL SYMPATHY NOTE BUT YOU CAN'T SUPPORT A FAMILY ON THAT."

TOUR EUROPA/*Beth Goldner*

IJUST WROTE MY FIRST novel, and finishing it felt like a violent storm had ended: tree branches strewn in the corners of my mind, wires downed, everything around me tired and gray. I decided to go somewhere else for a while, to run on new streets, so I chose Europe.

I am what psychiatrists call an obligatory runner. Simply put, I have to run every day. I have to get my heart rate up to 160 and sustain that for at least an hour. I have to feel the beat of macadam under my feet, monitor the ebb and flow of my pace. I have to sweat. The need to run started fifteen years ago, with a throbbing panic in my chest that nothing could quell. I had to take the panic somewhere, so I went to the local track. I was seventeen years old, and even before I started circling the gravel ground, I couldn't catch my breath. I knew nothing then about why I was panicked, where it came from, how it would travel in and out of my life. I knew only one thing: that I had to run.

I changed the silent *e* in *Europe* to an *a*, added the *Tour*, and suddenly my decision to run for two months on foreign soil seemed logical. It wasn't just a trip overseas, it was *Tour Europa*. Naming things makes them real. A person diagnosed with cancer doesn't really have cancer until they say aloud they have a *tumor* or a *malignancy* or *adenocarcinoma* or *melanoma*. The alcoholic is not really an alcoholic until he says, *My name is Robert and I am an alcoholic*. And the baby born or the puppy purchased or the trip taken is not really yours until you've named it. So I said it: *Tour Europa*. *Tour Europa*. *Tour Europa*. And then it was mine. I owned it.

I learned from my neighbor that Europa is also a moon, the sixth known moon of Jupiter and slightly smaller in size than Earth's moon. It was discovered in 1610, simultaneously and independently, by the Italian astronomer Galileo and the German astronomer Marius. Two Europeans, their heads tilted to the sky, trying to find something new.

Before I left for Tour Europa, I found a literary agent, a woman named Carson Van Volkenburg. She's one of those born-and-bred New York types: strident, ladder-climbing, a woman with great shoes and a barely detectable nose job who talks on a cellular phone incessantly. Carson knows how to sell things; she's a hawker. And if you want to accomplish anything these days—get a job, find a spouse, make a friend, publish a book—you've got to be a salesman.

"You know this experimental, stream-of-consciousness nonlinear thing is really making a comeback," Carson said, selling herself to me so she could sell me to someone else. And then the price tag: "If I can sell this thing, a publisher is probably going to want to cut it," she said. "It's too long, considering the market."

I left Carson to hawk and booked my flights. I had a $4,000 inheritance from my Aunt Kit, who died last year, enough to fund Tour Europa in a low-budget style. I bought two new pairs of running sneakers and four new running bras. I listened to my sisters register their concerns about the trip. They think that running across Europe is not exactly the next best thing in this thing called my life; but then again they never thought much of the previous thing—writing the book—either. They mean well, but all three of them are married, and married life can be comfortable and insulating to the point that something like writing a book or taking an overseas trip is cause for worry.

Cinque Terre, Italy
Cinque Terre, which translates to "five lands," is a cluster of villages along the Riviera Levantina.

These five towns—Monterosso, Vernazza, Corniglia, Manarola and Riomaggiore—are built right into seaside cliffs. The towns are about a mile apart each, but not connected by any road. There are only two ways to get from town to town: a rickety old railroad or an ancient footpath that climbs up and down seaside cliffs that are covered by olive trees and vineyards. I chose the footpath, which is rugged and gravity defying in some parts (200 feet up, with nothing but ocean and rock below, you find yourself standing on a path all of two feet wide) and easy and smooth in others. Along the way, you pass goats and the hearty men leading them; you pass octogenarian ladies in black dresses, with thick ankles and wide feet in unreliable shoes. Of course there are no guardrails, not even at the highest, most vertigo-inducing points. These are tucked-away villages in Liguria, where there are no such things as lawyers.

Walking along the curves of the path, you see the pastel dotting of the houses of the next town. You know what direction you are headed in. You breathe deeply and move forward, forgetting how frighteningly narrow the path is, how there is no guardrail, how you can slip from this dream and fall to your death.

I ran in Rome, where I started Tour Europa and where the streets were uneven. I ran in Florence, where the streets were lined with vendors selling leather and jewelry and handmade paper. I ran in Sorrento, a pink-and-brown seaside town, where the streets were wide and the air was damp from the Golfo di Napoli, the horizon lying out in my vision like a soft blanket. But now I am in Cinque Terre. I do not run in Cinque Terre on this narrow path with no guardrails. I am crazy, not stupid.

Depokate

My oldest sister is smart, knowing. She recites statistics like items on a grocery list. Before I left for Tour Europa, she had a new list for me.

"Did you know," she said, "that people with bipolar disorder, if left untreated, live an average of fourteen years less than the general population?"

"No, I was not aware of that," I replied.

"Yes," she said, "and they also have a higher rate of suicide."

"So you're saying I've got a half-decent shot—no pun intended—of blowing my brains out?" I asked.

My oldest sister, a physician, lives in Solanas Beach, California. She diagnosed me from 3,000 miles away, across the great landscape of America. I'm a textbook case, she claims. I am binary opposition running rampant. I feel high as the North Pole for months, and then I feel low as the South Pole for months; back and forth I travel. I am, according to her, of two too many poles.

"If left untreated," she continued, "the symptoms tend to get worse."

Maybe this is why I can't keep a boyfriend, I think. It's the answer to all of those unanswerables. I can only keep a relationship going for about nine months. I have it timed. Like gestation, a glowing nine months, followed by a quick and painful labor and then the baby named Goodbye.

"I think you should get a complete psychiatric evaluation, and if I'm right, I think you should consider the anticonvulsants instead of the mood-stabilizers. Depokate is really effective."

I am reminded that this is in the blood—these biochemical misfires rest snugly in our DNA. My sister rattles off another statistic about the hereditary nature of that which plagued our father (now dead), his brother (also dead), our paternal grandmother (dead too): "Family studies show that first-degree relatives of bipolar patients are eight to eighteen times more likely to have bipolar disorder than the general population."

Let those chemicals misfire, I think. Cars crash and people don't necessarily die. Life stumbles, sometimes recklessly, and it is okay most of the time. And of course she's going to say I have a disorder, that I've been manic on and off for what seems like forever. How else does one write a 600-page book? By being even-keeled? Stable and happy? Happy people don't sit down for two years, seven months and eight days and push through 600 pages, the same pages, the same story, the same sameness day after day, facing the unfinished, being married to it and with it in sickness and in health. Happy people don't worship things the way you have to worship something to write it for two years, seven months and eight days. Ask anyone who has worshiped anything—food or sex or stamp collections or shoes or presidents—how lonely it can be. Worship is a lonely and shitty place to be, and I don't want to be there anymore. I have come to Europe so I can find new ground, so that if I look hard enough, run fast enough, I can find a new moon.

Santorini, Greece

I arrive on the island of Santorini by the ferry, which I caught in Piraeus, just south of Athens. There are throngs of hawkers lined up to greet us, barking and beckoning, waving color photos of inns and guest houses, offering bargain prices, their English forced and choppy.

I walk across the dock, past the hawkers, looking for the local tourist office. I need to get a bus schedule because I am going to Kamari, a town on the southeastern side of the island, where, according to my guidebooks, there are black pebble beaches. A short, dark woman follows me.

"Five thousand drachmas for single," she says, trailing me with quick small steps, like a hurried squirrel chasing a fallen acorn.

"Five thousand. Where you stay? You stay with us at Hotel Maria. Five thousand drachmas," she continues.

"No, no, thank you," I say, trying not to look at her, feeling guilty for refusing her and her persistence.

"Come to Hotel Maria. Best beach in Santorini. Black pebbles."

Her words stop me in my tracks. *Black pebbles.*

"Are you in Kamari?" I ask, turning to face her.

"Yes, Kamari. Come to best beach in Santorini. Come to Kamari."

"How much?" I ask, already knowing her price but ready to bargain.

"Five thousand drachmas for single," she repeats. "But you take for four nights, I give to you for four thousand."

"Is breakfast included?"

"Yes, breakfast too. I take you there. I have car. I take you," she says. This Greek woman found me, hawked, and will now take me.

It is not easy to find a good place to run in Santorini. The streets are paved, but I don't risk running on them; there is no speed limit, and cars and jeeps fly by like loud birds. Running on the beach is difficult too. You sink in an unsteady way, constantly off balance from all of the pebbles, some small as a penny, others as big as the palm of a child's hand. I find the most difficult but only steady place to run: the mountain road of Ancient Thira. It is next to the beach and looks out over the Aegean Sea. The road, which goes upward forever, zigzagging back and forth, cutting sharp, has mostly foot traffic. There are lots of Germans hiking it, drinking from water bottles and slathering on sunblock. From the beach, they look like little ants; they think they can, they think they can. It is dangerously hot in the daytime to run the mountain road, so I get up each morning at Hotel Maria as dawn cracks, and I pass the woman whose hawking brought me to Kamari. She is readying the small dining room for breakfast, and we smile at each other. She shakes her head as if I am crazy, nuts, for running up the mountain road, a road that makes me mutter, *What the fuck was I thinking?* under my breath, a breath I struggle to find.

I am adding miles, new countries, new roads and towns to my life. With every breath and heartbeat and sweating mile I'm adding to my life, while the book that poured out of me like lava—slow and hot—is being shopped around, perhaps pages being cut. I am adding and subtracting in my life, and this is where I have found the balance. I know this now; this is balance.

Invest wisely
My middle sister told me to invest my $4,000 inheritance (she got the same one) wisely. I am throwing it away to run across Europe, she insinuated. This is a proper investment, I tried to explain, but she would not listen. She kept interrupting me, trying to sell me on treasury notes, junk bonds, blue-chip stocks, Europacific funds.

"I found my Europacific fund, just without the Pacific part," I said dryly.

She sees the certainty of money, its promise, its durability. She believes in it because it is unchanging; even if it fluctuates in worth, climbing up and down the stock market, it always has a value that one can rely on. She inherited the saving gene from our father, who paid in cash only, even for big items like a television or car. He wrote down expenditures in a worn looseleaf notebook, his tight, neat script filling line after line through the years, the ins and outs and ups and downs of our financial well-being. This steady, reliable treatment of money was in sharp contrast to the movement of his moods, to the steady unwinding, plateauing, movement back upward, at times dictated by whether or not he was taking his Lithium. In that unsteady world of his, we watched him move, a man, a solid provider, a husband, a father, a loving and tortured soul.

The year our father died—all of us were grown up and on our own by then—he was in the middle of planning a trip to Russia. Our father, the saver, was going to spend a month in another country. This type of trip was out of character, completely foreign to what we knew about him, a frugal and simple man unimpressed by foreign lands or foreign ways. He was going to Russia to find his distant relatives. Our paternal grandfather came to America when he was four years old, making our father a first-generation American. Our father wanted to go to Russia to find long-lost aunts and uncles, to find lineage and blood lines, to find towns and villages and people that linked him to where he was from, to find something to explain who he was.

York, England

About three hours north of London is the town of York. A large wall surrounds the town, protecting its streets, its courtyards and its mammoth Minster that looks like a tall, graying wedding cake. The thick city wall was built in the 13th century and is about 50 feet high. The top of the wall is flat, and wide enough to fit the span or five or six people. Walking along the top of the wall, which is accessible from various flights of steps, is something you just do if you are in York; it is free, a novelty, and you get a bird's-eye view of the town. You can spot the Americans on the wall: they walk hesitantly, a bit frightened, trying to create their own boundary because there are no guardrails. Their thoughts must be plagued by images of missteps and falls and broken bones and shattered spines. Maybe deep down they wonder, *Who could I blame if I fell?*

I run along the wall. I run with ease. I am tan and smooth, the seven weeks in Italy and Greece having touched my skin, leaving my soul full, my body bronzed, my head clear. Now, in Britain, the dampness cannot touch me. I am impenetrable. I run the wall because I can't just walk across things. I have to run because I am scared of how close walking is to standing still.

Running on the wall, I softly call out, "On your left," because I don't want to startle the walkers, but I want them to know I am coming, that I am headed their way. I hear people saying, "My word!" and "Would you look at that?" But I don't run fast or recklessly. I am just making my way through Europe in my running sneakers, and I am here to find new surfaces. I need to put this solid medieval wall—its substance and protection and fortitude—under my feet.

Jesus

My third sister found Jesus many years ago, at about the same time I discovered writing as a source of comfort for my hands and head, two body parts that seemed so connected when pen went to paper, so despairingly alone otherwise. Writing was a lot like running; it was something I had to do to get through that span of time when things were too far northerly or southerly or lacking an east and a west, lacking a course.

When my sister found Jesus, it was as if she had never known he had been there before. A Jew who converts to Christianity is the most Christian of them all, for she has moved from old to new—in Testaments, in faith, in lives. When I was writing the book, my sister told me I was obsessed. "The American culture glorifies and overrates the arts," she said, her voice like a wagging, pointing finger. Yet she is the one I call in the middle of a serious crying jag (they come on like a train: you can hear it slowly in the background, the horns blowing, "Stay out of the way," it calls, the sound getting louder and louder until the welling in my throat and eyes can't be held back anymore). I don't know why I call her when I'm in the depths of the southern descent. Maybe because she is always telling me that Jesus loves me, and even if I don't care that he loves me, it's good to know that someone does.

Sister number 3 sent me the New Living Translation of the Bible. ("Skip over the Old Testament," she told me. "It's the New Testament that you really need to get to.") She sent me a short book that I finished in one sitting, titled *More Than a Carpenter*. The author, a fact-finding journalist-turned-believer, claimed that Jesus was one of three things: He was either a liar, crazy or the Son of God. I called my sister after I finished reading it.

"What do you think?" she asked.

"Well, I think Jesus was a nut who was good with a hammer," I said, tired and in a mood. My sister loves me and worries, truly worries, about the safety of my soul, and she did not find my joke funny.

She sent me *TouchPoints*, a small paperback book enumerating God's answers to one's daily needs. *If you cling to your life*, Jesus says in the Book of Matthew, *you will lose it*. I called my sister a few days before Tour Europa and read this line to her.

"See, Dale," I said, "this trip is good. This is a good thing, because I'm not clinging to life."

"You're right, you're not clinging to it," she said, "you're just running from it."

I am running through it, and she can't see this. I am running in my life and through my life and across the world. I am running my life, you see?

Ireland and then Nairn, Scotland

I have just finished running in Ireland for ten days. I moved east to west, logging miles on inviting country roads, almost wearing out my second pair of sneakers. In Ireland there are road signs everywhere, wooden boards shaped like thick arrows, nailed into a single post. Each arrow has a town name and the number of kilometers left to get to it. Some posts have five or six arrows stacked like a totem pole, pointing in various directions toward various towns. Sometimes there are so many arrows that the directions one can take seem endless. Due south. Northeast. Southwest. A little to your left. A bit to your right.

My feet have touched Ireland's towns: Athy, Kilkenny, Cashel, the city of Cork, Blarney, Sneem, Dingle, Tralee. Ireland is small—two New Jerseys put side to side—so one day I hitched a ride to the tiny coastal town of Ballybunion. Seamus, my lover from college, grew up in Ballybunion. He told me about the bar his parents own there, a place where as a child he ate his morning cereal at a bar stool, while a neighbor would come in for his first pint of the day. After a run around Ballybunion, I stopped at the edge of town, where the land meets water. There stands the wall of a dilapidated castle from centuries ago. Just one solitary wall, a single bone of the castle left, barely surviving, yet strong and proud, erect, firmly planted, looking over the edge of the cliff to the water below, where the mouth of the Shannon River meets the cold and restless North Atlantic.

And now I am in Scotland, far north in the Highlands, in the town of Inverness. I am on my way even farther north, to Nairn. There are scenic walking trails in Nairn that I want to run on. The woman at the tourist office in Inverness gave me a bus schedule and told me how to get there. She told me to take bus number 47 to Allanfearn, then pick up bus 68 to Nairn. She told me about a small inn—cheap and clean—that is a short walk from the bus stop.

"Just head down Gordon Road," she said. "It's the road you'll be on when the bus drops you, and you'll see it, dear, just about a kilometer or so on your left. Lady Anne's House, it's called. The woman running it is Rose McBride. Tell her Lainie over in Inverness sent you."

I wait for bus number 47 and get on when it arrives. A light rain is falling. The bus is empty except for an older man, about the age my father would be now. He's there with his dog, a mutt that sits very patiently in the aisle, but with a frenetically moving tail. I smile at them both and sit in the seat directly across from the man, drawn in by the dog.

"I like your dog," I say to the old man.

"Yes, he's a good dog."

"What's his name?" I ask.

"Name's Brodie," the old man replies, smiling at me and petting the dog on the head.

I ask the man if I can give Brodie a treat. I have a pack of digestives—a bland type of cookie that is popular in England. I bought them strictly because of their name, *digestives*, which sounds like the antithesis of something you'd name a cookie, but at the same time, if said with a pompous British accent, makes all the sense in the world.

"Sure thing, dear. But I'm warning you, you give Brodie a treat and you'll be making yourself a friend for life," he replies.

The dog's ears perk up at the rustling sound I make digging through my bag. I finally come up with a cookie and offer it. The dog takes it gingerly from my hand.

"Headed to Nairn?" the old man asks, sizing up my backpack.

"Yes," I reply.

"Going to see Cawdor Castle?" he asks. Cawdor Castle is one of the well-known tourist attractions in Nairn.

"Well, no, not really. I mean, yes, I'm going to see the castle while I'm there, but I'm really going for the walking trails."

"Ah, yes, the trails of Nairn. Off the beaten path are ya, dear?"

"I guess you could say so," I reply.

"Well, keep in mind this. There's going to be a full moon tomorrow night. If you're going to be in Nairn then, you need to go over to Cawdor Castle at night. The way the light hits the small lake on the property—oh, you wouldn't believe it. It's like God is pointing his finger at you with those moon rays."

"I like moons," I say.

"I like moons too," the old man replies, petting Brodie, who is now looking back and forth from his owner to me, looking for another treat, approval, something.

"Have you ever heard of Europa?" I ask the man. He is a stranger, but is with his dog on a bus, and he already told me about a moon, so why shouldn't he know about Europa?

"Of course," he replies. "Galileo discovered it."

I am prejudiced, I know, because I am surprised; I think that some old man in the middle of Scotland probably doesn't know about things like the moons of Jupiter.

"I've never seen it," I say to him, "but I want to, someday."

"Did you know that the surface of Europa is made of ice?" the old man asks me. My hand is back on the dog's head; I'm looking out the window, where the rain is falling heavier, looking to the places I will run to.

"No, I didn't," I reply.

"Yes, the surface is completely covered in ice."

I imagine it is hard, nearly impossible, to run on ice. Maybe it can be done, though. Maybe you can run on ice slowly and not fall. Europe is not always easy to run on, the land not always conducive, but after a while the feel of the strange ground becomes reassuring, even if it is unfamiliar. The dog leans toward me, resting a wet chin on my tired thighs. My heart is opening on this bus headed north, north, north, almost as far north as I can go, headed to Nairn, where rain or shine I will run those walking trails and sweat and not stop until the course is finished. A dog has rested his chin on my thigh. A dog named Brodie.

"Underneath Europa's ice," the old man tells me, "there is an ocean."

Beth Goldner lives in West Chester, Pennsylvania. This is her first published story.

IN FACULTY BLOCK NUMBER FIVE/*Julie Rold*

MY NEIGHBORS WERE DRIVING me crazy with all their noise and gossip. The front doors of the rooms in our faculty block opened out onto one long, congenial balcony, like a motor lodge off an interstate, and my neighbors were forever hanging about and talking of the same things: the price of eggs, the state of their health and, especially, relatives who had gone south to Guangzhou and made a fortune selling ladies' rayon blouses. Only a good storm ever drove them inside. At night they woke me up calling to each other up and down the stairwells:

"*Ai!* Little Tiger! You asleep? Come play cards. Bring money!"

For six months I'd been living with them in a squat, raw concrete building—officially Faculty Block Number Five—where the college work unit had assigned us all a place to live. To show their enthusiasm for the government's new policies of "opening and reform to the outside world," the college leaders had painted the exterior walls of every floor a different color, from top to bottom, blue, yellow and green. It was about as festive as a mass of concrete could get. My own rooms were on the yellow, middle floor, which my neighbors claimed was the best. Living on the blue made for a hard climb with a load of vegetables from the market; the rats got in too easily through the drains on the green. In ancient China the color yellow was reserved exclusively for the palaces of the emperor.

I was the only foreign teacher in our work unit, the only one, actually, in the small town of Jingmen. It was many months before I was able to make out anything my neighbors said. When I first arrived, I spoke only a few set phrases of stilted, bookish Mandarin ("The smell of that dish is quite aromatic"), which sent my neighbors into hysterics, but for those first few months it was new to hear them laugh at me; everything was exotic and exciting. I would hear them jabbering away in the local dialect, and it was easy to assume that what they were talking about was also exotic and exciting. I confess it was hard not to be disappointed when I began to understand them.

"Be patient," I often told myself. "It's not them—it's you. You don't understand enough." I was twenty-four, pretty, slightly inclined to think of myself as ardent. I was still waiting for a moment when the differences between my neighbors and me would fall away, or at least seem smaller. I longed for some intimate thing to pass between us—

something sacred, significant. I wanted just one of them to say something wise and for me to respond in perfect Mandarin, "Yes, yes! How true! I have often felt that way myself." But as I listened to my neighbors day in and day out, I couldn't help but have my doubts that this would happen. There were times when I was convinced they had spent their lives at nothing but cooking, gossiping and gambling for small stakes.

Still, for the most part, I believed them to be kind. They worried a lot about what I ate and what I did with myself in the evenings. We wanted to like each other. Yang Lili, an art teacher at the college, lived on the green first floor of our faculty block with her husband, Gu, and their small daughter, Ya Ya. She was the same age as I, spoke decent English and was known throughout the college for her beautiful grass-style calligraphy. Several years before Ya Ya was born, the leaders had sent Yang Lili to study in Xian at the Fine Arts Institute. She was proud of having once lived in the city and of her English, which was by far the best of all of my neighbors, and which she liked to practice by giving advice to me.

"You have two new pimples!" she called to me late one afternoon. "That means too much fire in the belly. You should eat a bitter melon."

I was making my way across the shiny, packed-down square of dirt that was the front yard of our faculty block. She was sitting before her front door with a basin of laundry at her feet, eyeing me up as I came near.

"You are lonely," she announced.

"No, no . . ."

"Ya Ya is sleeping. Come and sit with me."

It was just before dinner, the time of day when Faculty Block Number Five reached the height of its sociability. Around us women were chatting to each other through open kitchen windows, out of which came the smell of vegetables frying in animal fat. Upstairs old men were lounging on bamboo daybeds and playing Chinese chess, and downstairs children were running around the lone plum tree in the center of the yard. Not long ago it had blossomed, but then girls stripped it to make garlands for their hair. Just opposite the faculty block was the students' dining hall, and beside that was the college dump. Hungry cats, too skittish to appear by the light of day, prowled the garbage mounds by night. They sometimes kept me awake when my neighbors didn't, yowling across the square.

"During the summer vacation," Yang Lili began, "I think you will visit your family in America." She didn't look at me as she spoke but was preoccupied with the collar of a shirt, which she was scrubbing below the water line.

"No. I'm sure I told you. My plan is to travel here."

"Americans like to travel," she informed me.

"Some of us do."

"Bob went to Hong Kong. You should go there as well."

This Bob had been the foreign teacher before me at Jingmen Normal College. Everyone talked about him, Yang Lili especially. She spoke of his skills in calligraphy; my colleagues in the English Department described his "lively" teaching method (for a foreigner, the highest possible praise); my female students talked about his love of ballroom dancing; the boys of how many points he had scored—twenty-seven—against the Math Department in some very important game of basketball. He and Lili still corresponded; she wrote him in English, and he wrote back in Chinese, his characters precise and delicate, a row of little cobwebs. Over the months, I felt I'd come to know him intimately. I'd conceived a great hatred for him.

I said, "Someday. Not this time."

"Where will you go?"

"To the southwest," I said. "Down to Kunming by train."

She rotated the shirt to start on the cuffs and conceded, "That is also a good place. We call Kunming the city of eternal spring. There are many scenic spots. You can see the great golden temple and the famous forest of stone."

"Really?" I said, trying to seem interested, though I had heard all this before. My conversations with my neighbors consisted of saying and listening to the same things many different times.

"There will be other foreigners in Kunming," she said.

"That's right. There should. A lot."

"That is good for you."

"Will you go anywhere?"

"Oh, no," she said, finally dunking the shirt into a plastic bucket of clean water. "There is no money. I am always here."

And I thought how this was truer than she meant, how every time I came across her she was sitting in that doorway with the washing or fussing over Ya Ya. I had never even seen any of her artwork, though once she had told me that at the bottom of her basin was a picture of a panda she had painted; she'd tilted it for me to see.

"That must be difficult," I suggested.

She wouldn't admit to this. "Our theory is that nothing is difficult if one's heart is right."

From the basket behind her, she pulled a small yellow dress on which there was a picture of a kitten. Below its paw, machine-sewn in English, were the words *The Cat*, and also in Spanish and French *El Gato, Le Chat*.

"When you return from Kunming," she added, "you must tell me all about it, for I have always wanted to go."

She started to wash the little cat dress, and we sat in silence. One good thing about the Chinese was that you could sit with them and say nothing and not feel awkward about it. Across the square the students were coming in groups from their dorms to the dining hall, carrying tin rice bowls and spoons. Yang Lili's questions started me off daydreaming about my summer vacation, not too many more weeks away. I had a feeling she wouldn't be much interested in hearing about what I planned to do. After six months in the most middle part of China, I couldn't have cared less about great golden temples or forests made of stone. My *Lonely Planet* guidebook said that down in Kunming the streets were lined with eucalyptus trees and the weather was always fine. Supposedly there were sidewalk cafes where they remembered how to make real French *café au lait* from days when Kunming was part of French Indo-China, and pancakes and hamburgers from the American and Australian packers. All I really wanted to do was hang out with other foreigners and watch satellite TV and have conversations at normal speed about things like music videos. Too, the guidebook said that Kunming was old and pretty and atmospheric—nothing like Jingmen—that the grand mansions of the French traders still stood about everywhere, fading and peeling in the sun.

Yang Lili had finished the little cat dress and paused to consider me. She tucked a few loose strands of hair behind her ear; her fingers looked especially clean and white against her dark head.

"You are lonely," she said again. "I will tell Gu to cook a fish for you." She began yelling for him.

My neighbors loved feeding me. This was one thing we did well together. They were proud of their cooking. It was a matter of personal honor for them, of preserving face. When they invited me over, they would serve up something with an impressive-sounding name like "Dragon and Phoenix" and always wanted to know if I had ever seen such a dish in America. I made a point of reassuring them many times, "In America, there is no such dish." This never failed to make them happy. Too, I ate whatever they put in front of me. I also felt proud when I heard them talking: "Sure, she eats anything."

This fish from Gu was a real treat, I realized. Gu came from Hong Hu prefecture in the central part of the province, where there was a very famous lake. Songs were written about it even in ancient times. It was maintained on all three floors of Faculty Block Number Five—blue, yellow and green—that Gu was a man who had a way with fish. He even had a special wok, which he'd brought all the way from his home village. It had belonged to his grandmother, and he'd made a vow never to wash it, as it was seasoned with the waters of Hong Hu Lake.

Gu emerged from their rooms in a sleeveless T-shirt and plastic sandals, with the stub of a half-smoked cigarette and with his hair standing on end. He worked night shifts in the Number One Blue Dye Factory and slept in the afternoons. Before the period of opening and reform, he had been the leader of the Indigo Brigade. Now he was called the "night manager." The lines of his hands and his cuticles were permanently edged in blue.

Yang Lili began to talk to him loudly, almost shouting, giving instructions about what he was to do. I was always amazed by how much more softly she spoke in English than she did in Chinese. Gu was a silent man. I could scarcely remember hearing him say more than a few sentences, and anyway he spoke no English. When Yang Lili finished, he quickly lit the end of his cigarette stub and headed toward the bicycle shed. He rode off across the square toward our work unit's main gates.

Yang Lili told me, "Gu is going to buy the most expensive fish for you."

"That is very kind," I said automatically, though I was preoccupied, watching a peasant who had come with a donkey and a cart to search the trash for bottles and tin cans. The peasant was tying the donkey by the head to the plum tree in our yard. It rubbed its muzzle against a branch, but when it turned I saw a long scar running down its flank. I worried the peasant might beat it. The Chinese could be cruel that way.

The news that Gu was going to cook a fish for me soon spread and caused a stir in Faculty Block Number Five. Neighbors were calling down to Yang Lili from the upper balconies and gathering around her to ask questions and offer opinions.

"Do the foreigners like Hong Hu–style fish?"

"How much is Gu going to spend?"

"Foreigners like milk and those foods which are sweet."

"How much is he going to spend?"

Yang Lili was pleased with this sudden chance to show off her English. All the while she kept at her washing, she translated everything for me, even when I understood and tried to answer for myself.

Soon Gu returned from the market, pedaling up to the faculty block with what looked like a rice bag slung over his back. The top end was tied with grass cord, and in the bottom something was moving. He leaned the bike against the wall, untied the cord and beckoned me with a jerk of his chin.

Inside, filling the bottom, was a great dark fish, long as my arm and as thick as my thigh. Steam rose from its body. It panted from the cavern of its gills.

"*Si tou yu*," Gu told me proudly.

Yang Lili translated, "The snake-headed fish." Then she added, "The most expensive of all."

I shuddered.

Gu dumped the fish from the bag. It lay on the concrete with its dark eye upon me, its gills flaring, wheezing like an asthmatic. The neighbors closed in about us, curious to see. One young man poked the fish with a stick and stomped on the walkway next to it to make it thrash around. I stroked my finger down its side, wanting to comfort it. Gu went to the kitchen for his knives.

He came back with a new cigarette burning in one hand and a square-bladed cleaver in the other. He put the blade down on the concrete walkway and the cigarette between his lips. Then in one smooth motion he squatted, puffed, picked up the fish and banged its head against the side of the faculty block. It fell with a wet smack and lay motionless. Gu squatted again and began to scrape off the scales with the back side of his cleaver.

"Is it dead?" I worried.

"Of course! Dead!" proclaimed Yang Lili.

"But maybe it's only stunned."

Yang Lili said something sharply to Gu that I didn't understand but that made all the neighbors laugh. In the next instant, Gu lifted the cleaver high and—

Thwak!

He hacked the fish head off below the gills.

My heart gave one hard thud and then seemed to stop completely. Gu picked up the fish head by the bony lip and carried it inside, returning quickly to resume his scraping. Those little fish scales were flying and falling around my feet. I felt squeamish: a foul taste was rising from my stomach to the back of my throat—I can only describe it as tasting like the smell of water warming in a ditch. For a moment I thought I was going to be sick, and I might have been, only the neighbors were watching me and I was anxious for my reputation.

By and by, I collected myself and felt all right again. It was better without the head, and soon I was even able to watch Gu and notice that he handled the fish quite well. I saw how the deep blue of his nails matched the markings on its back, how he smoked the cigarette without touching it and was mindful not to let the lengthening ash fall upon the flesh. He didn't say a single word as he stripped the scales and then sliced open and cleaned the belly. Only after he finished and scored the sides with tiny crosses did he say, *"Tai hao le,"* and pat the fish to show that he was pleased with it and himself.

At last he rinsed the body with clean water and lifted it carefully, holding it before him as if he were ready to place it on an altar. The fish drooped and dripped between his hands, leaving a trail of droplets along the concrete walk. From the doorway I watched as he laid it in his waiting wok and poured rapeseed oil over its side.

Most of the neighbors had gone, returning to rooms in the faculty block to prepare their own evening meals. Gu was chopping spring onions, ginger, a shock of coriander. I tried to chat with him in Chinese, asking him about the names of the things he was using, but he only smiled into his wok and shook his head. I couldn't make him understand.

"How many boyfriends did you have in America?" Yang Lili asked. This was Yang Lili's favorite topic of conversation. From Bob, I suppose, she'd gotten some notion that Americans had wonderfully exciting romantic lives that we loved to talk about.

"I've told you, Lili. I had one in college. There's no one now."

Yang Lili translated this for the other women. They contemplated me carefully, without blinking, as she hung the trousers on the line.

"Bob had many girlfriends," Yang Lili told me.

"I know."

"One day," she continued, "he got seven letters from America. All from different women! It was so interesting! Whenever there was a party in the dining hall, all the Chinese girls wanted to dance with him. Once he went and only ugly girls were there. The next day he told me, 'Lili, I won't dance with anyone who isn't as pretty as you. What a pity you are married!' He was very charming."

She repeated this in Chinese to the other women. Shading their small mouths with their hands, they giggled for some time at the expense of all those ugly girls at the dance.

"How is it that you lost your boyfriend?" Yang Lili asked. "Did you often quarrel?"

"No."

"Then that was your problem. You were too polite. We have a theory: 'Beating is loving, cursing is caring!'"

To demonstrate, she began to yell over my shoulder, teasing and taunting Gu inside. He flipped his fish over with a pair of chopsticks. The oil hissed in the Hong Hu wok. He erupted in a hot burst of syllables, more than I had ever heard from him, rushed at Yang Lili and made a show of waving his cleaver in the air.

Yang Lili laughed, delighted to have gotten such a rise out of him.

"I told Gu," she explained, "that he is not such a great chef, that he is too vain about his skill. The real chef is that old wok of his granny's. With such a wok, anyone could make a delicious fish—even a peasant from the western desert!"

Just then, from somewhere inside their rooms, Ya Ya began to howl.

"Anyway, you are pretty," Yang Lili added, gathering up her laundry things. "You should have a boyfriend—or many!"

"We're not all the same, you know," I told her. "Not every American has dozens of lovers hanging around."

She made no reply, just hurried in to Ya Ya, taking the basin of purple wash water away.

Gu was nearly finished with the snake-headed fish. Everywhere there was the smell of onions, ginger and coriander. He brought out a table, chairs, three rice bowls, several bottles of beer and a series of cold dishes that he'd also made for me: tomatoes sliced and sprinkled with sugar, twice-fried peanuts, tangerines in syrup, pickled bitter melon. Soon Yang Lili returned with Ya Ya on her hip. She was a fat toddler in an Easter-pink suit; her little wrists, especially, were rolled with flesh as if she had rubber bands around them. Yang Lili sat down again, this time putting Ya Ya instead of the basin between her legs. She brushed Ya Ya's hair into two hornlike pigtails and tied them up with blossom-colored ribbons. I supposed Yang Lili had been trying to encourage me, telling me that I was pretty. She'd only succeeded in making me feel irritated, self-conscious and morose. I was still desperate to defend myself, and my fellow Americans too, against the specter of Bob. I gave a high-minded speech about the dangers of stereotypes. But Yang Lili was so preoccupied popping twice-fried peanuts into Ya Ya's round mouth that I couldn't be sure she was listening.

There was a great sizzle from the kitchen. In the next moment, Gu was bringing out the snake-headed fish.

That fish was gorgeous—a masterpiece. Immediately I forgot about defending myself. It lay amid foliage of spring onion and coriander on a platter of China-blue porcelain. You could just glimpse its crisp golden flesh beneath the feathery shadows of the leaves. Most amazing of all was how natural the fish looked, how in its element, swimming along sideways in a savory pool of red pepper, garlic and ginger as if it had never known water but had been born to live out its days in Gu's special Hong Hu sauce.

Overcome, I resorted to one of those flatteries from my phrasebook in formal Mandarin: "Gu *Xiansheng*. The smell of this fish is very aromatic. Your skill level is very high."

It worked. Gu nodded in acknowledgment, wiping his bright face with a clean cloth.

"I poured warm water for you," Yang Lili said to me. "Go and wash your hands inside."

The concrete kitchen was damp and clean. Gu had just wiped down the tile and mopped the floor. His Hong Hu wok lay cradled on its gas burner, its inside black and bright. A metal basin had been left for me on a cement ledge next to the cold sink. I peered down through the rising steam and saw a picture on the bottom—the one Yang Lili told me she had painted before Ya Ya was born—of a tragic-eyed panda and its baby among leaning stalks of bamboo. And there, with my hands in the warm water and those pandas staring up at me and the smell of onions and coriander still in the air, I thought of the fish waiting for me, and I was touched. A rush of the finest kind of feeling came over me, for Gu, Yang Lili, all my neighbors—for humanity. It passed through me instantly, a lick of loving feeling coming from the center of me to my arms and legs, and was gone again. I reached out for a greasy-looking bar of soap, and that's when I noticed the snake-headed fish head in the sink.

It was lying on one side with its dark eye rolling, its gills flaring, its bony mouth opening and closing against the grout. It was still alive! A clot of black blood and brainy bits ran from its head down the drain. Suddenly, it flopped!

I was dizzy and something was pounding in my head—I guess the hard echo of my heart. I don't know how I made it back outside. I was confused, not sure if I'd already fainted or was just about to. But neither Yang Lili nor Gu noticed that anything was wrong. She was pulling flesh from the fish's back and feeding it to Ya Ya. He was thrusting a pair of chopsticks at me.

"Chi ba!" he said, smiling down on his fish, his cheeks shining with pleasure as if he had just swallowed a piece of gold.

My arms and legs were trembling. A single heavy drop of perspiration sprang from my armpit and rolled coldly down my side. I started with a sugared tomato instead. It bled on my rice like a wound. Next to me, Ya Ya was consuming bit after bit of fish flesh, with her front teeth showing—a baby ogre.

Gu thought I was being polite, not starting with fish because I didn't want to seem greedy. He reached with his chopsticks, pulled off several large hunks of it and placed them in my bowl himself.

The Hong Hu sauce dripped off the flesh. I saw little gritty things scattered over my rice, like those dark bits in the cold drain.

I gummed my fish a little, spat back into my bowl.

"Be careful of bones," Yang Lili said.

I put a smaller piece in my mouth, gagged it down with a sip of beer. I was about to be sick. My cheeks blazed from all the blood beating to my head. Water leaked from the edges of my eyes. I tried to speak, but only a belch came out.

Yang Lili had stopped feeding Ya Ya. Gu's golden cheeks had grown pale. Only Ya Ya was moving, squirming between Yang Lili's legs, reaching for the platter, asking for more fish. Suddenly angry, Yang Lili slapped her hands. She burst into hot tears. Then she began speaking in a low voice to Gu—the softest I'd ever heard her use with him. Ya Ya was screaming now, and I couldn't make out anything. Gu was staring at the platter of fish and on his face was that perfectly blank, expressionless look the Chinese assume when they are overwhelmed. Finally, Gu took up some fish in his blue fingers. He sniffed it once, twice, placed it on his tongue.

"*Huai le!*" he shouted.

"Spoiled!" Yang Lili translated.

"No, no!" I cried, but it was already too late.

Gu had grabbed the platter and was running with it across the square, rushing beyond the donkey and the plum tree toward the side of the dining hall. Ya Ya was crying so loudly that Yang Lili was forced to take her inside. Ready to burst into tears myself, I watched Gu fling the headless snake-headed fish in its Hong Hu sauce onto the garbage mound.

Afterward we picked at the cold dishes—Yang Lili, Gu and I. I attempted to make a confession.

"I'm so sorry—"

"When you buy a fish, do not go to that old woman with the very round face."

"Lili!"

"She cheated us. She will cheat anyone. Remember!"

Up and down, the neighbors were watching us, their faces dull, impassive, scarcely distinguishable from the concrete walls of the faculty block, as if they'd metamorphosed into one great silent beast with a thousand pairs of eyes.

Since that time I have often wondered who was most anxious to save face.

"The fish had some disease," I declared.

"Yes, yes! It had to be."

"This happens in America too."

"Gu says his grandmother once bought a sick fish like this."

It was full twilight now. The shadow of the plum tree had been absorbed into the square. Gu left us, heading off to his night shift at the dye factory in coveralls that were the same color as his hands. His work would not end until 4 A.M. But Yang Lili and I sat out for hours, telling all the neighbors how we'd been cheated, forcing them to vow they would never buy fish from the old woman with the very round face again.

There were all the sounds of the early evening—the radios blaring on different stations, people arranging games of mah-jongg, growing noisier still as the sky went black. But sometime after midnight it grew quiet, as quiet as I'd ever remembered it.

Those hungry cats, their bellies full for once, didn't need to howl.

Julie Rold lived and worked in rural China for three years. One of her stories appeared in *Scribner's Best of the Fiction Workshops* in 1997.

" NOW, NOW, MS. ELLIOTT, YOU KNOW VERY WELL THAT SHREDDER IS ONLY FOR PAPER."

ANGEL TONGUE / *Charles Simic*

Theresa, do you remember
That dive filled with smoke
Like a house on fire
Where nightly we huddled
In one of the rear booths
Reading to each other from a book
On the mystic way of life?

Days, all prim and clear-eyed,
You went to work in a bridal shop.
It had bars on its window.
The two mannequins in white
Had tense little smiles for me
Every time I dropped by
While you stood behind them.

We played an elaborate game
Of hide and seek with words
And our hearts while feigning
To find clues of divine presence
On streets steeped in shadow.
I recall the sight of your lips
Quivering from the cold

As you spoke of light so fine,
So rare, it lights the very light
We see by, in the meantime,
Your eyes were open so wide,
I hurried closing them with kisses,
While you talked of mystic death
With the tongue of angels.

BURNING EDGAR POE / *Charles Simic*

O the late days of autumn,
The wind's blowing
Charred book pages
Out of a neighbor's chimney
Scaring the blackbirds.
They can't tell their own
From the flying soot
In the saffron-colored sky,
And neither can I.

LOOKING FOR TROUBLE / *Charles Simic*

Didn't know I was doing it.
Had the notion I was living
A nice, quiet life
Patting the children on the head,
Going for a long Sunday drive.
In short, thriving.

Useless words. My smile faded
The day I found a man asleep
On my doorstep. Why? I said
Stepping over him carefully.
I spent the night making trips
To the door, trying to hear him
Breathe. At daybreak,
I made tea and took it to him,

But he was gone, leaving behind
His hat. Surely not far, I figured,
Walking out in my robe and slippers
Into the snowy street,
Peering into doorways as I went.
The cup and the hat in my hands

Made me seem even goofier,
Entering an alley where two
Of them slept. One stirred,
Pocked his raw eyes out of his rags
Puzzled. What did the other fellow
Look like? I wondered,
Backing out, distancing myself

While recalling how years ago
An elderly, well-dressed man
Came up to me in the street
And said I'm the spit image

Of his long dead brother.
Well, what do you reply to that?
I didn't. I just scrammed.

THE TUNNELING / *Charles Simic*

Prisons secured for the night.
Thousands lying awake out there,
As we too lie awake, love.
The blurry whiteness at the ceiling
Of our darkened room
Like a sheet thrown over a body
In the ice cold morgue.

Do you hear the one tunneling?
So faint a sound, yet so close,
It could be inside one of our walls.
I bet, he's left behind in the pen
A stand-in dummy or two propped up
On the pillow, just the way we are,
When the turnkey comes around.

MISS X / *Charles Simic*

It's her I want,
Who's got me
In her scissors' hold,
Down cold.

And clips me
Down to size
Every time
She bumps into me

On the street,
Veering
On her high heels
Still going clip, clip.

MADGE PUT ON YOUR TEA KETTLE/
Charles Simic

We are being hoodwinked,
That's pretty obvious.
The blue sky, the apple trees in blossom,
The lone sparrow
Nonchalantly hopping back and forth
In front of the tiger cat
Sprawled on the new grass.

There's nothing to worry about,
The lazy afternoon says.
Every shadow sits in silent study
Of some empty spider web.
Two ants hauling a dead cricket
To a cricket cemetery
Have stopped to take a long rest.

Charles Simic is a Pulitzer Prize–winning poet whose most recent collection is *Jackstraws.*

WILD IN THE WOODS: CONFESSIONS OF A DEMENTED MAN/*Floyd Skloot*

My twin, the nameless one, wild in the woods
—John Berryman, "Dream Song 255"

I AM DEMENTED. I have been clinically demented for a decade, ever since contracting a virus that attacked my brain in December of 1988. I display dementia's classic "multiple cognitive deficits that include memory impairment but not impairment of consciousness" and am totally disabled. You might never know, just looking at me.

There are, however, a few tips to the naked eye. My brain damage manifests itself in specific motor malfunctions. So I walk like Phillip Dean in James Salter's classic 1967 novel, *A Sport and a Pastime*, who in a bad moment "feels awkward, as if the process of movement had suddenly asserted all its complexity and everything had to be commanded." This is an accurate description of how I feel when I walk. I have to think about every step or else the whole process of walking breaks down. Like Dean, I walk "as if made of wood," only I do it that way all the time. If I bend to pick up a dropped coin, I will probably fall over. I can be tripped by a gust of wind. Few of my shirts are free of permanent stains from spills or splashes, and there are squiggles of ink on everything I wear. Watch me accidentally ladle the oat bran I've just cooked into the sink instead of a cereal bowl or struggle to affix the plastic blade attachment guide to my beard trimmer. See me open the pantry and stare into it with no recollection of what I was after an instant before, or start a bath by rubbing soap over my still-dry body. Play cards with me and wonder why I discard an ace just after you've picked up an ace off the pile or suddenly follow the rules of poker while we're playing casino. Try to teach me how to operate a new microwave oven or program an unfamiliar calculator. If the cat moves across my field of vision, hear my conversation stop as I forget what I am telling you. If I ask you to pass the "steam wheels" just wait a moment till I correct myself and request the "cream cheese." If we drive together and I tell you to turn left, be sure to turn right.

Dementia is a loaded word. To health professionals, it refers to "a precipitous decline in mental function from a previous state" and has clear diagnostic criteria. But to almost everyone else, it refers to doddering senility. Either that or craziness; the dictionary offers "madness" and "insanity" as synonyms. Dementia is the Halloween of illnesses, a horror mask, a nightmare affliction, its victims akin to Freddy Krueger or Michael "The Shape" Myers. It is so fearsome because it is so transformative. The demented are seen as out of control or out of touch, as zombies, given over to primal impulses. Plug "demented" into a search engine on the World Wide Web and you get referred to sites like "The Demented Pinhead Figurine," "Lunatic Lounge, the Home of Stupid Human Noises" or "The Doctor Demento Halloween Show."

We decry what we fear. We shroud it in myth, heap abuse upon it, use language and gesture to banish it from sight or render it comic. By shrinking its monstrousness, we tame it. So a new disease such as AIDS is known first as the gay cancer, or Chronic Fatigue Syndrome is known first as the yuppie flu, officially trivialized, shunted aside. And there is little we fear so much as losing our minds. Synonyms for "demented" are "daft," "deranged," "maniacal," "psycho," "unbalanced." Or, more colloquially, "bananas," "flipped out," "nutty as a fruitcake," "out of one's tree." The demented are like monkeys, it would seem.

I became demented overnight. Sudden onset is one factor that distinguishes my form of dementia from the more common form associated with Alzheimer's disease. For the Alzheimer's patient, who is usually over sixty, dementia develops slowly, inexorably. Mine developed on the night of December 7, 1988, without prelude and without time to prepare, momentously, the way it does in people suffering strokes or tumors, a bullet to the brain or exposure to toxic substances such as carbon monoxide. For me, it was how I imagine the day some sixty-five million years ago when a huge meteorite struck the earth, turning summer to winter in an instant. Not that I noticed right away.

When I woke up in a hotel room in Washington, D.C., after a long flight east, a taxi ride from the airport, a quick run around the mall and a light dinner, I simply felt sick. Though I noticed that it was almost impossible for me to tie my shoes, that I could not quite get the hang of shaving myself and that operating the elevator was a bafflement, I could not make sense of these observations. My notebook from the seminar I had come to attend remained empty of notes; I spent most of the time upstairs in bed. For six weeks afterward, I thought I had a terrible flu and that the confusion and mistakes, the inability to find my way back to the office from a coffee break or to sustain an idea during a meeting, saying "adequate" when I meant "accurate" or calling my "cubicle" a "crucifix," were connected to this bad bug I had caught. What it felt like was a gradual lowering of the blinds or one of those slow-motion descents of a shaken sheet as it softly rides the air down to cover your body. One day, driving on a familiar stretch of I-205, headed for the doctor's office, I had to pull over onto the shoulder and stop driving. I did not risk driving again for six years. I could not fill out the forms needed by doctors or insurers. Armed with a plastic cup, I walked to the bathroom to give a urine sample, used the cup for a quick drink from the faucet and returned to the examination room having forgotten to pee at all. I could not remember the doctors or what they were telling me, could not describe the history of my illness without notes, could not find my way back from the examining room to the waiting room.

Have you ever been delirious? Gripped by high fever or certain brain infections, diseases or injuries; after too much to drink, sniff or snort; after too many pharmaceuticals or too long a run, people can lapse into delirium. It is a short-term mental state characterized by confusion and disorientation. Most people have been there. Dementia resembles delirium in the same way that an ultramarathon resembles a dash across the street. Same basic components, vastly different scale. If you've run delirium's course once or twice in your life, try to imagine a version that never ends.

In May 1989, six months after becoming ill, I was examined by Muriel Lezak, associate professor of neurology and psychiatry at Oregon Health Sciences University. Dr. Lezak, acclaimed author of the 1983 Oxford University Press textbook *Neuropsychological Assessment*, conducted exhaustive tests with an empathy and tenderness that moved me to tears. She found extensive problems in my ability to learn and remember, a tendency toward slowed processing, fragmented visual recall and an overall "difficulty in keeping track of ongoing mental activity." To her, I appeared lost within the thickets of my own thought processes. My responses struck her as "very fragmented into bits," and these bits "were scattered rather helter-skelter as [if I] had seemingly lost sight of the original overall plan," all suggestive of a "significant visual learning deficit." I could not put things together, could not make sense of what I saw. She found that I had "great difficulty in organizing and synthesizing visual material when the burden of making structure" was upon me. She summed up our session by saying, "Mr. Skloot no longer is automatically accurate in handling basic arithmetic or writing tasks, as one might suspect he normally would be."

You never dream of hearing such things said about you. But dementia is a biological catastrophe whose essence is intellectual diminishment, and I had diminished all right. Big-time. My IQ was down about 15 percent. Unable to exercise, metabolism gone haywire, my body weight was up almost as much. I was, in many ways, so unrecognizable to myself that I dreaded looking in the mirror, confusing what was happening

inside my head with what might show itself outside. People kept saying I looked good. The hard edge from rigorous training for marathon
running and long-distance racing was gone; I looked softer, which
apparently was not a bad thing. I *was* softer. I was also slower. I felt
denser, tamped down, compacted. I lived with greater stillness; I had
time, had an emptiness where there had always been fullness—of mind,
of purpose, of agenda. I had so few defenses against the world—not
only because my immune system was scrambled but because I found
myself more emotionally open—that I felt utterly exposed.

A process had begun that required me to redefine myself, to construct a new sense of who I was and how I dealt with the world as an
intellectual shadow of my former self. It would be years before I could
make much headway. Fortunately, my dementia does not appear to be
progressive; at least it has not gotten worse over the last decade and is
classified as static. I got where I was going fast and have stayed there,
as though beamed down. Now I had an opportunity to reconfigure
myself. At least that was one way to look at this. Becoming ill afforded
me the chance to discover and align my emotional state with my new
biological state.

The word *dementia* has its root in the Latin *dementare*, meaning
"senseless." Yet I have found my senses heightened following the loss
of intellectual force. My responsiveness to odor is so strong that sometimes I think I've become a beagle. Intensely spiced foods—Indian,
Thai, Mexican—taste exaggerated in their richness; I can become
exhausted and confused by eating these cuisines. My skin often tingles,
sometimes for no discernible reason, sometimes in response to the
slightest stimulus. The same process that stripped me of significant
intellectual capacity and numbed my mind seems to have triggered a
corresponding heightening of sensory and emotional awareness.
Sometimes this can be a maelstrom, sometimes a baptismal immersion.
Forced out of the mind, away from my customary cerebral mode of
encounter, I have found myself dwelling more in the wilder realms of
sense and emotion. Out of mind and into body, into heart. An altered
state.

This is actually biology at work. Dementia is, after all, a symptom of
organic brain damage. It is a condition, a disorder of the central nervous system, brought about in my case by a viral assault on brain
tissue. When the assault wiped out certain intellectual processes it also
affected emotional processes. I am not talking about compensatory or
reactive emotional conditions; I mean the same virus zapped certain

emotion-controlling neural tissue, transforming the way I felt and responded, loosening my controls.

It has not been customary to recognize the neurology of emotion. For centuries, at least since Descartes famously wrote, "I think, therefore I am," in his 1637 *Discourse on Method*, scientists have tended to focus their attention on the seemingly measurable mental processes of memory, thinking or language production. Emotions, on the other hand, were thought of primarily as distractions to mental activity, difficult to assess objectively, either from within or without.

But in the last two decades, neuroscientists have made it clear that, as John E. Dowling says in *Creating Mind: How the Brain Works*, "feelings and emotions—fear, sadness, anger, anxiety, pleasure, hostility, and calmness—localize to certain brain regions." Dowling notes that "lesions in these areas can lead to profound changes in a person's emotional behavior and personality, as well as in the ability to manage one's life." This is what has happened to me.

Intelligence is only part of the story of human consciousness. The longer I dwell in this new, demented state, the more I think intelligence may not even be the most critical part. I have become aware of the way changes in my emotional experience intersect with changes in my intellectual experience to demand and create a fresh experience of being in the world, an encounter that feels spiritual in nature. I have been rewoven.

This concept of emotion turns Descartes upside down. It also gives a clue about where to turn within the wilderness of dementia. After all, when one way through the wilderness is blocked, survival dictates finding an alternative way. For me, since the softening of intellectual powers coincided with an intensification of emotional response, the way through this wilderness seemed obvious.

I noticed almost immediately after my illness began that my emotional condition was as altered as my intellectual condition. It was apparent in small, everyday experiences that had never touched me deeply before, such as being moved to tears by seeing an outfielder make a diving catch, hearing the opening chords of a favorite nocturne, feeling the first spring breezes on my skin as I stood on the porch, observing my dog's yawn or finding a grapefruit in the refrigerator, neatly sectioned by my wife and wrapped in plastic for my breakfast. I could also erupt in tears over the least frustration—trying without success to decipher a menu, to replenish the lead in a pencil, to operate a new boom box. It was apparent as well in the emotional upheaval that accompanies chronic illness, with its attendant loss of companionship and livelihood, freedom and diversion. I would look out my window, see joggers clomp by and, unable to run myself as I used to every day, be filled with a despair I once would have suppressed. Although I had nothing but time on my hands, the least delay in a bank or doctor's office would irritate me beyond all rationality. The gift of a portable phone from my former colleagues, with a note saying they hoped it would let them talk with me more often, shattered me with joy. Sometimes the emotional upwelling was embarrassing, as when the opening chords of the overture to *The King and I* sent me into a torrent of ecstatic tears. The arrival of two acceptances of my poems from literary magazines also broke me up. I was turning into a sentimental slob.

This was not merely a matter of being victimized by emotional storms. There was also disinhibition, a new freedom to express the sentiments I was feeling. At first I was swamped with ungovernable emotions, but I soon learned to swim within them, even to surf upon them. My relationship with my daughter deepened. Love and passion entered my life for the first time in decades. My brother's advancing terminal illness, which took his life in the summer of 1997, was something I could face openly with him after years of estrangement, spending time in his presence, crying with him, finding for the first time in decades the possibility of sharing the warmth we felt for each other.

Losses in my intellectual capacities are clear and measurable, the kind of losses that can be evaluated and scored. Changes in my emotional life seem every bit as great. But, perhaps in part because my form of dementia is not as grave as that of Alzheimer's sufferers, these changes offer a counterbalance to my mental losses. I feel differently, but in many ways I feel more fully, more richly. It is as though I have been given an area of psychological life in which to compensate for what is missing.

In the spring of 1993, I married Beverly and moved to the woods. This is something I could never have imagined myself doing. In fact, it is the opposite of what I thought was needed after getting sick. Logic dictated that I stay in the center of things, close to friends, doctors, services and entertainment. I should live where anything I might need was within walking distance. To do otherwise, I reasoned, would be to further isolate myself, and illness had isolated me enough already. It never occurred to me that city life could have a deleterious effect on chronic illness, or that it represented a clinging to old ways, or that the time had come to consider a new way of living, since brain damage had changed so much about me.

I believed in the importance of staying connected to the city, even though my intuition was urging me elsewhere. For instance, the first act of independence I had performed, about eight months after getting sick, was to spend a week alone at the Oregon coast in a small room overlooking the sea. The motel was called the Ocean Locomotion, though stillness was its primary attraction. I could walk the hundred yards from my room to a colossal piece of driftwood shaped like a davenport, plunked just beyond the tide line, and watch the breakers, the zany behavior of gulls or the sunset. Occasionally a ship would drift across the horizon. At the time, I could not have rationally explained why it felt vital for me to leave the city and be alone in nature. But I was drawn there and knew that being away from the city was good for me. Back in Portland, I lived for a year in an urban townhouse close to the Willamette River and spent several hours every day sitting or walking on its bank, pulled there, trying always to find more and more deserted sites. Still, I remained in the city till 1993.

By then Beverly had entered my life. I knew that in 1989 she had purchased twenty acres of hilly forest land in rural western Oregon, built a small, round house in the middle of the site and been living there by herself ever since. In time, she took me to see it.

The place, located two miles outside a small town of 1,100 and fifty miles from the nearest urban center, is so isolated that the closest neighbor is over a quarter of a mile away, and that neighbor is a vintner who does not even live on the winery property. The land is officially a tree farm, its rocky and irregular acreage filled with Douglas fir, oak, maple, the occasional wild cherry. Beverly left it rough and harvests nothing. The landscape is laced with blackberry vines, wild rose, hazel and poison oak, and what has been cleared for gardens is under continual assault from what remains wild. A winter creek cuts through the middle, and during its months of loud life there is also a lovely view south into the Eola Valley through naked trees. Some mornings mist rises from the valley floor, climbs the hillside, blankets the house for a while and then leaves a blazing sky behind, the whole show like a short drama entitled Hope. Some mornings cattle and horses call from the small farms at the base of the hill; once a llama that had gotten loose found its way up to the house, trailed by a massive billy goat with one broken, off-center horn.

I learned that nothing here obeys the rules imposed on it. The ground is hard, basaltic, unforgiving. Beverly dug out a small pond, working her pick and shovel like a convict, lined the hole with plastic and filled it with water plants that the deer ate almost before she could get back inside the house and clean off. They stepped through the plastic liner in their zeal, so she replaced it with a smaller, preformed pond liner, and the deer now use it as their personal drinking fountain. She allowed a friend from work to keep bees in a small grove for a season or two, but the hive failed, and now there are only wild bees on the premises. This is a place that does not tame, that fights back at efforts to diminish it.

When we discussed the possibility of my joining her, the idea of living in the country was appealing to me for several wrong reasons. A lifelong urbanite, I was born in Brooklyn, New York, raised there and on Long Island and have spent much of my life in cities. Not just in cities but in apartments. At the time Beverly and I began to be together, I was living in a new apartment building downtown, right in the middle of Portland's hubbub, walking distance from the bookstores, theater, concert hall, artsy cinema, restaurants, the Safeway. For nature, I had the Willamette, two blocks to the east, so polluted that the Environmental Protection Agency keeps threatening to add it to the Superfund cleanup list.

I still equated the city with self-sufficiency. But after spending a few weekends at Beverly's place in the woods, I began to consider escaping the frenzy, fleeing the noise and congestion. It would always be difficult for me to think clearly, but being surrounded by urban commotion made it worse. I felt scattered. I had come to see that it was impossible to truly slow down in the city. It was impossible to find harmony between my surroundings and my newly diminished self, reined in, slowed down, isolated from the worlds of work, running and community that I had always lived in. There was too much stimulation, too much outer life for a person in my situation. I had nothing but time on my hands, yet was living where time seemed accelerated. I needed an emptier place, pared down, humbler: a home that fit my circumstances.

But of course, rural life is hardly empty. My isolated, quiet, dull, out-of-the-way home of the last half decade is actually teeming with life. It offers life in its immediacy, to be experienced without the mediation of thought or explanation, and gives time to contemplate. You don't need to be quick, just open and responsive, to get what this hill is about. Dwindling well water, the delicate system by which electricity is delivered to us, the boundaries established for herbs or flowers or vegetables—the human imprint is fragile and contingent. Yesterday as I was writing this very paragraph, the power went out in a gust of wind and took along my thoughts. It takes rigor and flexibility to hold on, a dedication of soul, but the rewards are worth it. I had seen *myself* as dulled and emptied too, so it has been instructive to be reminded of how much life goes on beneath surfaces that appear quiet.

One spring night shortly before we got married, Beverly and I dragged her mattress outside and hauled it onto a platform made from a couple of chaise longues. We protected ourselves with an altar of citronella candles and a down comforter and prepared to spend a night under the stars. This was a first for me. Nice and peaceful, arm around my sweetheart, gazing up at the constellations, impressed by how much I could see. Then the action began. Bats swooped to catch the bugs. Owls started calling. I could hear deer moving through the woods just to the east of us, frogs in the pond. A skunk sashayed underneath our chaises and headed toward the compost pile. My first response was the fear of a city boy stalked, then laughter and soon a joy so vast that I felt caressed by it.

There are some days, when Beverly is at work and I am here alone, that I do not speak aloud at all during the daylight hours. Yet I am not restless or bored, I don't yearn for the city, and this is not an exile. Till I got here, gave up my city home and began learning how to be in these woods, I did not really understand how much I needed to live like this. Functioning now at a more appropriate tempo, looking closely at the world I live in because there is not much else to do, I understand more about what has happened to me.

When the coastal wind blows hard through the trees and I see them swaying, I lose my balance, even in bed, because the damage to my brain has affected the system by which I hold myself in place. To retain balance is work for me. It requires a focus on what holds still. I need to stop thinking altogether to do it right. Seeing those trees every morning also reminds me that this is a land of second growth. The timber on much of our hill was harvested many years ago, and I live within the density of what grew back. It is a good place for me to live, a workshop in survival, in coming back from damage.

A person doesn't escape to a place like this. It's not exile; it's home.

I am not getting any better. But I am also not getting any worse. At fifty-two, after eleven years of living with static dementia, I have discovered just where that leaves me. Since I cannot presume that I will remember anything, I must live fully in the present. Since I cannot presume that I will understand anything, I must feel and experience my life in the moment and not always press to formulate ideas about it. Since I cannot escape my body and the limits it has imposed on me, I must learn to be at home in it. Since I can do so little, it is good to live in a place where there is so little to do. And since I cannot presume that I will master anything I do, I must relinquish mastery as a goal and seek harmony instead.

The short, grizzled guy living atop the Amity Hills looks like me and for the most part seems like me. He goes out in a storm to bring in a few logs for the wood stove; he uses the homemade privy balanced between a pair of oak trees when the power is out, which means the well cannot pump, which means the toilet cannot be used; he has learned to catch live mice in his gloved hands in his bedroom in the middle of the night and release them unharmed in the woods; he sits in an Adirondack chair reading while bees work the rosemary and hyssop nearby. He is my twin, all right, my demented self, wild in the woods, someone I did not know I had inside me.

Floyd Skloot's essays have appeared in a number of journals and been included in *Best American Essays*.

THE WOMAN WHO SAID NO/*Lucy Ferriss*

HE WAS PUTTING ON HIS SHOES when he told her. "Samantha wants a contract."

"A what?"

"Contract. Or something. She wants me to write something down."

"What kind of something down?"

"It should say that if I ever have sex with someone else again, our marriage is over."

They were both sitting on the edge of the hotel bed. "And you said?"

"I'd think about it."

Marian traced the print on the bedspread. It made a complicated geometric pattern, like Rubik's cube or a pair of those twisted nails that should come apart easily but don't. "How long do you have to think?"

"I don't know. She came up with the idea last week."

Marian ran her finger down Joe's back, lithe and muscled under the slippery cotton of his shirt. A quarter of an hour ago she had lain behind him, curled on the bed, and thought how similar one back looks to another—shoulder blades, trapezoids, the knotty rope of spine. That she was not Joe's first affair was part of his attractiveness for her: she needn't take him too seriously. "Well," she said, draping her arm over Joe's narrow shoulder like an old friend, "that's really between you and Samantha, isn't it?"

"Yeah, I suppose it is. I shouldn't bother you with it."

"But if you sign a contract and keep seeing me, you'll be in deep trouble," said Marian.

"I'm already in deep trouble."

"I think I'd want to break off if there was a contract on file." Marian drew away, was sitting cross-legged on the bed. "Then again, if you refuse to sign it she'll know you're up to something."

"That about sums up the possibilities."

Joe smiled, and Marian touched a lean dimple on his cheek. "So what are you going to do?"

"Stall. What would you do, counselor?"

Marian stood and began to dress. She was a tall, thin, freckled woman with gluteals far sexier than her slight breasts, and for that reason alone she kept her back to Joe as she slipped back into skirt, bra, blouse, hose. "She doesn't mean to catch you," she said, her eyes on the ray of December light that slipped between the heavy maroon curtains.

Joe had picked this hotel, a cheap, all-season place up a winding road at the New Hampshire border. "If she wants you to sign a contract like that, it means she's expecting you to be tempted, right?"

"She knows," said Joe, shaking out a sock, "that monogamy is not my strong suit."

"But she's also thinking you would tell her about it. Given the signed contract. And that by choosing to tell her, you'd be choosing to end your marriage. Which isn't at all, I think"—she turned around, her blouse half buttoned, and leaned over him to smell his curly hair— "what you're doing here. With me."

He didn't answer that one. He made her take her clothes back off, so that she was late and messy that day, getting back to work. And though she believed that what Joe wrote down for his wife was no business of hers, Marian Lewis was a lawyer and knew the ins and outs of contracts, the loopholes and the parsing of phrases, so the subject wouldn't quite move off her agenda.

She had met Joe at a party in Boston. No, not quite. First he had come up to Peterborough to report on the state senator's fabulous divorce. Then returned to check facts. Then in November Marian had driven her daughter, Lisa, to Boston for sectional finals—girls' fourteen-and-under tennis—and stolen away from the match to a cocktail party, and there he had been, popping baby quiches into his mouth like a starving man.

There was always the chance she might have said no. The other times she had, in so many words, said no. Instead, under the ficus tree in the Boston loft, she had been the one to kiss Joe—on his neck, under his right ear. If she hadn't, he'd have kissed her. Or tried to. But she could have said no, and then he wouldn't have tried again. Sometimes, sitting in conference or driving through late-winter snow, Marian pictured herself saying no. Then suddenly it was as if she were living parallel lives, the life in which she'd said yes and the life in which she'd said no. And the lives were so much alike, even she had trouble telling them apart. Like those pairs of pictures in the puzzle books the children used to read, where you strain to find the ten differences between the pictures.

"Sometime you'll have to tell me," Joe had said, lying naked next to her on the hotel bed near the state border, "what you are doing here."

"I was hoping you'd tell me," she said, and blew on his chest, which had a thicker mat of hair than her husband Edward's and smelled like salted butter.

Throughout that winter Marian carried her affair inside her like a secret taint of blood. It came to her at odd moments, like when she'd dropped her son, Kurt, off for hockey and was on her way through wet snow to the mall. Turning the corner at the light, she'd think, I'm fucking a man not my husband, and a little rush would come between her legs.

Sometimes it would not come, and there were only the words, I'm fucking a man, so that Marian could consider them there in the slowly lightening days. I'm involved with someone outside my marriage, she tried sometimes, and she liked the way that sounded—as a line she might use on someone she was confessing to, if she were ever to confess—but she preferred to remind herself that what she was doing was fucking Joe.

The terrible thing, assuming she could find nothing wrong enough in her marriage to justify adultery, was that she was there out of frivolity; she could find nothing wrong enough in her marriage to justify adultery. She did it because she got away with it. Or worse, she did it in the hope that Joe would fall in love with her, would leave his pretty zoologist wife for her, would work to persuade her to leave Edward.

And of course she wasn't going to leave Edward, so this hope was mere vanity.

Marian was not a pretty woman. She had set her sights on Edward because of his beauty—his nose alone gave him the edge over Joe, who was snappy-looking at best—and because he sang. A lovely, dark-chocolate baritone. Songs from *Camelot* and *West Side Story*; he'd sung "Maria" to her on their first date, in law school, instead of the more obvious one about the librarian. Even now he told her all the time how beautiful she was. Her small, neat ass, her milky breasts, her slim hips and long waist. After fourteen years he remarked with wonder on what others might have called a stringy figure.

Joe never told her she was beautiful; he did not believe, she surmised, that she was. He only fucked her, and with such grace and urgency that she could not think of anything else while they were at it.

She had to be careful not to transfer Joe's style of lovemaking over to Edward. For instance, if she put the tips of her fingers into Edward's mouth for him to suck while she was straddling him, he'd have stopped what he was doing, torn her wrist away from his face, and stared a confession out of her. Or if she'd let him put a finger into her anus, the way he used to want to and she'd never let him. She let Joe do anything.

Joe was an investigative reporter. Generally he covered murders, also gruesome auto accidents and political scandals. He'd interviewed Marian in the first place because she had represented the senator in his bid for divorce. They discussed the ethics of prenuptial agreements, the ethics of politics, the lawyer-client privilege, the ethics of marrying money. In retrospect, Marian thought, they'd both come off as remarkably ethical people.

"What if you wrote," she tried the next time she met Joe, at a ski resort where he was investigating a crime of passion committed by the cook, "that infidelity on your part would be grounds for divorce? There's a lot of wiggle room in 'grounds.'"

He tried to grin, but it didn't last. They were drinking Scotch, which he always brought along. Marian had been lining up their legs, which were almost exactly the same length, only Joe's were more muscled and dark with hair. "That's like Clinton dismissing oral sex," he said, swirling his drink. "It could squeak by in court but not in anyone's conscience."

"I haven't come up with much else."

He put his hand, the one with the ring, on her thigh, rubbed a damp spot with his thumb. "It's not your job to, counselor," he said.

There would be nothing legally binding about it, of course. Joe could write, *Evidence that I am having an affair with another woman will mean the end of our marriage.* He could write, *On learning that Joe is having sex with another woman, Samantha may choose to end the marriage.* Samantha would spot the slippery language in both those versions. Their condition was the affair's coming to light, not the affair itself, and the second one put the burden of proof on Samantha.

This marriage will continue only on the condition that neither partner has sex with anyone outside the marriage. The second his penis penetrated Marian, Joe's marriage would end. Would he then need to rush home and tell Samantha that their union had ruptured? Could the end of a marriage be one partner's secret?

Marian began to consider Samantha a very clever woman. She was relying on Joe's faithfulness, not to her but to the words he set down on the page.

Twice in January Marian saw Joe, and they didn't mention the contract. Meeting Joe could be tricky business. He drove up her way on short notice, following the news, whereas her days were tightly booked. Marian handled what she labeled "price-tag divorces." It wasn't the prettiest field of law, negotiating settlements between people worth seven figures each, but because these people enjoyed the privilege of contacting their attorney at home, she was likewise able to construct a flexible schedule for herself. Her assistant, Pearl, who had grown children, was sensitive to Marian's need to keep tabs. If she started out of the office without mentioning where she was headed, Pearl was sure to pull out her notepad. "You'll be in range?" she'd say. "You won't forget your four o'clock? Sure you don't want me to have that material faxed?" The surprising thing, Marian sometimes thought, was not that she was morally willing to commit adultery but that she had the brain power left over to concoct the appropriate excuses.

After the second winter rendezvous, two months went by with nothing but e-mails. Joe was covering a murder trial on Cape Cod, a fisherman who'd strangled his boss with fishing twine and thrown him overboard in a net. It was bleak on the Cape. Joe's wife wanted him to drive home every night, ninety miles. *What about the contract?* Marian wrote. Meaning, did he have another lover on the Cape?

We're working on wording, Joe wrote. *If it weren't for you,* he wrote, *I'd have no problem with the thing.*

Meaning he had no other woman, at the moment. Marian found herself grinning as she drove Lisa to practice. "What's so funny, Mom?" Lisa asked. She was a muscular girl who resembled her father; when she lost a match, which she did often enough, she sucked in her lower lip for a long minute, then shrugged and flipped her racquet up.

"Nothing, honey. Just something someone at work said."

"What? Is it a joke?"

"Sort of. A grown-up joke."

"You can tell me," said Lisa. "Dad lets me watch *Seinfeld.*"

"No." Marian worked hard to straighten her mouth. "It's not that funny, really."

Things are better at home, Joe wrote when the Cape Cod trial was over. He was looking for an assignment in New Hampshire. Maybe she had some legal business in Boston?

Did you ever sign that contract? she wrote.

In reply he wrote a very long, funny e-mail about a man who'd been caught slaughtering pigs on his balcony in South Boston and selling the meat. He tacked on a P.S. to say that he missed her hands on his ass and another P.S. to note that things were still pretty smooth at home.

Meaning that Samantha had decided to drop the whole contract idea. Well, it was a stupid idea. Judging from Marian's clients, if you had to resort to a legal document beyond a marriage license to keep your husband from straying, you might as well forget the whole thing.

Of course, Marian didn't know Samantha. She'd heard that Samantha worked with large cold-blooded animals at the Boston Zoo; she was competent and affectionate and came home stinking of snake. Which did not seem to be the source of Joe's compulsive infidelity, though surely it didn't help. Marian pictured Samantha as all the things she wasn't: small, rounded, fair, faithful. Lying awake next to Edward, she thought of Joe's loose, almost hairless testicles resting against his wife's plump thigh.

Spring arrived early in New Hampshire. Mud season came and went in a week. The streams swelled. Crocuses gave way almost instantly to tulips and daffodils, and the trees leafed out dangerously. Edward's schedule—he was a tax attorney, mostly for small businesses—picked up, and Marian cut back to help more at home. By April, despite the e-mails and a couple of office phone calls, she had almost become the woman who had said no. Lisa persuaded her to pound balls together on the town courts as soon as the thermometer went above forty degrees. Kurt broke his arm falling from his bike in the muddy slush, and Edward spent his evenings helping his son write left-handed home-work. When the kids were in bed, Marian and Edward spread out a map of the Canadian Rockies and started sketching a plan that in-volved summer backpacking and sightings of moose. "Younger than springtime are you," Edward sang when she won the state senator's case. "Gayer than laughter are you. Warm as the winds of June are the gentle lips you gave me."

Edward's face was a flawless oval, his ears small, his nose so sharp and firm it seemed to lack cartilage. Approaching to kiss her, he held his mouth slightly open, his tongue already at his lips, so that she thought of being licked by a dog. "Please," she giggled at the song.

"Please what? What can I do to please my brilliant wife? Would you like a nice slow backrub? My hands on your delectable thighs? Hm?"

As if it had happened to a close friend, Marian remembered making love with a man who never praised, never asked how he might please her, who created pleasure with the force of his desire. "Everything you do," she said to Edward, injecting a sultry tone, "makes me feel nice."

The next week her computer brought a note from Joe. He'd landed an assignment, he wrote, a utilities scandal up by Bristol. He would be leaving in the morning, a two-day trip.

Did that give her enough time?

She would think of something, she wrote back. And assigned that task to the woman who had said yes, while she went on with the day's work.

That night the rain started late and changed over to sleet in the small hours. The kids prepared to leave with Edward for school, Kurt hold-ing his plastered arm close to his chest as if the sleet would dissolve it, Lisa lugging her racquet. "Be careful!" Marian said to them.

"This sucks," said Kurt.

"Be over in a day," said Marian.

"In Florida," said Lisa, "they're wearing halters by now."

"In Florida," said Edward, "tax lawyers are the earth's scum."

"So do divorce," said Lisa.

"And leave your lovely mother? Perish the thought," said Edward.

"Dad, I meant . . ." started Lisa, but then she saw him wink at Marian. "Jesus, let's go," she said.

Whistling "April, Come She Will," Edward fitted on his sunglasses, a perverse trick he always pulled when the weather turned gray, as if to fool himself into thinking that the shades were what made the day gloomy. Marian didn't remark. She didn't like to talk much when she was going to see Joe. Each phrase, each bit of daily business, made her aware of the deception. Breathing, she felt a bubble at the center of her chest.

Then her family was gone from the street, and she pulled together papers, snapped off the coffee machine, and took herself to work as if the only disturbance in the day were the stuff coming from the sky. From the office, she phoned Joe at the *Globe*. "Just making sure," she said.

"Weather's lousy, I hear," he said.

"An indoor day." She tried to make her voice sound suggestive, but instead was reminded of a playground aide planning recess.

"We can check in at that little hotel," he said, "at two o'clock."

"The one in the mountains? Is it open?"

"Eager for our business," he said. And then, dropping his voice, "Samantha's on again. About the contract."

"Oh, dear." She sat at her desk. "I haven't come up with a good solution to that," she said. "Have you signed anything?"

"Not . . . well, not really. I've been fiddling with it."

"So bring what you've been fiddling with. I'm a lawyer; I *do* contracts. Maybe we can find something you can live with. I mean, not that I care. But it's important to you."

"Thanks," he said. He sounded edgy.

"So we're still on."

"Oh, yeah. Yeah. As close to two as I can make it."

They hung up. Marian's hands were sweating. She rose and went to the window of her office—six stories up, the highest building in Peterborough. Before, when she had arranged to meet Joe, the confirming phone call had resembled foreplay. She'd known precisely what her alibi was. She'd been living her day already as though the Marian who was not having an affair really *was* going to the law library in Keene or the coffeehouse in Exeter. The Marian who spoke with Joe just before meeting him was usually the shadow Marian, the one who'd said *yes*. Today, though, the sleet had spoiled things. Today, the Marian who had said no had answered the phone, had made the arrangement as if it were an item on the schedule Pearl so carefully kept.

She spent the morning on the phone with an attorney in Portsmouth, hammering out details of a custody arrangement between an airline pilot and his pediatrician wife. She represented the husband, who wanted weekends, summers and holidays; the wife wanted Christmas. The children were two, four and five. She stayed in for lunch. Outside, it had begun to sleet again, the daffodils bending under the weight. Joe was driving north by now. Edward was tucked into his home office, humming through the numbers. At ten minutes past one Marian left a note on Pearl's desk: *Gone shopping, back by four.* She would forget her cell phone. People did sometimes. They wandered off, they got distracted. Such was the stuff of which movies were made. Marian had always worried under the surface about the jobs and families and ordinary futures of the characters in movies, whose lives seemed to happen only when they slacked off.

But she could explain it all away, for this one time.

Ice had crusted on the car. She stood toe-deep in slush in spring shoes and scraped. Around her in the parking lot, people hugged their thin coats, hoisted umbrellas. In the car she turned on both heat and defrost and waited until warm air was blasting her wet toes, then pulled out of the lot and headed east. She had expected, she realized as she paused at the first light, to be stopped—to run into a client, or Pearl asking what on earth she meant, shopping in this weather. *Why, Marian, you never shop!*

The sleet changed over to rain, then back to sleet. Cars were fishtailing in the fast lane. Marian had the windshield wipers going double time, like snake tails lashing. The defroster blew at top heat; the air in the car was like a desert. Here and there cars had pulled over, their drivers huddled inside or seeking shelter at one of the taverns along the way. Bushes in full bloom dragged on the ground like dresses tossed aside. At the Allenbury exit she turned onto Oxbow Road, which wound around a long hill toward the motel. This was what you did. You drove ridiculous distances in awful weather to fuck in a cheap motel and give flimsy excuses about it later. Oh, she loved it. Joe with his sharp chin, Joe with his hand making her damp before she could get her clothes off. The car climbed. The Marian who had said no dropped behind..

And yet. If Edward had asked her. If he had said—which he never would, because he would never know—but if he had said, "Write me a contract," she would have written it in five minutes. And called Joe. And said, "It is over." Who waited for such things? Who could sign such things and go on with the betrayal?

The motel smelled of coffee and carpet cleaner; the lobby was so poorly lit that at first she didn't see Joe, lounging by the hostess bar with a Styrofoam cup. "Hey, beautiful," he called in a low voice.

"Where's your car? Am I late?"

"Around back. No."

"I left my cell phone at the office."

"Clever girl."

She'd approached him and now they kissed, each of them tipping their faces exactly the same amount. Joe had put the cup down and slipped that warm hand under Marian's raincoat to her waist. He was wearing reporter's clothes, brown leather jacket and a loose-weave shirt. "So what's this case?" she asked him.

"Tell you later." He had her hips pulled to him; she could feel his erection. With his free hand he brought forth a slim plastic card. "Room 204," he said. "Same as before."

"Poet," she said. And tried not to be embarrassed by the oblique stare of the small, neatly coiffed woman behind the reception desk as they mounted the stairs at the back of the lobby.

They made love quickly the first time. Marian had worn clothes that were easy to remove, and their bodies coupled as though making sure they still fit. Joe brought out the Scotch and fetched plastic glasses from the bathroom. She liked to watch him move, from behind—the fine set of his hips, his small bare feet. She had come, but so quickly that it seemed an accident, and in her mind's eye she still saw the sleet battering her windshield, the tire marks of skidders on the road. "So tell," she said when they'd clicked cups, the plastic only whispering, "about the contract."

"There's not much to tell." He smiled his roguish smile.

"You didn't bring anything?"

"No."

"You said she was on about it."

"She's been anxious." He paused. "I'm gone so much. We talked about my changing over to editorial."

The Scotch burned down Marian's throat. Water, that's what she'd really like. "You signed it," she guessed. "Didn't you?"

"No!" He swallowed his Scotch, a little too quickly she thought. "Haven't even got the wording hammered out. That's not so important, anyway."

He put his plastic cup down on the pressed-board side table and moved lower on the bed. Taking her foot in his hands, he began to massage the ball and arch. As he bent his head, she could see a bald spot the size of a poker chip. Marian leaned back against the headboard.

"That trial on Cape Cod," he was saying, "was about the bottom of the barrel. I mean, the murderer was schizoid. He should have been in the mental health system a decade ago. And they were all dirt poor and alcoholic except the Hispanics, who aren't really fishermen. They're cocaine runners. I felt slimed, just covering the thing. Knocking out the sensationalist prose, getting it in under the word count." He moved his hands to her Achilles tendon, stretched her calf muscles. "I've got to change my life, Marian," he said.

She was only half listening. The foot felt delicious; the other one waited eagerly for its turn. But something wasn't right. "The contract," she said again. "I mean, are we really talking about a contract?"

He looked up at her dreamily. "Don't be a lawyer," he said.

She shut her eyes. He was doing her toes now. When he'd done both feet they would make love again, more slowly and with greater intent. If Joe was lying, if he had signed a contract, he might have done it yesterday or last week—or last fall even, before they began. He'd meant to break it to her slowly because he wasn't ready to give her up yet. For Joe, a contract with Samantha would imply—for no good and certainly no legal reason—a certain grace period. Before the conditions actually 'locked in. By the end of, say, May, when he was prepared to part from Marian, he would admit to having signed the thing.

On the other hand. He'd taken up the left foot now, thank God, his thumb on the arch. On the other hand, there may have been no contract at all. Neither requested nor proffered. He mentioned such things to women to give himself an escape hatch. When he was ready to end the affair, he counted on his co-conspirator's sense of decency. The minute he claimed he'd actually signed the contract, whatever woman he was with would feel obliged to break off.

"You can tell me you signed it," she said, her eyes shut. "I won't ask about wording."

"Jesus, Marian. Can you just stop about the contract?"

"It's not my contract."

"*Exactly*. I'm trying to tell you something else."

He was, too. Ever since the phone call yesterday, Joe had been trying to tell her something else. Only it was sleeting outside, bending the newly leafed branches, and they might let school out early, and her husband would sing to her, and what was she doing here?

"I can't say yes," said Marian. Unexpectedly her eyes filled with tears.

"I haven't even asked yet," said Joe. He'd let go of her feet, was kissing her legs, moving upward. She reached for her Scotch, finished it.

"I need a drink of water," she said.

"In a minute." He was at her belly now, nipping the tender skin with his teeth.

"I'd rather," she said, letting him pull her flat on the bed, "that there be a contract."

"I'm going to ask you," he murmured against her skin, "to change your life with me."

"I told you. I can't say yes."

"I haven't asked yet."

He turned her over onto her belly. Against the warm sheets all the places he'd nipped her were buzzing. He moved down and licked between her buttocks. She looked at the wide, low window—they hadn't drawn the curtains, nothing but woods outside—where sleet still flung itself. Lisa, she thought. Kurt. Edward. As if they were out there somewhere, slogging through the cold muck, the downed branches. People she knew, who knew her, the other Marian. Then Joe's penis was between her buttocks, his hand on her breast.

"No," she said.

"It's new for me, too," he said. She heard for the first time the fear in his voice. His cock pushed forward a little. She clenched, then released, and the tip of his shaft entered her.

She was fucking Joe. Joe was fucking her. There either was a contract or there wasn't. She would let him do anything, those were the terms. It made no difference, no obvious difference, in the rest of her life. Marian repeated these phrases to herself while Joe kissed her between her shoulder blades. Then he pushed in further, and began moving.

She groaned. She didn't form any words. His hand moved down, between her legs, and one finger went inside her where his cock wasn't, while the others moved among the folds of her labia, her clitoris. He pushed his penis in further, moving, really fucking her there now, and a queer taste filled her mouth, and she wasn't even sure she was Marian any more, and with a shock she came. Only then, after a few more thrusts, did he pull out—he had gone deeper than she thought—and spilled warm across her lower back, with a catch in his throat as he let go, and his gamey fingers in her mouth where her lips held them.

They lay hot on the white sheets. After a minute, Joe rose and went again to the bathroom, and came back with a plastic cup filled with water. Marian drank, the strange taste still in her mouth. Then she lay on her back. On Joe's thigh, her hand barely trembled. He was not handsome, she thought. His face wore its lines hard. In late middle age he would take to combing hair over his bald spot, giving attention to his sloping forehead, his hook nose, the creases in his neck.

"I don't have an assignment in New Hampshire," he said. "I wrote a contract and then tore it up. I left Samantha."

Marian didn't say anything. Clumsily, propped on an elbow, she finished off the water. If "left" meant "was kicked out by," there was nothing in Joe's Scotch-roughened voice (he would never sing to her) that called his innocent, clever wife to account. Raising herself up, Marian put her arms around Joe. There was no difference between his smell and hers, both of them violated and rank and intimate.

"Did I hurt you?" he asked.

Against his shoulder Marian shook her head, but then had to say it. "No, Joe," she said.

"No what?"

He was a person now, to her. That was the awful part. "You didn't hurt me," she confessed. And felt with the intensity of a spring storm how she would drive back down the mountain, tires slipping, unable to resist the sleeted road that ran between no and yes.

Lucy Ferriss is the author of four novels, most recently *The Misconceiver*.

THE COLD WAR / *Eric Pankey*

My mother nods off. A lit cigarette
Elegant between her long fingers.
The arm of the divan riddled with burns.

Lightning, out of sync, preens the maple.

What is the square root of *yesterday*?
How did I solve for the door ajar?
There's no end to it, my father would say.

My mother nods off. A lit cigarette
Elegant between her long fingers.
The burns like islands on an oily sea,

The obsolete map of an archipelago
Where the Bomb was tested year after year.
There's no end to it, my father would say

And ask me to warm up his drink.
The unknown, the variable we call *it*.
Upholstery smoulders more than it flames.

Lightning, out of sync, preens the maple.

BYGONES / *Eric Pankey*

What is the past but everything:
The *not-there* between memory
And foreground, between suffering
And a moment's hardened amber?
Still, each word gives way to silence
And I must reinscribe this scrawl,
This impermanent graphite ghost
As signature on these torn scraps.
In the end I will be voiceless.
The earth that held me down will hold
Me once again, unforgiven,
Without a plea. Once, I listened
And heard far off the fire break
Ignite with the song of crickets.
I heard a cold wind at loose ends
In the brambles and witch hazel.
I heard my brother say his prayers,
Not as rehearsed words enacted,
But with a child's solemnity.
I heard the snap of a dog's jaw,
The thud when the truck knocked it down.
I heard the refrain, *I ain't got*
No home in this world anymore,
Stuck as these lines stick in my mind,
But the rest of the song was lost:
Each unsaid word driven in edgewise,
A silence etched by burin and acid.

THE ANNIVERSARY / *Eric Pankey*

1.

The constellation Virgo harbors a black hole at its center, but tonight I see the moon, ordained, a basilica of salt, mouthing its one secret like a saw-whet owl, and all that might be culled, collected, and classified beneath it, named as a disposition of objects, as a taxonomy, an order, a genus, or subject matter, is smeared with this salvaged and chalk-dry light, this fine- grained and corrosive distillate, this heirloom dust that gathers on the pearl button of the glove, its little satin noose.

2.

When I said, "But tonight I see the moon," I did not tell the whole truth, for I have not even looked outside, but have relied on the conventions of memory, and with a word or two the moon, like a body under siege, wears thin outside my window, the moon forages in the attic, the moon is hauled up like a broken whetstone from a well, for that is what I do with a word or two: avoid scrutiny, avoid measuring the lead weight of my own heart.

CENOTAPH / *Eric Pankey*

1.

In the shallow domain of light's fitful flare,
An aviary of silt and minutia drifts:
Pinpoints of citron, lilac, and sulfur,

Chips of shell-pink, a medusa's plume and ruff,
Coral cleaved and sundered, its dust offcast,
A constellation untied from its mooring.

How close the splintered sun that bracelets my wrist.
I reach down through to the edge of my seeing,
Beyond the fan vaulting of bladder wrack,

Through eel grass, through fallow shadow realms,
But I cannot pull you back to the surface,
You who are the body of confession,
The cold weight of water that unearths a grave.

2.

The night above you is a capsized hull:
No air finds its way through the caulked seams.
How long did the crescent moon trawl in the wake?

How long before the wake itself collapsed?
Before *North* and *South* held the same compass point,
Marked the same unfathomable distance home?

Nothing can hold the body for long.
Burned by salt's caustic, ropes would frazzle
And a canvas shroud, rived and flayed,

Would let loose the dark matter of its cargo,
Thus I offer only provisional words:

Each a winding sheet of reef wind and white wash,
Each a tattered disguise for the travesty.

3.

From a distilled essence of quartz and rose,
From a gramarye of psalms and waves,
From strewn stones and a hazel rod,

I have built this empty tomb for you.
Let its fretwork of shadows be your raiment.
Let thunder's phosphor light your way.

Grief is weightless and hard-shelled
Like a seed carried on an updraft,
A seed set down on hostile soil.

I have built this empty tomb for you,
Which the tide will bury and not exhume.
Sleep as silt sleeps in its dark fall and depth.
Sleep as silt sleeps in its dark fall and depth.

UNDERDRAWING / *Eric Pankey*

The wind-brindled marsh surface,
The dunes overthrown by flood tide,
The length of Salt Island Road to its dead end,

Are now a charcoal stain burnt beneath zinc and titanium,
The abandoned gestures of a night's edge.
Nonetheless, a fish hawk hunkers beneath the downpour:

A smudge beyond the blown rain, a ragged effigy
Of nothing I can honestly name. Yet in my idleness,
I ravel the hermeneutics of talon and wingspan,

Of updrafts, windsheer, and angles of descent.
I wipe the glass, but it fogs again. I wipe the glass,
But soon cannot see through the marks my hand has left.

TO THE MAGPIE ON THE ROOF OF THE MANGER / *Eric Pankey*

You hid each star but one in a shallow shadow box,
A relic-filled cabinet of curiosities,

And let the wind rifle the tinder. And let the wind
Refurbish the straw, the stalls, and the dovecote's
niches.

What happens to a moment held captive, a moment
Torn away, ransacked from the dull continuum?

In your beak, you hold a marble in which the
world—
Shrunken, drawn long, upside down—is as round as
this world

That deceives us with horizons and vanishing points,
The parallel rows of grapes that touch in the distance,

The *far away* where all is drawn together at last.
From here, I can even see myself in the marble—

Bent, distorted, the sky below me a blue pit
Over which I hang headfirst, confused like the damned.

Eric Pankey's fifth collection of poetry, *Cenotaph*, is due out in January 2000.

SCIOTO BLUES/*Bill Roorbach*

IF YOU MOVE TO COLUMBUS, Ohio, from Farmington, Maine (as I did three years ago to take a job at Ohio State), you will not be impressed by the landscape. It's flat there—as I write I'm back in Maine, escaped from Ohio for a third summer straight—and the prairie rivers move sluggish and brown. In Maine you pick out the height of flood on, say, the Sandy River by the damage to tree trunks and the spookily exact plane made by ice and roaring current tearing off the lowest branches of riverside trees. In Columbus you pick out the height of flood on the Olentangy or Scioto Rivers by the consistent plane attained by 10,000 pieces of garbage, mostly plastic bags, caught in tree branches.

Always in the months after I moved, I was looking for a place to run my dogs, Wally and Desmond, who are Maine country dogs used to the unlimited woods. We started on a subsidiary athletic field at Ohio State—long, kick-out-the-jams gallops across mowed acres, lots of barking and rumbling—then leashes to cross Olentangy Boulevard and a parking lot, so to the Olentangy River (my students call it the Old and Tangy), where "the boys" swam hard just across from the Ohio Stadium, known as the Shoe, in which the football Buckeyes famously play.

By the time the U. started building the gargantuan new basketball arena in the middle of our running field, the dogs and I had found Whetstone Park, a big urban preserve a couple of miles upstream, just across the river from Highway 315, which at that point is a six-lane, limited-access highway. Really, Whetstone's a lovely place, well kept, used in multiple ways, though not much in winter, always the sounds of 315 in the air like a mystical waterfall with diesel power and gear changes. There are athletic fields, a goldfish pond, picnic areas, tennis and basketball courts, an enormous and important rose collection in a special area called Park of the Roses, just one section (about three miles) of an all-city bike path, tetherball, speed bumps, a library branch (in satisfying possession of my books) and fishing spots on the Olentangy River.

Which runs through Whetstone after a scary trip through a couple of suburban towns (Route 315 its constant companion), through a dozen new developments and several parks, past at least six shopping malls. Indeed, the detritus at its banks in Whetstone is emphatically suburban. Plastic grocery and other store bags of course dominate, festooning the trees in various colors, the worst of which is the sort of pinky brown that some stores use in a pathetic attempt to imitate the good old kraft paper of the now fading question, "Paper or plastic?" The best colors are red and blue, because at least there's that moment of thinking you see a rare bird. Garbage bags are part of the mix, too, but heavier so lower in the trees.

Plastic soft-drink bottles come next in sheer numbers. These things float best when someone upriver has put the cap back on before they're flung out of a car window. Or perhaps not flung but only left beside a car in a parking lot along with a neat pile of cigarette butts from the emptied car ashtray. Come to think of it, these bottles are probably seldom thrown directly into the river. Their walls are thin, so plastic bottles aren't always the long-distance travelers you'd think. Cracks let water in, and silt. The bottles don't end up often in trees, either, because they are light enough and smooth enough for the wind to knock them free. They are everywhere.

Tires occupy their own category and come in two sorts: with and without wheels. Those with wheels are heavy, but float, so they end up high on logjams and in trees; those without wheels get caught up in the silt and mud and form strange, ring-shaped silt islands or, buried deeper, show just a little tread as part of a sand bar.

Next are car parts other than tires. Like bumpers and doors and hoods. These must be dumped at riverbanks, is my guess, off the edges of parking lots built too close to the water, then carried by floods. Occasionally, too, a whole car gets into the water and slowly demonstrates the second law of thermodynamics: all things seek randomness. Entropy continues its work, and the car spreads downstream.

Aerosol containers make a strong showing in the river, those former dispensers of paint and freon and deodorant and foot spray and whipped cream and so forth. Indestructibly happy bobbers, these canisters are capable of long trips, clear to the Gulf of Mexico, I'm sure, and before long into the oxygen-free, Lake Erie–sized dead zone the Gulf now boasts. But some do get up high in tree crotches and last there for years—decades if they're of stainless steel. WD-40 as a product gets a special mention here, for the paint on the outside and the oil film on the inside keep these cans alive and recognizable for years, wherever they roam.

Newspaper and other print matter turns up but disappears just as fast, leaching what it leaches into the water. A special category of printed matter that I ought to mention is pornography, which I often find high and dry, the park being its entry point into the river. *Juggs* was one magazine I happened across. It had many photos in it of women who'd had obviously harrowing operations. Also, some kind of trading cards that featured various young women naked. These I discovered clipped neatly by the bark flaps of a shaggy hickory at the eye level of a large adolescent or small man, footprints and dribbles beneath, the whole gallery abandoned after the riparian onanist had done his work.

Other items: prescription medicine bottles, but not in abundance; mattresses, common, usually appearing as skeleton only, that is, the springs; pens of endless varieties, mostly ballpoint, ubiquitous, some working; twisted shopping carts; tampon tubes of pink plastic made by Johnson and Johnson (plenty of these, from flushes, giving lie to the idea that sewage is well managed upstream); guard rails; lengths of rope of various types; lengths of cable, mostly Romex; joint-compound buckets (but these are fast fillers and sinkers and join the silt banks permanently with their tire friends and broken glass bottles).

Glass. Any glass that turns up, except tempered, as in windshields, at least turns back to sand, squandering its legacy of power and fire. The rare complete glass bottle with lid does float by, but these are goners, baby; first rock they encounter and it's *smash*, step one toward beach glass for kids to find. Eyeglasses you'd think would be rare, but just in the last year I've found three pair, lenses intact.

Planks. Now, planks hardly count, being trees, but often planks have nails, which hardly count, either, come to think of it, being iron. Then again, planks are often painted, so they do add to the color stream— what's that purple? What's that turquoise? A bright yellow board I once saw up in a willow, was particularly startling.

Pieces of Styrofoam are important in this trash system. There are blue pieces often enough, occasionally green, but white is most common. Everywhere are the tiny cells that make up the product—billions of bright spheres, with samples worked into every handful of mud. Cups, sure, but these don't last long. Coolers predominate. Then chunks, which must come from packing materials. Then even bigger chunks, unexplained on the Olentangy, though nowhere as big as the huge chunks found on beaches on the seacoast in Maine, parts of boats or floats or who knows what. And oh, yes, speaking of beach flotsam, boat parts are common too, even on rivers, and even in the Olentangy. Fiberglass boards, not too big, or rowboat seats, or canoe prows, rarely. This is not a sport river.

Though there are fishermen, and there are fish. Catfish and bass, most notably. The fishermen leave their own class of trash: broken fishing rods; lots of line tangled in branches above; bobbers hanging from power lines; lead sinkers. Lead is poisonous, of course, so a special mention. Also lures sometimes, hanging as well. Or just plain hooks in a branch, with dried-up worms. Left by little boys, mostly, though lots of retired men like to fish the river. Also men who don't look old enough to retire, maybe some of those guys who have I'd Rather Be Fishing bumper stickers on their bumpers.

The fisherfolk also leave packaging for hooks and snells and bait and so forth. American Eagle is one of the brand names you see frequently in the mud. And Styrofoam bait cups are just everywhere, their lids not far behind, these packed by local concerns, sometimes with an address printed along with the logo so that I can mail the shit back to them (yes, I'm a crank). They may not be responsible for their customers, but they should care where their names turn up.

Some of the other garbage comes with brand names, too: Budweiser, Wendy's, Kmart, Big Bear, Dow Chemical, General Electric, Goodyear, to name just a few. All these big names sticking up out of the mud! It's like some apocalyptic ad campaign!

Now for the less tangible. Apart from the major chunks in the Old and Tangy River, there is the smell, and the smell must come from somewhere. It's not horrible or anything, not even pervasive, but when the dogs get out of the river there's not only the usual river smell—mud and oxygen and hydrogen and fish and pungent organic rot—there's something else, one notch below healthy on the dial. My amateur analysis is as follows: equal parts motor oils, fertilizers and straight human shit. Also shampoo and detergent, the faintest sickening edge of perfume.

Which leads me to the foam, good bubbly stuff that can stack up to two or three feet high and is sometimes wishfully called "fish foam." But fish foam hasn't the density of suds, not at all, and smells like fish rather than perfume.

I mean, the river is a junkfest.

That's the Olentangy before it gets to campus, and before it gets to the large skyscraper downtown of Columbus. And Columbus is big—bigger than you think, an Emerald City that pops up on the prairie. It's the biggest city in Ohio, population about 1.25 million inside the Greater Columbus loop of I-270. The city's official slogan should be It's Not That Bad, since that's what people tell you, over and over. I think the actual civic slogan is More Than You Dreamed. True. And that huge school where I've just gotten tenure: 60,000 students, 15,000 staff, 5,000 faculty. Something like that. A city within the city. The Olentangy flows right through campus, unassaulted except by lawn chemicals and parking-lot runoff and frequent beer vomit on its way to the Scioto.

Columbus's two main rivers meet at Confluence Park. This is not really a park at all but some kind of convention or catering facility on city land, probably the result of all kinds of inside deals. I took the dogs there once in my early search for dog-walking paradises. Confluence Park was hard to find. There are so many roads crisscrossing each other and exit ramps and overpasses that you pass the place ten times before you get to it, a scavenger hunt of signage, and then when you finally get there, it's just another parking lot next to the river. Oh, and the catering facility and its big dumpsters overflowing with whatever party has just come through, making someone a nice private profit on public land, is my guess. And meanwhile, plentiful homeless people have pulled all the liquor bottles out of the dumpsters for years, getting those last drops, then creating a midden of broken glass down along the water. No park at all, just a steep, rocky, trash-strewn embankment forming a point of land where our two protagonist rivers mightily meet, the greater silt carry of the Olentangy coloring the greater water volume of the Scioto. Here the Olentangy gives up its name, and the two are one: Scioto.

Which flows through the big city under several bridges, looking like the Seine in Paris (the Seine is a dead river, by the way, fishless, oxygenless, killed, unlike the Scioto). But the Scioto is not a navigable river like the Seine; the Scioto's only four feet deep and heavily ensilted. I won't say much about the replica of the Santa Maria that floats here, trapped in a specially dredged corner under the Broad Street bridge in a 500-year anniversary testament to a man who never reached the Midwest but gave his name to our fair city nevertheless.

Anyway, just below town the river pillows over a containment dam a couple of hundred yards wide, a very pretty fall, really, the funny river smell coming up, men fishing, bums and bummettes and bumminas lounging, bike path twisting alongside, highway bridges, rail bridges, turtles on the warm rocks in spring, egrets, herons, seagulls, swans, kingfishers, beavers, muskrats, rats.

And no dearth of trees to catch the trash after flood! Maple, ash, cherry, gum, walnut, oak, locust, sycamore—on and on, dominated thoroughly by cottonwoods, which in the spring leave a blanket of cottony seed parachutes in a layer like snow.

The parks once you pass below the city are a little tawdry—poorly cared for, placed near the police impoundment lot and the railroad yards and light industry and a complicated series of unused cement ponds that once surely were meant as a sewage-treatment facility. Oh, also in sight of the practice tower for the fire department, which trainers douse with kerosene and burn for the recruits to put out.

On the northeast bank of the river is Blowjob Park, as one of my students called it in a paper, which I found because it is at the very end of the bike path. The path ends at a parking lot where lonely and harmless-looking men sit in cars gazing at each other and waiting for liaisons. The city sometimes arrests these men in courageless raids, not a homophobic act, says a spokesperson, for the men are said not to be gay exactly, but married guys looking for action of any kind, loitering and littering and certainly dangerous so close to the impound lot and the defunct sewage-treatment plant.

When I moved downtown, downriver, to German Village, a turn-of-the-century neighborhood—now trendy—of brick buildings, restaurants and shops surrounded by what some Columbusites have called slums in warning me, but which are just further neighborhoods, with less and less money apparent, true, but with plenty of lively children and sweet gardens and flashes of beauty along with the ugliness (which isn't much worse than the general ugliness that pervades this prairie city and its suburbs) . . . when I moved downtown, I brought the dogs over there for a walk and a swim, two of their favorite activities. Down below the dam, I nodded to men fishing, and the dogs raced happily, and it wasn't bad. You go down below the dam and the riverbank is broad and walkable in dry times—this first walk was in autumn—and you see good trees, remnants of the hardwood forest, and chunks of concrete under the Greenlawn Avenue bridge and rebar wire and yes, examples of all the junk listed above, particularly those plastic grocery bags in the trees, but fifty-five-gallon drums as well, and broken lawn chairs used for comfort by fishermen and abandoned when beyond hope. Also some real dumping—an exploded couch, perhaps thrown off the high bridge, and some kind of switchboard with wires dangling, and a filing cabinet with drawers labeled Contracts, Abstracts, Accounts Payable and Personnel. It would not take much, I thought at the time, to figure out what local business all this came from. Might be fun to return it, but a lot of work. And probably they paid some asshole to cart the stuff to the dump, some asshole who kept the dump fee and emptied his truck off the Greenlawn Avenue bridge.

And down there too was the large concrete bastion of a culvert, labeled with a sign: Caution, Combined Sewer Overflow. In other words, when it rains, get out of the way. And if you think Combined Sewer Overflow just means rainwater washed off parking lots, listen: in the rich, dried mud right exactly there, the dogs and I hiked through 1,000, no, 10,000, plants I recognized (and you would recognize, too, at once) as tomato vines. How did so many tomato plants get sown? Well, tomato seeds don't readily digest, generally pass through the human digestive tract unscathed. You get the picture.

And the doggies and I walked that sweet fall day. After the bridge it was hard going, a rocky bank strewn with valueless trash, but also bedding and clothes, particularly male underwear for some reason. It wasn't too pleasant, and getting steep, so I turned back, but not before noting that across the river there was much parklike land, sandy soils under great canopy trees. Dog paradise. How to get there?

Wally and Desmond and I hiked back to the car, drove over the Greenlawn Avenue bridge (it looked very different from above), and found the entrance to what is called Berliner Park. I was excited. There were baseball fields and a basketball dome and a paved bike path along the river (a discontinuous section, as it turned out, of the Olentangy bicycle trail that also passes through Whetstone Park, mentioned before), and many footpaths to the water.

In the woods along the river there was the familiar trash, of course, multiplied enormously by the location just below the city and just below the dam. Here's how it gets there: rain falls, perhaps during one of the many thunderstorms Columbus enjoys. The parking lots puddle, then begin to flow, carrying gasoline and oil and antifreeze of course, but also cigarette butts and cigarette packs, chaw containers, pop bottles, aerosol cans and many tires, just simply whatever is there. The light stuff gets to the river fast. Tires move a few feet per rainstorm, but they eventually make their ways to the river or get stuck trying. Shopping carts probably have to be actually thrown in, but shopping bags get there two ways—flow and blow. Kids' toys are carried downstream just like anything else. And what can't float waits for a flood. Anything can ride a flood! Anything at all!

It's a mess. In fact, the part of Berliner that lies along the river is so bad that most people just won't hang out there. That leaves it open to what I call lurkers, men who lurk in the trees and know that my two dogs mean I'm a dog walker and not a lurker, and so not to approach. My dogs have even learned to ignore them, and I have, too. To each his own.

Except for the one lunkhead who threw a rock in the path in front of my wife, but he seemed just developmentally delayed, not malicious, and with the dogs along, gentle Juliet felt safe enough but hurried up out of his purview.

And once I found a note—poignant and plaintive, a personal ad aimed directly at its market, pinned to a log: "Loking for love. Grate Sex. Call me up or meat heer, meet hear."

During one of our weekly phone talks, I told my mother about Berliner and all the trash. She said, Well, why don't you and a couple of your friends get together and go in there and clean it up?

She's right, of course. It's easy to complain and not do anything. But,

Jesus, the flow of garbage is so great that my friends and I would need to work full time till retirement to keep up just with the one park. Perhaps the city could hire a river keeper. I do pick up this bottle and that can, and fill a bag now and again. It's the least I can do. Yes, the least. Okay, I'm implicated here, too.

Downstream a little farther there's another storm-sewer runoff warning and the vile smell of unadulterated, uncomposted shit. The bike path goes on. It's not a bad walk once you are past the stench, which takes a minute because there is also a honey-truck dump station right there, which you can see from the path, a kind of long pit where the septic-tank-pumping trucks unload. This stuff has a more composted reek, a little less septic, so there's no danger of puking or anything. The dogs run on, free of their leashes because there isn't ever anybody around here except lurkers. The dogs have no interest whatsoever in lurkers, and they love nothing more than a good stink. The path ends at a six-lane highway spur-and-exit complex, but not before passing a stump dump and a wrecking yard, 10,000 or so crashed cars in piles. Also a funny kind of graveyard for things of the city: highway signs, streetlight poles, unused swimming rafts, traffic cones. It's not too inviting under the highway bridge; it's frightening in fact, but if you keep going there's a fire ring and much soggy bedding, a bum stop, and above you, up the bank and past a fence or two, the real city dump.

Here we (dogs, Juliet, myself) most commonly turn around and head back. I guess I'd be hard-pressed to convince anyone that it's not that bad walking here. Really, it's not that bad. The dogs love it. But they do get burrs, and Wally, the big dope, insists on diving into the reeking storm-sewer runoff, so we have to make him swim extra when we get upstream, where the water's cleaner. And note: the city's been working on the pump house. Lots of new valves and stuff, and the smell is really much less, if just as bad. I mean, I'm not saying no one cares.

It's a nice place under the crap. The trees are still trees. Up in the trees, the Carolina wrens are still Carolina wrens. And the wildflowers are still wildflowers even if they grow from an old chest of drawers. And the piles of stumps are pretty cool to look at. And the great mounds of concrete from demolition projects, too, reminding me a little of Roman ruins. And the sky is still the sky, and the river flows by below with the perfection of eddies and boils and riffles and pools. And the herons are still herons, and squawk. And the sound of the highway is not so different from the sound of the wind (except for the screeching and honking and sputtering). And the lights of the concrete plant are like sunset. And the train whistle is truly plaintive and romantic, and the buildings of the city a mile upstream are like cliffs, and I've heard that peregrine falcons have been convinced to live there. And the earth is the earth; it is always the earth. And the sun is the sun, and shines. And the stars are the stars, and the sliver of the waxing moon appears in the evening, stench or no, and moves me. So don't think I'm saying it's all bad. It's not. I'm only saying that the bad part is *really* bad.

One fine blue day after much spring rain, Juliet and I in joy take the dogs down to Berliner Park, oh, early spring when the trees are still bare (but budded) and all the world is at its barest and ugliest, every flake of the forest floor, every fleck of litter and offal visible, and the turtles are not yet up from the mud.

We get out of the car next to a pile of litter someone has jettisoned from their car (Burger King gets a nod here, and Marlboro), and walk down the dike through old magazines and condoms to the dam to watch the high water of spring roaring over. In fact, the normal fifteen-foot plunge is now only two feet, and the water comes up clear to the platform where we normally stand high over the river to look, laps at our toes. There are boiling eddies and brown storms of water and the unbelievable force of all that water smoothly raging over the dam at several feet deep and twenty miles an hour. You would die fast in that water, not because it is so very cold but because of the supercomplex and violent pattern of flow.

Juliet and I stare through the high chain-link and barbed-wire fence into the boiling maelstrom, absorb the roar wholly, lose our edges to the cool breezes flung up and the lucky charge all around us of negative ions as molecules are battered apart by this greatest force of nature: water unleashed. It's a moment before we see the flotsam trap, where an eddy returns anything that floats—anything—back to the dam and the blast of the falling river. And the falling river forms a clean foaming cut the length of the dam, a sharp line, a chasm; the river falls so hard and so fast that it drops under itself. Great logs are rolling at the juncture. Whole tree trunks, forty feet long, polished clean of bark and branches. Entire trees, a score or more, dive and roll and leap and disappear, then pop into the daylight like great whales sounding, float peacefully to the wall of water, which spins them lengthwise fast or sinks them instantly, and disappear only to appear twenty feet down-river, sounding again, all but spouting, roaring up out of the water, ten, fifteen feet into the sky, only to fall back. Humpback whales they are, slapping and parting the water, floating purposefully again to the dam. It's an astonishing sight, objects so big under such thorough control and in such graceful movement, trees that in life only swayed and finally, after a century or two of wind and bare winters, fell at river's edge.

And then I see the balls. At least five basketballs, and many softballs, and two soccer balls, and ten dark pink and stippled playground balls and forty littler balls of all colors and sizes, all of them bobbing up to the wall of water, rolling, then going under, accompanied by pop bottles of many hues and Styrofoam pieces and aerosol cans, polished. And a car tire with wheel, floating flat. This old roller hits the wall of water and bounces away slightly, floats back, bounces away, floats back, bounces away, floats back, is caught, disappears. Even the dogs love watching. They *love* balls, especially Wally, and are transfixed.

The tire reappears long seconds after its immersion, many yards away, cresting like a dolphin. Logs pop out of the water like titanic fishes, diving at the dam head-up the way salmon do (in fact, you see in the logs how salmon accomplish their feats: they use the power of the eddy, swim hard with the backcurrent, leap—even a log can do it!) among froth and playground balls and tires and bottles with caps on, balls and bottles and tires ajumble, reds and blues and yellows and pinks and purples and greens and blacks, bottles and aerosol cans and balls, balls and tires and logs and tree trunks and chunks of Styrofoam, all leaping and feinting and diving under and popping up and reappearing in colors not of the river: aquas and fuchsias and metallics, WD-40 blue and Right Guard gold and polished wood and black of tire and crimson board and child's green ball and pummeled log and white seagulls hovering, darting for fish brought to the tortured surface in the chaos of trash and logs and toys, all of it bobbing, the logs diving headfirst at the dam, the balls rolling and popping free of the foam for airborne flights, and tires like dolphins, and softballs fired from the foam, and polished logs, and a babydoll body, all of it rumbling, caught in the dam wash for hours, days, nights of flood, rumbling and tumbling and popping free, rolling and diving and popping free, bubbling and plunging and popping free.

Bill Roorbach is the 1999 winner of the Flannery O'Connor Award in Short Fiction. His work has appeared previously in *The Missouri Review*.

THE INTENTIONAL DECEPTION/
Anton Chekhov, translated by Peter Sekirin

ZAKHAR KUZMICH DIADECHKIN was having a New Year's party. The idea was to celebrate both New Year's Eve and the birthday of Malania Tikhonovna, his wife and the mistress of the house.

Many people were there. All of them were serious, respectful and sober; not one scoundrel among them. All wore pleasant expressions and held respect for their own dignity. Some were sitting in the living-room, on a long sofa covered with cheap vinyl. The landowner, Gusev, and the owner of the nearest grocery store, Razmakhalov, were there. They spoke about bribery and drink.

"It's so hard to find a man," said Gusev, "who doesn't drink nowadays, a serious man. It's hard to find a man like that."

"And the most important thing, Alexei Vasilievich, is law and order."

"There must be law and order. Right here at home, so many bad things are happening. How can you establish law and order?"

Three old women were sitting in a half-circle around them, looking at the men's mouths with amazement. They looked, astonished and awed, at the two men talking about such clever things. Gury Markovich, their in-law, was sitting in the corner of the room, looking at icons. Suddenly, a soft noise came from the lady's bedroom. There, some younger boys and a girl were playing bingo. The bet was one kopeck. Kolya, a first-year high school student, was standing next to the table, crying. He wanted to play bingo, but the other children would not let him. Why should a young boy play if he did not have a kopeck?

"Don't cry, fool! Why are you crying? I think your mother should beat you."

"I have beaten him enough," sounded the mother's voice from the kitchen, "you bad boy. Varvara Gurievna, pull him by the ear."

Two young girls in pink sat on the mistress' bed, which was covered with a cotton blanket that had lost its original color. A man, twenty-three years old, sat in front of them, a clerk from the insurance company. His name was Kopalsky, and his face reminded one of a cat. He was flirting with them.

"I am never going to marry," he said, looking dashing and adjusting the tightly fixed collar on his shirt. "A woman is a wonderful thing for a man, but at the same time she can ruin him!"

"But what about men? Men can't fall in love. They can only . . ."

"You are so naive! I don't want to be cynical, but I happen to know that men stand much higher than women when it comes to love."

Mr. Diadechkin and his elder son, Grisha, were pacing from one corner of the room to another, looking like two wolves in a cage. They were burning with impatience. They had already had a couple of drinks at dinner before, and now they wanted another. Diadechkin went to the kitchen. There, the mistress of the house was covering a pie with powdered sugar.

"Malasha, the guests would like some more snacks to be served," said Diadechkin.

"They'll have to wait. If you eat and drink everything now, what am I going to serve at midnight? You can wait. Get out of the kitchen and don't get in my way."

"Can I have just one small shot, Malasha? You won't even notice it."

"What a man! Out of the kitchen! Out! Go talk to our guests! You're not wanted here, in the kitchen."

Diadechkin went out and looked at the clock. It showed only eight minutes after eleven. There were fifty-two minutes before the long-awaited moment. The waiting was terrible! Waiting for a drink is one of the worst things. It is better to wait for a train for five hours outside in the snow than it is to wait for a drink for five minutes. Diadechkin looked angrily at the clock, took a few steps across the room, and moved the big hand five minutes ahead. And what about Grisha? Grisha was thinking that if he did not get a drink then he would have to go to the pub and drink by himself. He was not ready for that.

"Mother," he said, "the guests are upset that you're not serving them any treats. This is no good. You want to starve them to death? Give them a shot."

"Wait for it! It's coming soon! Don't hang around in the kitchen!"

Grisha slammed the kitchen door noisily and went to look at the clock for the hundredth time. The big arm was merciless; it was almost at the same spot.

"This clock is slow," Grisha said to himself, and moved the big hand seven minutes forward.

Later, Kolya was running past the clock. He looked at it and started to calculate the time. He was waiting for the moment when they would start crying "Hurray," but the hand of the clock seemed to be motionless. He got very upset; he climbed the chair, looked around furtively and stole five more minutes from eternity.

"Do you want to see what time it is now? I am dying with impatience," said one of the young ladies to Kopalsky. "The new year is approaching, and it brings us new hopes and new happiness." Kopalsky made a bow and ran to the clock.

"Oh my goodness," he murmured, standing by the clock. "It is such a long wait, and I am so hungry. I can't wait to kiss Katya, as soon as they cry 'Hurray!'" Kopalsky came back, then returned to the clock and shortened the old year by ten minutes. Diadechkin drank two glasses of water, but the burning inside did not stop. He paced around all the rooms. Every time he went into the kitchen, his wife pushed him out. The bottles standing on the window were tearing his soul apart. What should he do? He had no power to resist. He jumped at his last chance. He went into the children's room to the clock, but he saw a scene that disturbed his heart. Grisha was standing in front of the clock moving the minute hand.

"What are you doing? You fool! Why are you touching the clock?" Diadechkin wrinkled his forehead and cleared his throat. "What are you doing? Nothing? Then get out." He pushed his son away from the clock and moved the big hand a little forward.

"There, now there are 11 minutes until the New Year." Grisha and his father went to the hall and started setting the table.

"Malasha, the New Year is coming!" Diadechkin cried to his wife.

Malania Tikhonovna came out from the kitchen to check the time. She looked carefully at the clock. Her husband had not lied to her. "What am I going to do?" she whispered. "The peas for the ham are still sitting in the oven raw. What am I going to do? How can I serve it?"

Then, after a short pause, Malania Tikhonovna moved the clock backwards with a trembling hand. The old year received another twenty minutes back.

"They can wait," said the woman, and returned to the kitchen.

Peter Sekirin has published a biography of Dostoevsky and two translations of major works by Tolstoy. Another Chekhov story translation appeared previously in *The Missouri Review*.

Daniel Woodrell

Daniel Woodrell is the author of six novels, including *Under the Bright Lights, Woe to Live On, Muscle for the Wing, The Ones You Do, Give Us a Kiss* and most recently *Tomato Red,* for which he received the PEN Center West Award for the Novel. *Woe to Live On* grew out of his first published story of the same title, which originally appeared in *The Missouri Review.* It has since been made into the motion picture *Ride With the Devil,* directed by Ang Lee and starring Skeet Ulrich, Tobey McGuire and the singer Jewel. His other novels have earned numerous honors and awards as well, with three of them being named to the *New York Times* Notable Books of the Year list.

Born in the Ozarks in 1953, Woodrell was a high school dropout before joining the Marine Corps. After the marines, he worked at several manual labor jobs until eventually receiving his MFA from the University of Iowa. He has currently returned to the area of his family roots and lives in West Plains, Missouri, with his wife, writer Katie Estill. This interview was conducted by Kay Bonetti, Director of the American Audio Prose Library, in the summer of 1999 in Columbia, Missouri.

An Interview with Daniel Woodrell / *Kay Bonetti*
edited for print by Jo Sapp

Interviewer: I see ties in your work both to the Ozarks in Missouri and also a city that sounds suspiciously like St. Charles, Missouri. Are there connections? How much of the geography of St. Bruno is St. Charles?

Woodrell: St. Bruno has things in common with several places that actually exist. It's overwhelmingly comprised of fictional aspects, but the general notion of it is influenced by the north side of St. Charles. The geography is similar. The fictional town is much bigger than the actual town. It's as St. Charles was when I left there in 1968. The street that is now the tourist street is where we used to go and get winos to buy booze for us when we were twelve or thirteen. They used to live in the coal bins back there behind those buildings.

Interviewer: You grew up there?

Woodrell: Yes. I was born in the Ozarks. But we moved to the city for my dad to work, and we lived in St. Charles.

Interviewer: Was this part of the post–World War II back-and-forth migration of people from the Ozarks to St. Louis for work?

Woodrell: Yes. Ninety-five percent of my family disintegrated between World War II and Korea, in terms of living in the Ozarks. They just all took off—the ones who hadn't already run toward Detroit in the thirties. I'm the only male left down there.

Interviewer: So you eventually returned to West Plains to live because it was home?

Woodrell: Yeah, it's been the center of home for our family since before the Civil War. When we said "home," that's where we meant. But we didn't often live there. We only spent vacations and holidays there until I was an adult.

Interviewer: Was your mother a teacher?

Woodrell: No, but she did teach all of us to read before we went to grade school, so I was already a pretty good reader before I ever went off to school. She had kind of a fetish about that. I also was born with various illnesses that kept me bedridden at different times. I just read stacks and stacks of books. My intestines were in a ball and they were not where they were supposed to be, and so were corrupting each other. I couldn't eat at times. Once they discovered what it was, when I was twelve or thirteen, and then did an operation, I became totally healthy.

Interviewer: Has that childhood experience had any impact on your sensibility?

Woodrell: I may have gotten a little too used to amusing myself. I can be by myself for great long stretches pretty happily.

Interviewer: What's it like, living in West Plains and being a writer who's pretty well known all over the country? Is it hospitable to your writing, or do you feel isolated?

Woodrell: You can certainly get your privacy there. Some of the well I draw from is all around me. There's not much replacement for walking over to a cemetery and seeing your own dead ancestors from 1870 and so forth buried there. It definitely gives you another sense about the ground you're standing on. I know we're not exactly up to date with the popular culture of the time. I see it on TV, and I see it when I go to New York. But it doesn't seem to penetrate the actual daily life that I lead in West Plains. The isolation is good for my writing, although I do sometimes wonder what will happen when the books really get read.

Interviewer: You went to school at the University of Kansas in Lawrence. How did that happen?

Woodrell: I was a high school dropout; I went into the marines the week I turned seventeen in 1970. I wasn't paying much attention to the war. It just sounded like . . . fun. I got a GED while I was in the marines

"There's not much replacement for walking over to a cemetery and seeing your own dead relatives from 1870."

and got out. My parents lived on the Kansas side of the state line then. I declared in-state residency and went to Fort Hays State College first and then eventually ended up at KU.

Interviewer: Who did you study with at Lawrence? What did you major in?

Woodrell: Allen Lichter, Chester Sullivan, people like that. James Gunn. I had a Bachelor in General Studies. That allowed me to take all the lit courses I could cram in so I actually managed to get more lit credits than I could have as an English major.

Interviewer: Is that when you started writing?

Woodrell: That's where I really began to get serious. I'd always vaguely had it in mind to do. I think it was third grade when I went public with my desire to be a writer. At KU is when I decided to dedicate myself and see if I had anything or not. I was twenty-three by then. I was in Lawrence for six years. Often hitchhiking around for months at a time and then coming back to see if I could enroll again for the GI Bill. There was a year where I allegedly did straight MA work at Kansas, but then I dropped that and I was admitted to Iowa.

Interviewer: Who did you study with there?

Woodrell: Bharati Mukherjee, James Alan McPherson, Jack Legget, Lynne Sharon Schwartz. I took "Forms" from Barry Hannah—I know I'm leaving people out. It was a crucial time for me. I'd been in Kansas writing hard for quite a while and totally into it. I quit college in Kansas for two years just to read the reading list that Hemingway recommended in his "Notes to a Young Writer" or whatever it was

"Every book I write, once I hear the tone it starts coming."

called. I loaded trucks and read those books, so I was full-tilt into it, but I had no sense of where I would stack up. At Iowa everybody was from all over the place, so you got a sense of whether you really had legs or not. The faculty in general didn't teach. They responded thumbs-up or thumbs-down to whatever you handed in. But your fellow students' conversations were very educational.

Interviewer: Where did *Woe to Live On* come from?

Woodrell: As I said, my family's been from around Missouri since way before the Civil War, and I grew up hearing these anecdotes about the Civil War in Missouri, just enough to get me interested. I didn't really begin to look into it until I was at KU. The research library there is very good on the subject of the border wars. I began to dive into memoirs, letters, everything I could get. I came across these odd facts about the war in this region—such as a black man riding with Southern bushwhackers. The uniqueness of that began to bring it all into focus for me.

Interviewer: Did you start the book when you were in Kansas?

Woodrell: No, I wrote a short story at Iowa. *The Missouri Review* published it, and I tried to start the novel several times. Initially it was a whole different cast of characters. That never seemed to work for me, and I put it aside and wrote *Under the Bright Lights*. Then *Under the Bright Lights* looked as if it was not going to sell, and we didn't have any money, and I said, "If I'm only going to get one more shot I'm going to make it *Woe to Live On*." Halfway through that, the first book sold.

Interviewer: So you started *Woe to Live On*, put it aside and wrote *Under the Bright Lights*. On the surface I can't think of two more different kinds of endeavors. What on earth happened?

Woodrell: I began to hear the voice again of the narrator of *Woe to Live On*. Not to be too mystical about it, but there's some kind of musical thing to it. Every book I write, once I hear the tone it starts coming. Originally I kept trying to do *Woe to Live On* from the point of view of this woman and her children caught in the exodus, the diaspora from Missouri, because that interests me a great deal. But I wasn't happy with what I was getting. Something wasn't in tune with it. That was the version I set aside and pulled out.

Interviewer: That was the Texas diaspora, mostly?

Woodrell: Yes. Most people went to Texas. Then I moved to Arkansas because of the cost of living. All of a sudden Confederate flags were all over the place. When you went to have a drink with people this wistfulness about the war and everything still lingered, and all of a sudden the voice of Jake Roedel came back to me. Actually I think I wrote it in six months. It just went, once it happened.

Interviewer: In *Woe to Live On* you've got a "dutchman"—that is, a German—and a black man running around together with the bushwhackers. The German immigrants were traditionally with the Union. Was this a conscious choice on your part?

Woodrell: Yes. Your allegiance would go to another human being without parsing out the larger world politics of the human being you were loyal to. In this instance both the black man, Holt, and Jake Roedel are loyal to individuals who happen to be on the Southern side. Their personal loyalties supersede any political notion. I always think back to when I was seventeen and went into the marines and had no particular feelings about the larger political context at all.

Interviewer: It also gives them the means to grow, emotionally and psychologically, within the course of that tale, doesn't it? The fact that they're just a little on the outside. More than just a little on the outside. Roedel has to prove himself over and over—that he's not bad for a dutchman. You've mentioned the historical precedent of blacks running with bushwhackers. How many of the bushwhackers were of German descent?

Woodrell: You see a few German names in the rolls here and there, but I'm sure they were ninety percent pro-Union. This issue of blacks in the Confederacy is actually beginning to get a lot of coverage in the last year or two because researchers are coming forth with some of the facts, which are that at the end of the war they were trying to raise all-black companies in the South, for instance. I'm not saying this was a good thing or anything, but it's an interesting thing.

Interviewer: Probably because there wasn't anybody left to fight by that time.

Woodrell: That's right. The mistake they made was not including Southern blacks in their armies from the beginning. The truth is that the mix of people who were around at the time, they were all going to be involved in the war in one way or another. There were Native American groups from Oklahoma riding with both sides also. Pretty prominently, actually. The Chinese curse, "May you live in interesting times," came into full effect with everyone in the region.

Interviewer: Tell us about the bushwhackers. Where did they fit in terms of the larger picture?

Woodrell: Quantrill at times claimed he was officially commissioned. Whether or not he really was, I don't know. And Joseph Porter had probably the biggest band of irregulars in the state until he made a mistake tactically and got penned in against the Missouri River over here. I believe he had about two thousand men, and quite a few of them got killed. The rest fled in different directions. But he was ruined as a force. I don't think too many of them were officially acknowledged by the Confederacy after Lawrence. They didn't want anything further to do with them after that. Before then they were more than glad to have them along in Westport, in Lexington, et cetera. They were just like the Serb militia ethnically cleansing Kosovo. They were cleansing the countryside of pro-Unionists, or undecided even.

Interviewer: Why didn't they just go and join the army? Was it because of the border wars situation?

Woodrell: I think so. They'd already gotten accustomed to a certain amount of irregular military outlook toward Kansas. And they didn't want to get far from their actual home and kin, either. They needed a community that would let them hide, and home was where you could do that. The Union forces, the first ones who came in, made a horrible mistake in the way they treated people. One of the commanders wrote a letter to Lincoln saying, "We are making rebels out of

"I began to be smitten with the sounds of those voices and then just made up my own variations."

---

good loyal citizens everywhere we pass." A lot of these guys who went rebel were either neutral or inclined toward preserving the Union at the outbreak of the war.

Interviewer: People say that the border wars of the 1850s were the pre–Civil War civil war. Did the bushwhackers actually start forming in the '50s, before the war itself?

Woodrell: The sentiment was there. They may not have been very well organized until after the official outbreak. The estimates on how many of them there were are just all over the place, from a couple thousand total to maybe ten or fifteen thousand at different times. A lot of guys would go out and ride on one or two scouts and then go do something else.

Interviewer: Did you write from notes at all, or did you give yourself what George Garrett and Mary Lee Settle call a "historical memory" to write out of?

Woodrell: I read and study and think enough to feel like I can inhabit the time well enough to tell the story. Then I don't keep beating myself up with facts from research.

Interviewer: I love the device of the letters in *Woe to Live On*. Are those drawn from real letters that you read?

Woodrell: One of the things that comes up when you research the Civil War is that a lot of people, even if they weren't perfectly educated in terms of spelling and punctuation, just seemed to write good letters. So I began to be smitten with the sounds of those voices and then just made up my own variations. They also give a sense of the humanity of

---

"One of my biases as a writer is that I'm definitely in favor of a lean narrative."

---

the others, because all the letters are stolen letters from Union troops. One of the things I discovered was—and this is so crazy that I'm surprised someone hasn't written about it—that the Confederacy continued to have mail delivery in Missouri during the war. It was just one guy who came up and snuck all over the place. He got arrested, caught, a couple of times. But he continued to deliver the Confederate mail into Missouri. I think he finally got caught and locked up for good in late 1864.

Interviewer: The whole war west of the Mississippi was a different kind of war. It was bloodier, it was longer, it was maybe more hurtful, but it had its own character; it had its own music. And it's been largely neglected by historians.

Woodrell: Missouri was under martial law longer than any state has ever been, and in the area I'm from, Howell County and Oregon County, three years after the war was over the revenge raids were still going at such a clip they had to temporarily reinstitute martial law. They appointed the leader of the regional Union forces to go straighten things out. I believe he straightened it out with an uneven hand. But he did straighten it out. My family, insofar as I know, were all on the Confederate side, but they were from northern Arkansas and southern Missouri, and my mom's father's line is from up around Kansas City. I grew up hearing about that and hearing references to ancestors who were bushwhackers, allegedly. That always greatly intrigued me. I realized when I went to research the border wars that the only book I could find was by Richard Brownlee from the Missouri Historical Society, which is still a really good, valuable book. There have now, in the last few years, been two or three more. When I lived in Lawrence I had to walk across Massachusetts Street all the time because I lived in East Lawrence, and that was the street that Quantrill burned down. There

---

was a marker in the ground near where I used to cut across the parking lot, and that was where twenty-one unarmed recruits were among the first people to be gunned down by the Missourians as they swept into town. That marker would remind you it happened, and that it happened right here, right where you're standing.

Interviewer: In fact there were several sackings of Lawrence. In the 1850s the bushwhackers tried to dynamite the Free State Hotel, and it was so soundly built that they couldn't, so they ended up just burning the inside out. What year was Quantrill's raid—the big one—in *Woe to Live On*?

Woodrell: August of '63. But there were also massacres in Missouri, as well, that aren't publicized at all. Before he died, Jo Shelby said the one mistake of his life was being a border ruffian before the war. He may have been trying to cleanse his image a little bit. But he may have meant it totally, too. It's hard to say.

Interviewer: I was trying to place it because *Woe to Live On* is so totally in the voice and mind of Jake Roedel that dates and other external facts aren't even mentioned. The reader is dropped down into some unknown time and place. You know you're in Missouri, and that's about it.

Woodrell: I think one of my biases as a writer is that I'm definitely in favor of a lean narrative. One reviewer said it might be the only Civil War novel he's ever heard of that doesn't even mention Grant and Lee.

Interviewer: Jake and Holt are transformed in this raid. They defy orders and show mercy. Did that have historical precedent?

Woodrell: Yes, very much so. Lots of bushwhackers left to join the regulars after Lawrence. Lots of them left before then, too.

Interviewer: There's a significant change in his sensibility as the book proceeds. Holt changes too; for the first time he identifies himself as a black person.

Woodrell: One of the interesting footnotes—one hears different accounts in different places—but one of the accounts is that there were two scouts on the raid to Lawrence, and one was a black man named Nolan whose handwritten letters, I believe, exist in the research library, and the other was a white guy named Fletch Taylor who ended up being a congressman from Joplin after the war. One-armed by the end. I thought that was rather fascinating also because there were quite a few black people in Lawrence, and yet the spy mission to scout for the raid didn't make him feel conflicted or anything.

Interviewer: But it did with Holt. He is not a slave, but he is George Clyde's best friend.

Woodrell: That's loosely based on fact. A George Todd, out of Kansas City, had a black man who was similarly close to him. That was Nolan. I don't know if he rode throughout the war with Todd or just a good chunk of it.

Interviewer: So you did model some of your fictional characters after real people?

Woodrell: I knew I was going to do fiction, so I didn't want to be constrained by, "Oh, really, in April of 1863, Bill Anderson was actually doing such and such." It's an issue I've never satisfactorily settled for myself—the use of historical figures. But I decided that since they weren't superfamous, I would just go ahead and make up my own characters for the Bill Anderson and George Todd roles.

Interviewer: You've hit the big time with *Woe to Live On*, which is one of the great ironies. Here's one of the finest novels written in the last twenty years, bar none, and it was out of print for years. Now it's been made into a "major motion picture," as they say, by no less than Ang Lee. Wow! How did that happen?

Woodrell: A woman named Ann Carey worked for a producer, whose name I don't remember, when the book was new. She read it because he was at that time considering something with this background. He changed his mind and decided to do something else, but she remembered the book. Years later she was working for the production company involved with Ang Lee. He was finishing *Sense and Sensibility*, and he said he wanted something that wasn't all about women and domestic worries. She remembered the book from ten years past and gave it to him. He apparently read it overnight and wanted it.

Interviewer: Where did they end up filming Lawrence?

"In the '30s scholars were down in the Ozarks because they were finding living Elizabethan language."

Woodrell: They used Pattonsburg, Missouri. It's just exactly like Lawrence. They actually put furniture in the buildings, so you weren't just walking by empty buildings. I was there for those days of filming the raid on Lawrence, and that was fantastic. They cut the Lawrence thing down to a certain manageable length, though for my taste it could be three times as long. But that's just me.

Interviewer: Were they able to leave a lot in about the family relationships?

Woodrell: That's what they start with, trying to make that clear. It's a social situation, a wedding. People are talking about the coming war and they're not all on the same side, and there's tension. One of the things they discovered in the research with an audience is that you can't assume the audience knows what you're talking about when you talk about the border wars; you have to find a way of setting the context.

Interviewer: How do you feel about them changing the title to *Ride with the Devil*?

Woodrell: I realized when I sold the rights that they're going to have to earn their money back. If they feel like my title just won't work, then they should change it.

Interviewer: How involved were you with the filming?

Woodrell: I saw a few days of shooting. And when the script was being written by James Schamus, he talked to me several times to see what I felt about any changes he might be making. I have no official interaction with the group.

"There's a lot of not very good crime fiction, some of which succeeds very well."

Interviewer: What did they do with that wonderful, wonderful, wonderful language of the book?

Woodrell: They kept as much of it as they could in the dialogue. I saw the cut with some screen writers who were visiting for another reason, and they were flabbergasted at the quality of the language—the neo-Shakespearean quality of the language.

Interviewer: How did you do that? I mean, reading diaries, reading letters from the period is not hearing people talk. Where did you get Jake's voice?

Woodrell: I don't know. Ever since I can remember, as I say, if I could get in tune. . . . James Lee Burke read the novel and sent me a postcard saying, "I believe your ancestors' bones were talking to you here when you wrote this, because it's coming from somewhere." That's as well as I can explain it.

Interviewer: Were there any Group One speakers still hanging around in the hills when you were growing up? People whose speech has not been fiddled around with?

Woodrell: Older people, yes, and the farther into the country you go, the more of them you'll run into. In the '30s scholars were down in the Ozarks because they were finding living Elizabethan language. I would imagine that's been really dented, but people there still have a myriad of pithy, colorful ways of expressing things.

Interviewer: Do you think you picked up Jake Roedel's voice from them?

Woodrell: I think I had the idea vaguely of Walter Scott because one of the notions that compelled the Southerners was this Sir Walter Scott kind of notion. When you read the accounts from the era, the use of language often has a relationship to that older form. It turns out I may have made one or two mistakes in usage, though. There were some slang words that actually may not have been in use for another twenty years or so. And the name of the primary female is Sue Lee, but apparently it wasn't until some years after the Civil War that Southern women began to often have two names instead of just Constance or Charity or whatever. It doesn't mean it never happened, but it wasn't as prevalent as it later became.

Interviewer: *Under the Bright Lights* is a very different kind of book. What led you to it?

Woodrell: I love crime fiction of a certain kind. The problem with crime fiction is that there's a lot of not very good crime fiction, some of which succeeds very well. I was reading all kinds of different writers who turned me on, from straight fiction and from crime fiction. Raymond Chandler and William McIllvanney and Hammett and Cain and so forth. I like those guys equally with anybody else. I was also really knocked out for a number of years by William Kennedy. So this idea of the rhythm and music and long, loopy sentences that have snappers in them at intervals—all of this began to really come to me. Coming from Missouri, I was introduced to Twain quite young, which I would tell parents is a mistake once you get past Tom Sawyer. Too much Twain too young and you've lost them. One of my all-time motivating factors in being a writer was Nelson Algren. Some paperbacks of Nelson Algren novels had covers that looked kind of sexy. So by accident I began to read Nelson Algren. He was probably the next real, serious writer I ever read. His lyricism has always stayed with me. My actual favorite is *Never Come Morning*. But *The Man with the Golden Arm, Walk on the Wild Side, Somebody in Boots*, etc. I had never finished a novel, and I said, "I'll take this and get going and see if I can actually finish writing a novel." Up till then I had finished short stories, of course, but never actually finished any of the novels I'd attempted.

Interviewer: You've written a trilogy that features the Shade family: *Under the Bright Lights, Muscle for the Wing,* and *The Ones You Do.* I get the sense that you know who these people's cousins are.

Woodrell: I felt very close to the family. The crime aspect was more or less an excuse to link things together as I really dealt with family issues. As a young writer I felt like that would be a good use of one aspect of the form, to take it and lead it over to where my true interests lie, although I'm not sure how much thought I put into that at the time. It was feeling more than thoughts.

Interviewer: Unlike the Shades, you have no French in your family, right?

Woodrell: No, I do. My grandmother was entirely of French-American descent and her family came from East Texas before the turn of the century. Where they were just before east Texas I don't know.

Interviewer: So using the Shade family wasn't entirely alien. It's the same background that you've been talking about.

Woodrell: I'm fragmented Irish. In the 1850 census of Woodrells in Izard County, Arkansas, which is just across the line, the census taker had put in parentheses next to them, "Irish." I don't think of Woodrell as an Irish name, but my research has shown that they had a habit of marrying Irish immigrant women for two or three straight generations. I don't think ethnicity carried much weight when you got out that far into the woods. Race might have, but ethnicity I don't think mattered very much once you got way out there.

Interviewer: Did you build a genealogy for the Shade family?

Woodrell: Yes, in my mind, they were like an imaginary family. I have two brothers, I'm the middle one. My dad was, when he was in stroke and interested, an excellent pool player. He'd been raised in very destitute circumstances and had in fact lived in a pool hall for a while as a rack boy.

Interviewer: Like John Xavier Shade?

Woodrell: They have several things in common. They looked almost alike. My father was quite handsome as a younger person and was a lot of fun to be around and a great storyteller. He was not irresponsible toward his family, though, like John X is, not at all.

Interviewer: And the maternal figure?

"I don't think ethnicity carried much weight that far out into the woods."

Woodrell: She's still alive. My mother's a fairly forceful person, as was her mother and as was my father's mother.

Interviewer: It sounds like you borrowed a little bit from the same family when you wrote *Give Us a Kiss*.

Woodrell: Yes. That's more like my mother's family instead of my father's family. The grandfather figure is the only figure I've drawn where people actually thought I'd come a little close to an actual person.

Interviewer: Who would that have been?

Woodrell: My mom's dad. Without the criminal history, but with a lot of the governing instincts, the boss qualities. Dominating.

Interviewer: The families you write about are often ones that mirror the history of this state: the insider/outsider, the legal/illegal, the crossover, a wealthy family in which criminal things are done, as in *Give Us a Kiss*.

Woodrell: This is one of the things I find interesting. My father's family was far lower on the social spectrum than my mother's family was, but there was no significant violence associated with them. My mother's family at different times have been quite successful and quite prominent, and there's all kinds of violence in their history. You think it's the poor side going to get out there and do something mean, and no, it's the side that already has something, and they want a little more.

Interviewer: You talk about your novels really all being about family. I'm interested in the edge, a real kind of love-hate sense that I pick up in terms of your roots and the conflicts. Are you conscious of that at all?

"I don't think you need any coaching at all to be violent."

Woodrell: I've become so as I've gotten older. It probably was a fuel I was running on all along but didn't really understand what it was until maybe the last five or six years. I came to realize that there are themes in my life that seem to pop up, and certain buttons that must go to something that really matters to me, and that's one of them. Even living in the Ozarks—it's not a fifty-fifty split, but there's a split in terms of an affection for it and disdain or something like it.

Interviewer: There's a theme of all the pain that families can cause, the damage that gets done in the name of loyalties in families.

Woodrell: Yes. That's where most of the deep things happen to you.

Interviewer: It seems to come down to the individual level, doesn't it, in your work. Jake Roedel's simple insight was that he had a wife and a baby and that was where his first loyalty had to lie. Out of that insight came his refusal to commit another senseless act of violence.

Woodrell: That may have been a young man's notion. I'm probably more cynical now. Sometimes I wonder if I am as hopeful as all of that, and then someone will point out to me that in your actual life you keep getting up and going on, don't you? It's as if there's some purpose to that. Why would you deny that to fictional characters?

Interviewer: One of the things that struck me, in reflection, after reading *Woe to Live On* a second time, is the age of these people, in terms of recent events, such as Littleton, Colorado. Does it surprise you that people are surprised by violence coming out of teenaged boys?

Woodrell: No, I think we've had this little pall of semicivilization set in and people lost track of the actual organic animal fact of young men coming of age. The average age of the bushwhackers was not quite nineteen. There were some as young as fifteen running around. One of the reasons the military wants young people is that you are so capable of violence without much forethought at that age. That's why the marines take seventeen-year-olds, historically. They often make pretty good fodder in the front wave. Because they'll go.

Interviewer: Do you think that mankind is inherently violent?

Woodrell: I don't think you need any coaching at all to be violent. Many, many times I've been surprised at who among the people I know turns out to be capable of the most violent behavior.

Interviewer: What drives you to write? Do you pay attention to the market?

Woodrell: That's a question a writer has to ask himself all the time. You think, "Well, look at that—that book made 1.2 million dollars. Now, couldn't I be a smart guy for once and do something like that?" As a totally self-supporting writer, I have no other source of income. There were certainly times when my mind would wander over toward whatever was prominently displayed in the bookstore. I've actually sat down and tried to write something that I thought some larger audience might like, but I can't write it. I can't stay interested.

Interviewer: Didn't your publisher hound you to keep writing in the vein of *Under the Bright Lights* instead of *Woe to Live On*?

Woodrell: *Woe to Live On* had an unfortunate timing because it was published before this renewal of interest in the Civil War. It wasn't in stores—no ads, no nothing. I assumed it had disappeared for good. But I felt proud of the book and glad it got published at all. Had it been some other time, it might have been more enthusiastically published.

Interviewer: How come you kept writing books in the crime vein? What was going on?

Woodrell: *Woe to Live On* barely got reviewed and didn't sell. I felt like I still had interests to investigate with those other books, so I did. But since I finished *The Ones You Do*, I have no further interest.

Interviewer: Have you killed off the Shades?

Woodrell: I don't think I could go back to them. People ask me all the time if there's going to be another installment. I have no plans to, at this time. I have a few too many ideas running around of things I think I want to write about.

Interviewer: What are you working on now that you're leaving behind the world of the Shade family and the country noir of *Give Us a Kiss*? Are you going back to writing from history?

Woodrell: I have several things in the hopper right now. One is more about Missouri history. Being from Missouri, I knew about the Civil War, but in other ways I didn't pay that much attention to the history of my own region. As I read more, I find more and more that I'm interested in. The diaspora. The town of Carlotta, in Mexico, for example. Missourians who refused to surrender at the end of the war went to Mexico to found their new empire down there. They supported Maximilian against Juarez. So they founded a town named Carlotta, after Maximilian's wife. It's down near Veracruz. They were immediately in the middle of another civil war. Shelby was one of the big guys in that, and General Sterling Price, and several congressmen from throughout the South ended up down there. They also did one in Egypt and Cuba and Brazil. The one in Brazil is thriving still. The one in Veracruz only lasted a few years.

Interviewer: There's a colony of Americans that refused to surrender after the war in Brazil? Southerners?

Woodrell: They refused to live under occupation, so they left the country and went to Brazil. I believe Jimmy Carter and his wife visited there once. The ones in Mexico lasted until about 1868. They picked the wrong side again. They went with Maximilian, and he very soon was shown to be a poor choice. There's an anecdote about how they made their choice about which side to go with—Juarez or Maximilian. And the anecdote is that Shelby or Sterling Price said, "Fellas, which side should we go with here? We're going to have to pick a side." They had actually been hoping to be kind of neutral. And allegedly one of the Missourians spoke up and said, "I really like them hats Maximilian's boys wear." If this is true or not I don't know, but this is what I've heard.

Interviewer: What about just language to you? To what extent is writing for you basically playing with words?

"The fun for me is when I get to sing, and I get to sing when I write those sentences. Language is the start of it all."

Woodrell: I wouldn't write if I couldn't get off on the language. I have in the past had people say, "Well, why don't you write a little flatter?" The fun for me is when I get to sing, and I get to sing when I write those sentences. Language is the start of it all. That's crucial to me, it's fundamental.

Interviewer: In this passage from *Woe to Live On* you write, "We were hardened youths by that point, warfare was what we knew. Though we were mostly still boys by civil calculations we had by now roughed up the Swami and slept where the elephant shits. Shocking us would have required some genius." Where does the expression "going to see the elephant" come from?

Woodrell: I'm not positive where it actually originates. It was a common expression in the Civil War though.

Interviewer: It's British colonial surely, isn't it?

Woodrell: I'm sure it is. It's simply a reference to "I have seen it all." And it may have passed over from the British armies.

Interviewer: And the turn you take on it here, "we've slept where the elephant shits," that just takes it off.

Woodrell: That's the way I see these boys. These are really rude boys, you know. And they are the type who are beyond the normal range.

Interviewer: Besides that, it's really funny.

Woodrell: Kind of. A lot of people had a problem with *Woe to Live On*, that there are laughs here and there. One of my favorite things is switching tones, and a lot of people criticize me for it. But I love to switch tones

"But I love to switch tones because life switches tones."

because life switches tones. How many times in your life you're laughing, it's all great, you're in love, and then, boy, two dances later your whole world's down around your ears. That's the way it happens.

Interviewer: I asked you earlier about changing the title for the movie. But where did you get the title *Woe to Live On*—which obviously the movie world can't deal with at all?

Woodrell: No. Universal said they wouldn't release a movie with "Woe" in the title. Sure as hell, somebody will do "Woe" something and it will be a smash. I've been asked that a few times, and I'm not positive where it came from. I often draw up a list of titles, and I imagine I ended up combining a couple of them to come up with that feeling. It has the feeling of the story to me.

Interviewer: It's so ambiguous. It can be turned every which way. Which word do you put the emphasis on?

Woodrell: It's a riddle; it's an enigma.

Interviewer: You've mentioned Mark Twain, who was obviously an enormous influence on you, for every reason in the world that he would be, given where both you and I are from. Mark Twain was so focused on language and dialect that he had trouble ending things. Do you ever have that same sense in your own work?

Woodrell: I put a pretty severe discipline on myself not to. Again it's just a general notion, but if something's not pertinent to the overall story I try to cut it. So by trying to exercise this discipline, I feel like I keep a connection with the story. Where it ends is where it feels right to end for me.

Interviewer: Have you taken any heat over the ending of *Tomato Red*?

Woodrell: I wouldn't say heat. That book has actually generated the most controversy. I believe people in New York might have misunderstood the point of it and been uncomfortable. There have been people wanting something more hopeful there, but to me it is kind of a hopeful ending. One of the bunch is going to get her shot in the world and life. She had to betray her class and her people to do it, but you do have to betray your class and your people to do it.

Interviewer: What about the senseless act of violence? Looking back, do you feel that's adequately prepared for in the course of the book?

Woodrell: I do, actually. I think if you're looking at the person that Sammy Barlach is, he lives an easily combustible life, you know, readily combustible. And at the time of that kind of pointless act of violence, quite a number of frustrations have come together all at once—a combination of fears and so forth—and he just reacts all of a sudden to the wrong impulse. That doesn't seem hard to believe at all, to me.

Interviewer: And the place that Doyle comes to, at the end of *Give Us a Kiss*, is one of my favorites. It's like he has never been more at home. He's sitting in jail, and . . .

Woodrell: He's not surprised really to end up there; he wasn't planning on it, but he's not too surprised. He thinks he's compelled or fated to act out his family dramas or follow in their footsteps. At some point he says he felt like his genes had him cornered. And in that set of circumstances he did what he felt the whole weight of history was pushing him to do.

Interviewer: Again, back to Mark Twain's influence on you as a writer. To what extent did the kind of problems with first-person narrative that Twain had affect you as a craftsperson?

Woodrell: Actually, I had a bias against first person for a long time. I thought, mistakenly, that it was a thinner way of getting at a story. For quite a few years in my apprenticeship I tended to avoid first person as much as possible. Now I've gone through a phase where I'm nuts about first person. To me, you just find the mind and heart of the person talking; and that's your plot.

Interviewer: But by definition Jake has to be the person he is now, at the end of *Woe to Live On*.

Woodrell: Well, he looks at his own past without squeamishness. He is willing to portray himself as he sees himself to have been, and to me that's a kind of great classical iconic person to be.

Interviewer: It's a transformed Jake Roedel who's telling us this story. Did you find that liberating, or was it difficult? You actually talk like it was a pretty easy book.

Woodrell: I had a real strong feeling for this. I was in the marines during the Vietnam War. It was just an accident I didn't go to Vietnam. I assumed I would, and I actually volunteered twice to speed up the process. But there'd been so many seventeen-year-olds killed and that was such bad PR that they said, "We'll send you to Okinawa till your eighteenth birthday if you want." That's when they were threatening me. I wasn't the best-behaved little gyrene you ever ran into. I was just a kid. I ended up on Guam instead. Actually, some older marines who'd been in Vietnam knew my captain was going to send me to Okinawa till I was eighteen so I could go to Vietnam, and they put me on an order for a quota of marines to Guam to "save my dumb ass," as they put it. Earlier the corps had tried to send me to a school, and I said, "I don't want to go to school. I want to be slopping around in the jungle on foot." They said, "No, you really don't." I said, "Sure I do." But older officers, all of whom were veterans, said, "No, they're not going to send you." Now how would I feel about that? I knew lots of guys who did go to Vietnam either while I was in or after. I've heard a lot of first-person reminiscences about various things. When I got my GED on Guam it was me and two sergeants, and both of them had chunks missing from Vietnam. We had a lieutenant from Mississippi, ROTC, who had never been to Vietnam, and he took special delight in messing with those who had. These men had literally been in Vietnam for breakfast and were still muddy and dazed, I think, by the sudden change in their circumstances. This Mississippi martinet loved to strut up and down in front of them and jump on them for their mustaches or sideburns or whatever he could find—unbloused boots—whatever regulation thing he had in mind that had no pertinence in the field. Watching him do that has always hung with me, because I could see in their eyes that these guys would just as soon kill him as whoever they'd been shooting at that morning.

"To me, you just find the mind and heart of the person talking, and that's your plot."

Interviewer: The thing that struck me about Vietnam was the remarkable way a person can invest that much of himself into an experience and be able to say afterward, "That was wrong." How brave the guys were who came back transformed for the better. It's really hard to look at something that bad and just accept the fact that, hey, it was not a good place for us to be.

Woodrell: Or the fact that you could have done it yourself. I understand that under a certain set of circumstances you're capable of almost anything. I recognize that. And yet one meets many, many people who insist that they wouldn't have. Which is pious baloney. I'm sure that was my unconscious—almost conscious—desire with *Woe to Live On*.

Interviewer: It must take remarkable strength of character to have gone through something like that and be able to assess it in the way that Jake Roedel can. In your head, how old is Jake Roedel when he's telling this tale?

Woodrell: In the short story he's an old man. But I just think of him as a mature man. This is one of the things about Vietnam, too, the idea that you're going to apologize for your experiences. That actually frustrates the aim and makes a person dig in deeper. I recognize that, if you're lucky, there's this honesty about your experiences. Clearly, where you went beyond where you wanted to go, you recognize that, but you also recognize that you're a human being, you're going to want to keep living and you're going to have to find a way of integrating this, and that's simply how I saw Jake Roedel.

"DID I WRITE IT MYSELF? HEY, I'M A KING."

THE LETTERS OF DJUNA BARNES AND EMILY HOLMES COLEMAN (1935-1936)

INTRODUCTION

Djuna Barnes once said she was the "most famous unknown of the century," though her writing and painting distinguished her, as did her haughty, cape-tossing gestures, auburn hair and acerbic wit. Born in New York in 1892, she grew up in a family that included a charismatic grandmother who was a journalist, salon keeper and theosophist. Her American father was a proponent of free love and her British mother an aspiring poet. When Djuna was five, her father's mistress joined the household, and Djuna's siblings and half-siblings were educated at home, where all the children were encouraged to write daily. The family split up for financial reasons in 1912, and Djuna helped support her mother and brothers by writing for the *Brooklyn Daily Eagle*. She was hired to write for the *New York Press* by novelist, critic and photographer Carl Van Vechten in 1913 and moved to Greenwich Village, where she shared a house with photographer Berenice Abbott, literary critics Malcolm Cowley and Kenneth Burke, Dorothy Day of the Catholic Worker Movement and a number of actors and artists. Her circle of friends was formed largely by the Provincetown Players, a theater collective that launched the career of playwright Eugene O'Neill and inspired Barnes to write her own final drama, *The Antiphon*, many years later. By 1921 she was on her way to Paris to write for *McCall's*. These early influences portended a life that could not be ordinary.

In Paris, Barnes was at the center of the expatriate group. She knew Man Ray, Sherwood Anderson, Ernest Hemingway, Edna St. Vincent Millay, Marsden Hartley, Sinclair Lewis, William Butler Yeats, Hart Crane, James Joyce, Natalie Barney, Gertrude Stein, Constantin Brancusi, Mina Loy and Edmund Wilson, but she was most impressed by the artist Thelma Wood, with whom she lived for eight years. When their relationship foundered in 1929, Barnes began to work with great intent upon *Nightwood* (1936), the dark and highly wrought modernist novel for which she is best known. Set in Paris and New York, Barnes' novel (which T.S. Eliot likened to an Elizabethan tragedy for its "quality of horror and doom") is the story of five tormented and tormenting cosmopolitan characters. Though she resisted self-knowledge, Barnes' work was significantly autobiographical and documents in a poetic style the struggles of an early-twentieth-century woman with the problems of freedom, sexual and otherwise. Her rage at betrayals by her parents and friends generated the tormented characters of the satirical *Ryder* (1928) and *Nightwood*. After being rejected by numerous publishers, the latter novel was eventually published by T.S. Eliot at Faber & Faber and the following year in America by Harcourt and Brace.

Emily Holmes Coleman was instrumental in the publication of *Nightwood*. Coleman was born in California in 1899, graduated from Wellesley College in 1920 and married in 1921. After the birth of her son in 1924, she spent two months in a mental hospital in upstate New York and later wrote about the experience in her 1930 novel, *Shutter of Snow*. Her poetry was published in *New Statesman* and *transition*, but she was better known for her literary zeal, keen criticism and volatile temperament. Coleman first met Barnes at Deux Magots in 1925 in Paris, where Coleman was society editor for the *Chicago Tribune*. They met again in 1932 at a rented country estate in England, where they and novelist Antonia White were guests of heiress Peggy Guggenheim. It was here that Barnes wrote much of *Nightwood* and Coleman kept an as-yet-unpublished diary that assessed Barnes in a way Barnes found too astute to bear. Though the two were judgmental of each other at first, they eventually formed a friendship that deepened after the 1934 death of their mutual friend John Farrar Holms, an erudite Englishman who was also part of their company in the summers of 1932 and 1933.

These letters are a small portion of the voluminous correspondence between Barnes and Coleman. We offer them as a sampling of an intimate conversation between two American women writers whose significance has been underestimated. The letters illustrate, too, the kind of intense literary dialogue that was typical among the expatriate writers and artists of the period. At the time of their writing, Barnes' novel had been rejected by Scribner, Simon & Schuster, Viking, Covici, Heubsch, and Boni & Liveright. Barnes was stranded in New York by the Great Depression, while Coleman was living in London. Their friendship was approaching its zenith as these letters traversed the Atlantic. Coleman's project was the publication of Barnes' book, which she greatly admired. Though her affection for Barnes is evident, Barnes was ambivalent about intimacy with anyone by this point in her life, and she resisted Coleman's efforts to lead her toward self-knowledge (Coleman's fervent soul-searching makes her, in retrospect, the more contemporary of the two). Barnes drifted from man to man after the demise of her relationship with Thelma Wood. Depression, which she had fought all her life, made her unwilling or unable to act much on her own behalf. She expected the generosity of friends to sustain her but resented having to ask. Coleman spared her this difficulty by arranging a lifelong Guggenheim fellowship for her. In return, Barnes occasionally opened up to Coleman in a way that she did with no one else.

At the time of these letters, Coleman was involved with Sir Samuel (Peter) Hoare. The difficulties in her relationship with the guarded Hoare were highlighted by her blossoming interest, both literary and emotional, in the much younger, married poet George Granville Barker. It was 1935, the trough of the Great Depression, a particularly turbulent time on both sides of the Atlantic. In America, the WPA was just being formed to provide jobs for the millions of unemployed workers. That September would see the assassination of Huey Long, while almost simultaneously in Germany Hitler's Nuremberg Laws went into effect. The following month, Mussolini invaded Ethiopia; there was war, too, in China, and the Spanish Civil War was on the horizon. On the personal front, also, it was a troubled time for Coleman and Barnes. Many of their friends had married and were preoccupied in various ways: one stricken with tuberculosis, two enduring the birth and death of their first child, most contending with meager finances. The two writers' conversation has an elegiac undertone as both women struggle to reconcile the brilliance of the decade just past with the approach of a future clouded by war and uncertain prospects for writers and artists. There are shadows here of who each woman would become: After two more visits to Europe, Barnes would spend many years in bitter seclusion in New York and die alone in 1982; Coleman's ardent soul-searching would result in a life-altering religious conversion. Coleman died on a Catholic Workers' Farm in 1974, thirty years after the most active period of her friendship with Barnes.

Barnes and Coleman were situated at a crossroads in the twentieth century. Their letters are artifacts of the time just before the advent of mass culture, a time when writers knew publishers personally and could hope for the careful attention of a T.S. Eliot. Before feminism articulated their difficulty, both women struggled with how to maintain a sense of self in a world bent on dismissing their intellects and sexuality. While technology was becoming the coin of the realm, Barnes and Coleman, armed with only typewriters and pens, navigated a distance between spirits and left a singular impression of the hunger that animates creative work and the loss and emptiness that often inspire it.

G.C. Guirl-Stearley

EDITOR'S NOTE

Because of the length of many of the letters, we have found it necessary to cut passages that were repetitive or of lesser interest to the general reader. Such decisions are, of course, subjective and often hard to make. Scholars should refer to Barnes' letters at McKeldin Library Special Collections at the University of Maryland at College Park and Coleman's at the University of Delaware Library in Newark, Delaware. The original letters excerpted here were all typewritten, and although they were part of an informal, unedited correspondence, they required little editing except for our abridgement and the insertion of annotations. Other editorial changes have deliberately been kept to a minimum in order to preserve the flavor of the originals. We have silently corrected misspellings and typographical errors. Except where they were egregious, the authors' eccentricities of punctuation and inconsistencies between British and American spellings have been retained. Underlined words and phrases have been changed to italics, but Barnes' occasional use of all capital letters for emphasis has been retained. All parenthetical words and phrases were parenthetical in the original letters; what little clarification we have added is indicated by brackets.

Footnotes and introduction are drawn from Phillip Herring's *Djuna: The Life and Work of Djuna Barnes* (New York: Viking, 1995) and Peggy Guggenheim's *Out of This Century* (New York: Universe Books, 1979). We thank Joseph Geraci and Herbert Mitgang, literary executors, for rights to publish the letters of Emily Holmes Coleman and Djuna Barnes, respectively.

---

7 Oakley Street, London, S.W. 3,
November 5, 1935.

Djuna my darling;

I got your sad little note as I was putting a letter to you into the box. How I wish you did not feel like this. I sent your manuscript to Eliot last night, having just read it through again, with a view to its form—and I took out pages [that] seem to be stories of the Doctor. However good they may be in themselves I know they will irritate Eliot. . . .[1] Whether he will take it or not I do not know. I was very sad as I took it to the post office. I am afraid it will have to be privately published. I don't think anyone will risk it. It is too peculiar a book. If Eliot turns it down I shall begin immediately (after trying Wishart and a few others) to get it privately published. . . . Once anyone loves this book they will do anything for it. I shall see that the book is published, if I live. . . .

If human art can draw blood out of a stone, I will draw interest from Eliot for this book. . . . I sit feverishly waiting for what he is going to say. I wrote him a letter of which I think he will never get the like again. All the brains I have, all the passion I have for your book, and the understanding I have of what it means through so many intense readings of it; all the love I have for poetic truth; and the injustice I feel for the suffering you have undergone to get this published, when junk upon junk is put before the world every day—I put into this letter. . . . The letter must excite him, if he is not a rock.

But when I read the manuscript again before sending it, I was very pessimistic; the first part, fine though it is, all about Felix—has nothing to do with the main theme of the book. You can't write about passionate feeling (Nora's) and scatter it all over Felix, Robin, Guido, the Doctor. *It can't be done.* Eliot will see this; it will madden him. . . . I'll send you the correspondence, when Phyllis types it in carbons. I must send it to Muir.[2]

Anyone with an ounce of creative talent—and many who have none at all—falls in love with your book, because they love the "light" in it so that they forget what form it is in. It ought to be as moving as Lear: it could be—in some state, where your gifts were harmonized. . . . The book is bound to get published, because England must be full of people who love it as Peggy,[3] John,[4] Muir, Barker,[5] Tony,[6] Sonia[7] and I do. (Sonia is raving mad about it, so that I had to send her my own copies of excerpts, she begged me so passionately for them). There must be some even in America. (Leonard, Polly, Muffin,[8] to say nothing of people more intensely fond of poetry than they are). So that if the book were privately published it would have its audience. . . . I do feel though that Eliot is the man who *might* risk it. It's just a question if writing so utterly different from his own kind, and having a lack which, to him, with his passionate longing for order, seems the worst lack any writing can have, CAN prevail on him, when it is that of genius. Barker agreed with me that if Eliot got the mss. of *Moby Dick* he would be likely to reject it. But if you took the bad parts out (a fourth or fifth perhaps) of *Moby Dick* it would be a complete book, the chase of the whale, his love for the whale; but your book cannot be made perfect by taking things out; it attempts so much—it attempts dramatic tragedy—and taking out can help it, but cannot improve the initial misconception, which was not to have taken the tragedy of Nora and Robin and made a central theme out of it. . . .

Dear Djuna, I don't want you to be discouraged. Whatever the faults of this book it is the work of a genius such as America has not yet produced, and all the world is going to know it some day, and you will be honoured; before you die if you do not die soon. In the meantime do not worry, because there are people who love you and believe in you—ones whom you have not seen, like Barker—and Peggy I am sure will help to get this book published if all recognized publishing firms fail. Your chief audience is in England, so I think it is best to try to publish it here: until you get a reputation by it. (If Eliot shows any passion for the book I will give him *Ryder*: such is his nature that he might like that because it HAS a form—though I personally do not like it). When you do get a reputation it is published in America without further trouble. I myself when I read the good parts feel that there's no use my continuing to write.

Your little letter moved me very much—are you better now?[9] You've been writing me letters so different from what you used to do. It's been really good for you to have someone to communicate with who did not want to listen to anything but the deep part of you. To say nothing of the touching letter you wrote Peggy, about dreams. It is certainly a joy to me, now that John is dead, to be able to write to someone who knows what I am talking about. Of course Sonia does up to a certain point: beyond that point only you go. How is Muffin? Of course I do not mean that he doesn't love your book; and wouldn't love it more and more, when he gets it into him more—when his glass is broken through. What are you doing to Elsa?[10] I do hope something. And what about your flat? Do you think you can get 80,000 francs for it, really?[11]

I have had a week such as I never had before. Barker was in London; he came here every day. His book fired me so that I could scarcely read it. It is absolutely different from yours, and from *Alanna*[12]—the first half—being poetic in an *inhuman* way. It is not profound, in a human way, like yours. (I'm sending you *Alanna* tomorrow). But he inhabits continually poetic worlds of such intensity that I cannot dare to think of them. Only Muir, sometimes in some of his poems, has been in them. His presence here stimulated me to write poetry so that I have been going around in a sort of dream, not sleeping, not eating. I cannot write now, because, now that your mss. is off, I must get at my own book, and fix the end of it up, and send it off. (It goes also to F. & F. through R. de la Mare. I shall of course not send my book to F. & F. until the decision has been made on yours.) Then I am going to write poetry. I can't think of anything else. I intended to do nothing else this winter. I did not know that an angel from paradise would be here to help me. I can't tell you what I feel about Barker. It is something I never felt before. I may be in love with him—it is more likely that I am entering, with him, into my own proper realm, of thought and feeling; worlds I entered with John in the abstract but never really. John always kept back—I suppose because of Peggy, because of sex—I don't know. We never touched each other once as Barker and I have touched already. Of course he is not as wonderful as John, I don't think he ever will be. I've just been looking at John's letters to Hugh Kingsmill[13] (they are here now, and I've barely been able to look at them, between Barker, and your book, and my own); at the age of 22 (Barker's age) he knew everything about people. His mind was as keen as Shakespeare's. Barker I don't think has an unusually keen critical intellect. He has of course a mind, and it may develop, but it isn't at all the calibre of John's. But perhaps because of personal, perhaps sexual reasons (I think I almost repelled John sexually, and that must have been an intense barrier) I never felt the letting down of the veil I have felt with Barker—though he is so reserved, introverted, and seemingly entirely covered with an adolescent shell. I hope he does not fall in love with me. I should find it terrible to resist anyone so almost myself. I don't want to think of these things. He has gone back to Dorset, he is very happy with his wife . . . He made me show him one or two of my poems. That afternoon I experienced such excitement that I nearly faint thinking of it. I don't mean that he thought they were successful, but he was in my world, and I was in his, for a few minutes.

I've finished the second part of his book. It is absolutely astonishing. . . . There is much you won't like. You can't fail to feel the power of the imagination which at last (after centuries it really seems in England) is born again in him. I am so happy that I know him; to know him and you seems to me as much as any human being could possibly need in this life. . . . Eliot, for some unknown reason, has recognized his genius; and given him great encouragement. (This is the most encouraging thing I know for your book). He has a long poem which is to come out in March here. He recited some of it to me. I don't even dare to think of it. It's so wonderful. Muir has seen it. Muir wrote him a letter about it which I never knew Muir could ever write. It is really as if one were beginning to live again.

My life with Hoare[14] continues the same. I have this flat, which I love so, and which brings life to me, and I have my writing, and the thought of you and Barker—how exciting, how terrifically exciting. I wish you were here. I don't think you could ever be happy, as I am. It is not your nature. Your book is the result of the most dreadful suffering. I think perhaps what I write that is the best (this book is only a practice) will come from the most intense springs of personal happiness in me.

Peggy was here, met Barker, thought him very young. She didn't get at him at all. He read poetry out loud to us. Peggy was lovely—like a bird she sat, twisting her head, frightened and delighted. He reads poetry like magic; the first human being I have ever met who does. He tried to make me like some of the young modern English poets. He has no commerce with them in his work, but is naturally interested in them—I am not. He is tall, with a round head, rather sloping forehead; a long beakish nose but not shaped like a beak—grey eyes, I think, which he squints up because he is nearly blind, through an auto accident. His mouth is small and very sensual, small, thick lips, I think; his chin recedes. His hair is curly. I didn't like his looks very much at first—though he is pleasant to look at. Tony and Phyllis think him beautiful. He has a very Oxford manner, and way of talking, which he has made up. I talked to him for positive hours about John. He was fascinated. I talked about you a great deal. I talked about your portrait of me.[15] It frightens me. What does it mean? I am 15 years older than he, and yet we met in the eternal world. . . .

I can't think of anything but Hoare—I know he would love me after it would be too late. I would be gone—I am mad—your picture—what will become of me and my horrible life? O Djuna if we are dead and buried on this earth it would be better than to try to make truth out of our lives. I am so frightened—dear—it all comes out—I dare not tell you. I don't know—I hope he does not care for me—will not—for he loves his wife—there would be no need—we could be friends, love in that realm—it can be done—must be done—don't you think—how can I tremble like this and dream through fear, no hope, only terror of my weakness and the thought that I could coldbloodedly hurt Hoare who is my life—dear Djuna what could I do—it doesn't matter now—he's gone and I shall write. So much to write. . . . This wickedness, not to love Barker, but to have made my life with Peter—I needed it so—but I should never have done it if someone can do this to me—should I? I believe that. O Djuna I shall begin to suffer now—I may have this little bliss first—I may have what I can, before this happens, as I—I can't write the words—I cannot say "It will happen." If he doesn't love me, that will save the *act*. It will not save me, who know what I am capable of. . . .

Ah, my Djuna! I am done. I am damned, at last—after these weeks of peace and deceiving happiness. If he doesn't love me, if I am a fool—lost in madness—can I stay with Peter? If he does not love me, will it save me Djuna?

Nov. 6

The mss. has arrived. Eliot's secretary sent me a very respectful acknowledgement. She said—"It arrived safely this morning."

November 22, 1935
111 Waverly Place
New York City

Emily dear:

I am very distressed by your last two letters. Your agony is such an ecstasy that I am really nervous about writing you as you ask me to, to tell you what I think.

To begin with I must repeat that I do not, and can not have your attitude toward sex itself. I do not think it monstrous and evil. You should not despise the key, which is what it is, to all we ever really learn. Now, in your case it seems to me, from what little I know of you, that in the sexual direction you have been cruelly starved, certainly so in your relations with Peter. Therefore that you should flounder about and clutch at the merest straw is certainly not wicked or immoral or any of those things you call it. The fact that you can be in love with Peter and yet turn to Leonard, and now to Barker is pretty conclusive proof that there is something monstrously lacking in your relations with Peter.

In any case I know from my experience with Thelma, that *no one* could have thrown me into any other arms, not even for the months when I had nothing whatsoever to do with her, not even after we had separated for a number of years, how many? two? three? I simply had no room for any other "terrible attraction," and that you have proves, it seems to me, that something is deadly missing. Certainly were you passionately in love with asceticism that would be another thing, if you wanted to be and had been a nun, and your whole passion was turned in that way, and your renunciation of the body was your largest passion and love, then I should say that you were now backsliding, but even so, I would have to say that considering the intensity of that backsliding there must be something *missing* in your relation to God. That you are going to hurt Peter is probably true, but the fact that you blame yourself for not waiting for Barker, merely means that Peter is not your true love, or how can you say it? Yes, you should have been pretty sure about Peter, about making him a "target forever," because he is as he is. But also his own character makes him, inevitably, a target, that is why he fought you so desperately. With T. and myself it was in this degree very different, she did not fight me, she wanted me (along with the rest of the world).[16] Peter really did not want his life touched, so in touching and in leaving him (if you do), you have hurt him badly, but it would seem more cruel, had he given in all the way, and laid his body down before you, he has not, that he has given in as much as he has is possibly more than another's quick and complete surrender, but the complete (tho possibly less difficult) surrender is what you want, what any ardent person wants. That you can be so swept away by Barker is a charge against Peter. It could not be called a charge, naturally, had he given you all the passion you desired, in that case the whole thing would be different. Therefore it is not like Dorothy and John, she gave him her very soul (or so I understand) and then because sexually he tired of her, he left her. Well dear, these things happen. You can't, you simply can't, put sex out of life, it won't have it—it's a law of nature, and how sinful it is to follow that law, well, that is the individual's problem, according to his belief. I do not say you may not have been wrong in forcing Peter, perhaps you were. *Perhaps* he has a *right* to be lifted up and slain, it may be what he needs. You can't know the pattern of your history and fate until it has been committed, and it's the lack of pattern in your life with Peter that's probably going to drive you into some other, even though of lesser value—with Peter you seem to mill and mill and make no design, and when that happens there is only one design to make, that is a bloody one. All this is arguing on only one point, Peter. As for Barker and his worth, and you and Barker and your worths, how in God's name can I know? I never saw the boy and I do not even know how he writes (which means so much more to you than it has ever meant to me in a personal sex relation, tho now perhaps I should also look for someone mentally my equal, I don't know) Barker may be the most idiotic person in the world for you, but best or most idiotic, that you can have such feelings about him remains a dangerous sign against what you hoped was life with Peter. I do not see how you are going to live forever with Peter if you can, every now and then, so dreadfully want someone else. I wonder if you would be "Cured" were Peter to take you to bed and keep you there? If Barker *really* is your "damnation," then by the same peradventure he is your fate, perhaps you were meant to be damned, I believe that what you most feel that you must do, no matter what the consequences, and if it damns you to Hell, then Hell is your home. Fanatics, and prophets, and lovers and poets all know their home when they find it, you have not found yours, so you are still turning and turning, and if Peter were your right torture, it does seem that you would be turning in that orbit, and not running off into another . . . *unless* you are simply being impulsive (you love poetry so much that you might follow that instead of your true love) and wanton and childish. This I can not know, *you* can, if you look into the matter clearly and with some of that cold blooded blue pencil faculty of yours.

Would Peter be exactly and only what you want *if* he would give in? Then can't you wait? You would have waited for John wouldn't you? And if Barker were our John, would you hesitate to give Peter up, no matter how he hurt? Now let us look at Barker. He is twenty-two, you thirty-seven—he is married and loves his wife, also (commercially) he has no money (so if you took him probably no one would help him— usual reaction—nor his wife—then what?)—let us make it all as dreadful as possible. From your description, he sounds as if he looks terrible, no chin and his forehead going to meet it, well looks don't matter anyway, except they give an indication of what we will suffer from. And you do not even know if he is in love with you, or ever will be. I can't tell you anything sensible on his side because I do not know him, and can't from someone's letters only. But from the sound of the thing, and taking you into the picture, I should say if you want your level safety I'd hold onto Peter like a drowning woman because if you walk in such ecstasy as your letters indicate very long, I do believe you would burst, or go mad, or something I don't like to contemplate, however, I never did much care for safety, and if you are seeking destruction in your own medium, Barker sounds like fate. On the other hand, remember that twenty-two and thirty-seven never meet, really, neither physically or mentally, they may seem to, but they just don't, unless thirty-seven is a child and twenty-two a man. Then it might be. I *have* looked at my portrait of you Emily dear, but what can I tell you that it does not? It really isn't a horror, nor something monstrous in a bottle. What is it that you truly want to be? Make a set of notes on that, outline what you think would be perfect for you. I don't know what you really want to be, I don't think you have clearly got it down in your own mind. How would you like to look, and act and be . . . think of it. . . .

I am having a beastly time myself, what with your news about my book, your news about yourself, Marian[17] two days off from having her stomach cut up for her child, and Louis, naturally, insane with apprehension, and now Mary[18] on the phone to tell me that one lung is gone, the other going, two months to live, and taking it like a prick. My God what strange blood Irish blood is. Her husband acting like a beast and a bastard, won't even bring her a sandwich, stinking drunk all the time, and *she* taking *his* pants off and putting him to bed. It's awful. Now the doctor has her thoroughly scared she is going to a sanatorium, in a room with another consumptive. . . . I can't bear to think of it, she said she wished at least her husband could stay sober long enough to take her, she did not want to go alone!! What a friend he is. Of course I told her I'd help her pack, and take her myself.

And as if this were not enough Muffin. I think it is hopeless. He seems ill and depressed. Been away now weeks, stays weeks more . . . talks about himself as if he were in the second person, and that person on his bier. My family is all that's left to complain about, just everything is shot to hell as far as I am concerned. Even my Paris apartment has not been heard of since, in spite of Saxon's[19] brag, and now the franc probably shooting down to god knows what. Last night my sweet brother (of course "in fun," so charming!) said I was "full of shit." Thelma here yesterday (she's broke!) said she did not like William James' *Variety of Religious Experience* as it was superficial and proved him ignorant, even of his quotations from St. Augustine; St. Augustine believing that evil was not a substance, but a swerving from truth, that James thought good and evil two substances, etc, etc. She also said Gromaison's *Life of Christ* the best (I must admit I never heard of it, or if I have, don't recall it. Have you seen it?)

Now dearest Emily as to the private publication of *Nightwood*. What do you think? It really is never very much use, does not get heard of much, unless like South Wind what's his name, you have a large reputation, or unless like Joyce, a Beach[20] to push it like fury and money and a library to help, as she had. Also I couldn't think of letting your father (Good heavens!) spend his hard earned money on it. Tony either, she hasn't any, nor you, nor anyone with three cents, only. *The Ladies Almanack*[21] cost some six hundred dollars, five hundred of which I still owe. Bob McAlmon[22] paid for it. I might be able to do as well with *Nightwood* if privately published as I did with the *Almanack*, but I doubt it, people were more willing then, by far, to get rid of their money. I met Alfred Kreymborg[23] on the street, he wants to see *Nightwood* (always admired my work, since the world began) and says it's just the right length for the *Caravan*[24] and if taken would automatically be published by Norton. So shall I let him see it? Peter has it now, Anne[25] wants to read it, have asked for it back, but have not heard anything about it.

Sonia, out of a clear sky, called me by phone one night several days ago, about eleven. I was asleep. Said she particularly wanted to see me, so I said all right, tho I would not have seen her had she not been your friend, as I am seeing no one except Mary, Fitzi,[26] Marian, all old friends and so do not get so on my nerves. Well, she took me to lunch the next day, and I must say that I was not very outgoing (got a bit tight, I've been on the wagon, you won't believe it, for over a month except for that lunch and one dinner). Somehow she annoyed me more than ever, this will make you angry, but I might as well tell you the truth, *we* both said how fine it was that someone was in the world who loved beauty as you do, etc, etc. Then she said you were not very happy. Then I asked what it was she particularly wanted to see me for, she said the death of her brother, and told me that. Must have been a monster. I really could not give her one ounce of what she wanted, which was you. My introversion and English blood simply curls up at the edges and *dies* trying to meet the original blaze at brightly burning backfires, and that's what Sonia is. She lives on other people's bodies like a phosphorous, and I never would bear that in a person. She told me you had sent her the excerpts from my book. There's nothing I can do to stop it, because you will do it, so there's no use talking about that either.

Emily darling, I don't know what to do or to say to you in your trouble, and then too I write knowing that between writing and answer there are some twenty odd days in which heaven knows, anything or nothing can happen. You ask the impossible. When you ask me what makes you a child, if anyone knew the answer to that, the world would end. "Can you help it that you do not grow up"? I do not believe so, Emily—tho knowing yourself a child is a long step.

Love & write at once
D.

---

7 Oakley Street, Dec. 4th

Dearest Djuna—

I can't imagine why I don't hear from you. I do hope nothing has happened to you. I can't think why you shouldn't have replied at once to my terrible letters. I wish I hadn't sent them—I'm sure I've worried you horribly. They helped me, in making me get things straight. At the moment the thought of Barker fills me with repugnance—more especially since I've had a letter from him about my poems. (He does know good poetry; but he exhibits a youthfulness which naturally bores me, since I'm out of it; I'm out of intellectual youthfulness at any rate). . . . Women like me are so mad, so unconnected with life—in the real sense—I was going to say that hence they have no meaning to the ordinary man; but Barker is not that ordinary man. He is very absorbed in his work, is writing a book on Poetry and Psychology! He is going to show it to Eliot when he comes at Christmas, first bringing it to my door. (If I haven't heard from Eliot by then I am going to get Barker to inquire discreetly. I say discreetly—*I don't want to hurry him up*. The longer he takes to reply to my letter the better, because that means he is conscientiously reading your book—which I am certain he would do anyway now). . . . I'm a little fed up with him now, or rather, fed up with illusions.

I was reading some of my letters to John (I have them all). They are so sweet. I've been reading Lawrence's letters. Some of them are wonderful. . . . I know he was a man full of envy, and worse than envy—unsatisfied ambition—power; and he kept on yelling how terrible people are because he was not conscious enough to face the differences between himself and them. (Djuna, there is some of this in you). *Consciousness is honesty*. If one wants the intellectual truth enough, it is made clear to one. I wish you would believe this, Djuna. Reading Lawrence's letters nearly breaks my heart. I read them first in 1932. Now 3 years later they are more real to me than ever. I looked up my letter to John about them, & his reply. My letters to John fascinate me. Such passion. I'm sure they were the best letters I'll ever write. They were childish in spots. But he got the best out. He's not alive now and I don't think anyone will ever get that best again. I read all his letters to me again. They are full of life, and thought. I'll show them to you. (Only about 10). . . .

Peter telling me all about Stendahl who must have been a charming man. Peter loves him because he was in the civil service & still had the guts to write. He was terrified of spies. (It was discovered after his death that he was right to be. Spies were after him all the time). He bound all his works in dossier covers, labeled falsely to put the police off. He had this secret life. (He loved the Italians, lived in Italy always). Peter read me some of the explanations (for the police, who might be searching) on his covers. They were terribly funny. It said one novel was about a man who married Charlotte Corday! (To put them off, to get them on to the French Revolution). I wanted to read some Stendahl—have always wanted to know his writing—but the aspect of him which would interest me (his presenting an evil person sympathetically—first time this was *ever* done) is not the aspect of him which would fascinate Peter. (How Peter hates reckoning with evil). But it nearly kills me to read French—even Stendahl's French which is entirely lacking in the sloppiness which drives me crazy in most French writing. (Strange, French is so much one or the other: Pascal or Romain Rolland). Stendahl modeled himself on the Code Napoleon! I don't know if it's a good or bad thing (Barker has it to the point of not knowing a word of a foreign language—can't learn it; you) but I don't really like—in fact suffer agonies reading—anything but English. The only exception to this is Dante. He is so much nearer my own poetic world than any English poet, that the gap is bridged. I don't think I could learn a new foreign language now. I mean, to read. (This is not true since I made rapid progress in Spanish in Spain). But really I wonder if I can read Stendahl. . . .

Lawrence was a much greater man than you know. If someone could go through his works and make an anthology from them, and from these letters, you'd see quickly enough. I know the bilge he wrote counts in one's estimate. As far as I have been able to see—with the exception of *Sons & Lovers* (and only parts of that—and that was not what he wanted to write) every book he wrote is unreadable. (Except [*Studies in*] *Classic American Literature*). He irritates me to the very point of madness. His prophet style, and the *extremely* unpleasant personal manner he has in some of these letters—as if he knew the truth but could not be bothered to reveal it—really puts me off terribly. But then when he is quiet, and peaceful, and will let himself *enjoy* life for one moment (a bit like you!), out come the most sweet and loving truths. . . .

I'm looking at a picture of Lawrence when he was 29. Before he got his beard. It is very true, and sweet, as he was then. It is an unmistakable "working class" face! Looks like a *very* intelligent, sweet British workman. The eyes are wonderful, much better than Stendahl's. His nose is coarse. He has that great English chin, which is so ugly and I think shows—must show—such a lack of proportion in a character—I know of no other single feature which is so physically unattractive to me—he did well to cover it with a beard. I think a small chin shows

---

character. (No chin at all may show the greatest character; look at the 18th century portraits—and I know a good example, Colonel Egerton—my Routledge publisher). I think a chin like this shows indecision. Do these points interest you? They do. Lawrence got a wicked look later in life. He got wicked. He got to hate, instead of to love. (There is a kind of hate which is right, & a kind which is false). *Why* he petered out no one knows. It wasn't only tuberculosis. Joyce has petered out. Look at Holms. Something terrible was going on then in Europe.[27] It has done Hoare in. Look at Eliot. Very interesting and awful this. (It has nothing to do with you and me, since we are American).

I wrote Muir a long letter yesterday about his new poems. I didn't think much of them. I started reading his *Chorus of the Newly Dead* again which he wrote many years ago. In spite of being like Tennyson and showing also the most commonplace acceptings of human cliches, it is in a frightening imaginative world. Nothing he has ever done is equal to it. I think he is done for. (Not for reasons that would affect the above; personal life, & weaknesses). I of course did not say any of this, but I think it's true. He has got a new lease on life, through going up there into Scotland. His poem is about that; but it's just statement, not imaginative. Not his own heavenly, strange, desperately beautiful poetic life. He is by the sea now, and says he can drink and drink it, till the end of his life—as he was brought up by it—in Orkney, you know—the very north of Scotland. He wrote so sweetly. I made Hoare promise to write him. . . .

I talked & talked to Hoare (who had not of course answered Muir's letter of last summer) & said he had no right to be so self-absorbed, to be stewing permanently in his own misery, to such a point that he could not lift one finger to help a starving man. (Muir might take things from him he would not from me; and there is no one else to help him). I don't know if he will write a decent letter. I said he must remember Muir is nearly 50 and hence must be treated with kid gloves (as I do not do you!) for when one is 50 and is doing what should be one's life work—in his case he has not done it yet—and when, as in his case, the chances are his real life work never will be written—the person criticizing, or encouraging, has got to take an entirely different tone than if writing to a young person. Don't you agree? . . . Hoare is really something strange. . . . When you see him here you may learn more, & then tell me things I can't know because I am so blind. . . . I don't EVER know what Hoare feels, at a given instant, if he conceals it by hurting my pride; or even if he does it by a mask. (He said "You can't tell from my face, but I can tell from my bowels.") I know what he feels in the long run. He is madly in love with me. He perhaps *never* will give it expression. When one is in love one is rendered stupider than ordinary. Everything the loved one says creates such an intense emotional reaction that you are occupied with that (can't help being, it's so awful) and so have not the detachment to enable you to know *why* they said it. Also, when one is in love one has such a sense of inferiority—one is so vulnerable. This also throws the judgment off. You know this, of course. To begin with Hoare and I started about as stupid (about people) as any two mortals could ever be. (Especially intelligent ones). We could have been led around in a ring & got prizes. The letter I sent him telling him I was going to leave Deak[28] (in January 1931), and his reply, which I saw recently, are classics. He was aged 35 and I was aged 32. Really prizes. So it's not to be expected that in 4 years we'd have come to perfect understanding. Added to this the fact that we are God's *holy* opposites. If ever two people were opposite. . . . Nothing should be put to him straight out. *Immediately* he retires. I should keep him guessing. Sonia told me this 4 years ago. I ought to know it by now, yet I keep on bashing my head against the wall of his fears. They are impenetrable. . . . What is imbecilic about me is that regularly, at least once a year—that which I did last year, in NY—it was the 5th time—now I've done it again, in a much more frightening way—I put it to him to make a decision. Just what he CAN'T do. . . . The satisfaction of this physical part (since we're both madly starved—I've NEVER had any satisfaction—3 months with Bianchetti,[29] and that not half what I wanted it to be) I should think would burn us both up. But until it can happen I *must not* force it. . . . Barker will want to sleep with me some day. If he does, and should love me—could I resist? Well I don't know. . . . At the moment he irritates me for being young, not knowing people; and *I* irritate me much more for being young. God damn it. (O Djuna perhaps I am getting sane).

Much love to you, darling. WHY haven't you written? (Are you sick?) . . .

PS: I've been finishing a very funny poem about a man who killed himself (all abstract), which I "received" in about 1931; it just came, 4 verses, didn't know what it meant. Showed it to John years later wanted me to finish it. Never could. Now Barker likes it the best of all & thought of one good word to replace two bad ones. So I went on, about 20 verses. Don't know what it is like. I want to finish one about Melville or Ahab—called *Ahab on Land*—which I think you'll very much like. Must get it done for you—feel it is your meat. Also *actually* worked on my book today—have got these two miserable creatures into Pt. III. They are now in England (having come laboriously up from Italy; it took them some time). She is pregnant now, the poor dear. (This is not me). I like Pt. III the best. I like the long sentences. The chapter on horses is in it. This will please you, I should think. I took a chapter out of the beginning of this London part & planted it smack at the end. Seems a great innovation. Do not know if it's right. . . . I really DO need to get this book aired out. No one has seen it but Tony. Have been leading a very lonely life this week. Ate eggs, as you and I used to do. New York, it seems so far, so far away. Was I ever there? I don't think I was ever. I think of the snow coming outside my window there.

Peter and I went to the Tate gallery on Sunday (it is the "modern" gallery here). There was a Van Gogh there I never saw before—a field, with flowers very carefully done, really in wonderful ways. Not his usual possessed madness (like those cypress trees), but calm. The madness all right—absolutely original—but controlled—what one wants. (You know in 1932 I saw in The Hague in a private collection 200 Van Gogh paintings; mostly mad, not in a good way. I wish I could see them again). I never will forget our going to that exhibition in New York. You made me see things I never noticed—you looked so *finely* at every smooth detail, so lovingly, like an anguished painter. You know there are six Sassettas now in the National Gallery (which I think is the best gallery in Europe) here; they bought them when I was in America. We saw a Sassetta in the C. Club—the magi going down the hill. These Sassettas are ravishing; the life of St. Francis. I long for you to see them with me. There are 2 would really fetch you. The N.G. has wonderful things—2 Francescas better than any in Italy. I can't forget that picture in the Metropolitan of the man looking through the window. I gave it to Peggy. I want another one. Some day if you're ever there perhaps you would get me one. Love to you, dear.

Djuna dear, I've just got your letter. It has brought me tremendous comfort. It is an icy cold day. I sit in front of my fire and read, write and do my book. I *sit* here the whole day. I send Mrs. Stafford—Hoare's char—out to get food. I never go to the cinema or see any one except Tony, Phyllis & Hoare, & Peggy when she comes. This week I've seen no one but Hoare. Your letter I love you for, for some reason (I know one can't *tell* anyone else what to do—one may clarify; but as you say I already have the situation pretty well clarified not entirely though). . . . It's because it shows a real understanding of me. I wonder if I have so real a one of you. . . .

Well dear enough about me; what about your life? I have loaded this on top of you; you have been so sweet; responded as no one could. I wish you could come to England. Answer this: what do you feel about coming to Europe without Muffin? Your money stops in March, does it not;[30] then Peggy might do something—I think. I have some influence with her. How should I use it? She understands that you can't live in America, but thinks (as I do) that you would not want to leave Muffin. Probably you shouldn't leave him—unless you are certain he could follow. At any rate I'm quite sure Peggy would be willing to give you $100 a month. I don't know how she would feel about a visit. Would you want that—and then go back? I don't think this would be satisfactory, would it? Better make a clean break, when you do come; set up your lares & penates here. I feel that with me & Peggy in England you could stand it. There are others too you might get on with; less offensive than Americans—I think. (I find anything better than American ignorance & slow wittedness). I don't know how you would live; am trying to be practical. Certain things would drive you crazy (accustomed to & loving Paris as you have been). But I feel that where the people are we like best there the heart can accommodate itself. . . . Nothing of course could be worse than New York. You know that shit. (Funny I have the strangest imaginative associations with New York, from last winter—nothing to do with the apes & imbeciles;[31] I think of it in heat and in cold; get odd feelings from the snow fluttering down over the roofs outside my window at the Earle (I *loved* that room). Also very odd feelings from the heat—your mother's house and people's voices ringing outside in those houses across the way, that hot evening). Hence, Paris eliminated (you can't live where you have no friends & where there are memories of friends), there is nothing left but London. That of course would decide that (were you to leave Muffin—or even come with him I should think). The problem is your getting accommodated to London. I must think of everything you would hate. But this is a trifle premature, & really solves nothing. What to do about Muffin is your trouble. I well understand it all. He's so like Muir, and in some ways like Hoare, that yet he is *really* like Muffin, that's the trouble. (As far as your book goes I should not worry at all. I am going to get it published. *And you know I will*. It may mean waiting some more). You sound very despaired about Muffin. You don't tell me why . . . I know so little. What is it you don't get—you too don't get enough. (With me it's sex, perhaps something more too. Yet if Peter "put me in his bed and kept me there" I feel I could bear anything—anything). Perhaps you too will turn. When the worm turns the other worm moves—to get out of the way, or to get in the way.

About Sonia. I'm sorry she bothered you. She is very sensitive to people, but was stupid in this instance. I hinted to her last spring that you could do without seeing her. I probably was too cryptic, since she is so sensitive & I didn't want to hurt her. I know what you say. I know all of it. What can I say except that I've known Sonia for years—that she does *not* flatter me—(or even understand me)—Peter has the idea she sits at my feet, someone told me Sonia was a "disciple" weakness (mine). She is not a disciple, though I could do with some. . . . I can't help pitying someone like Sonia. I know you—and Hoare—and Peggy not so much—can't pity anyone; you despise everyone. You may think this is a Christ complex. I simply cannot help giving out anything I've got to someone that needs it. . . . What can I say? The only thing is not to inflict [Sonia] on people who can't stand her. I didn't mean to. I absolutely hinted (very difficult since she's so sensitive & admires you so much) that you didn't care to see her. It's dreadfully hard to tell that kind of truth to anyone like that. She certainly didn't enjoy the lunch. I'm sure you won't hear from her again. About my sending her your book—the excerpts. I don't want to get mad with you now, after this wonderful letter. But this really makes my blood rise. The only thing we ever fight about is this!! The beastly selfishness of it. How *can* you Djuna? Why do you write at all? And your writing is not appreciated by so many people that you can afford to be snooty with someone who genuinely loves it. That good writing is reserved for a chosen few: well, I don't see it. Love and beauty are for those who want it. I see that the trouble is that you think of the book (as ever) as *yourself*. You don't want Sonia to have *you*. Well, your book is no longer you—it is an entity apart from you. Do not keep it from those who may get life from it. I don't think you would if you exercised you imagination.

Goodbye darling—thank you for this letter. I haven't answered it yet—I will (God knows I will!)

Emily

Dec. 9, 1935

Dearest Emily,

Thank you for Barker's book.[32] I received it some days ago, and read it at once. I wrote you about it, but decided not to send it, as it was in pen and looked as if you would never be able to get through it. And besides I could not finish it as I have been having so much trouble through my friends. First I had to see poor Mary Blair off for the Tuberculosis League in Pittsburgh—one lung completely gone, the other touched, and her case ninety nine per cent hopeless. Doctors gave her from two to four months to live. She looked so thin and scared, the cheekbones hollow and shivering, and her eyes bright as fire with fear and with a gay Irish determination to laugh it off. Then one morning December second, at two I got a hurry call from Louis, saying he was in the Harbour hospital about fourteen hours earlier than Marian had thought to go, as she had been taken with pains that they thought were labour. I got up, was asleep, and dashed into a taxi, got there before the caesarian was over, I could hear her screaming a floor above, Louis jumped like "the lopped leg of a frog," I pretended it couldn't be Marian. He jumped and turned green at every sound, the steam in the radiator, the flapping of a curtain, everything and anything. He had woman blood, most men do not take on that bad. Well, the upshot is that they have a son, seven pounds four, named Michael. Marian in great pain the first three days, doing better now. But I am still in a collapse, and Louis just coming out! The older I get the less able I seem to be to take anything emotional, literally on the flat of my back for two days, and still a week later depressed and low in spirits and weak feeling physically. All that time I had no word from Muffin, just when I needed it (Ah the history of the world) partly because his last two notes were so *inutile,* so brief and so about nothing I wanted to hear that I was furious and did not answer, and then as I had not the energy later to write he got the idea I did not want to hear. Now I have the sweetest letter from him, he is *about the nicest human being in the world,* and so darling to admit a change in feeling is what I mean. He says that now he has mailed back *Nightwood* to me he begins to see "what it is, really splendid. Generally writers write books, yours is born. That everybody who reads it should have different opinions about it is like when people stand before a newborn child and try to fathom its soul and its future. And the measure they have is their own size." I can't tell you more about him, because my hand refuses to write, but the moving finger writes upon the wall. I do not know if she knows or not, she pretends not if she does. Personally I believe she is doing it out of cleverness, to know a thing brings it to a head, she does not want this to get anywhere above the waist, any man can live that distance down she imagines probably, and with some justification. He is still away. I have almost forgotten what he looks like. His letters seem to come from a great distance which only I calculate.

Now in re Barker. I asked an Englishman here, one Peter Jack (critic on the *Times*) if he knew Barker and his work, and if so what he thought of him. He threw up his head and said "You don't have to take that young man seriously, one of the advance guard." I asked Geoffrey Gorer (do you know him? An Englishman, author of *Africa Dances*[33]) what he thought. "Ah" he said in that devastating English that sweeps away even God when it wants to, "a geyser of sentimentalism, beauty you know, and suicide and despair and all of that, and all of it lovely, too too lovely. He can't stop talking." So there my dear are two English opinions! I can't say what I think of him personally as I have never seen him, but I can see what he writes. You ask me not to mention any of his faults as you know them, but to tell you what I love. Because his faults are a strange virtue. In spite of every sort of thing which he does and which I dislike, all the posturing and smart alecky business, in spite of the "precious" subject and the consequent feeling of slight nausea which things of this sort, when written of briefly, in a "thin purple folio," in spite of all this—there is something that comes authentically through, as if it were a watermark stronger than the ink that overlies it. It is as if a Greek tragedy had been found by him in an old loft, over which he has written his own thoughts, but through which the faded ink persists. Undoubtedly he has strange knowledge for so young a boy, not as tho he himself were great, but as if he had come from some place where greatness was—in the presence of the precocious, we always say, will he just peter out because the strength does not seem to be in the person himself, but in some value that life from death gives. I am not an impassioned critic like you, I am much more like Peter Neagoe so will say no more, tho I know it will enrage you.

You know, I don't even want to write letters anymore. I *have no energy at all*. Sometimes I can't even lift the telephone tho it's ringing, I can't be bothered. I think there must be something physically wrong with me, it can't all be mental and I don't know what to do about it. It were exactly as if the words "Heavy with years" were literally true, I am weighed down. Probably it is a reaction from all the trouble now in the world, the coming war, apparently war all over the place, the smell of death is already hanging in the clothes of the nations, and why, what sort of people would we all be if not depressed, and a strong sense of futility over every impulse to create. Create, what for? A schoolteacher said the other day that she could barely get through her hours for depression, she could not take any pleasure in teaching children who were destined for cannon fodder. Can you blame her?

I do not know what to say in regard to Peggy's willingness to do something about me. I won't know anything about Muffin for days, he is supposed to return on the fifteenth but he has said nothing about it lately, so I presume she is going to keep him on. I want to talk to him first, not that that will make much difference I fear, he does not know what to do or what to say, and so he stays just where I found him, and waiting and waiting does no good as far as I can see, but I must give us this last chance, that is to see what he feels now, when he returns, if anything, above his usual gentle affection. Damn gentle affection! But I don't, as a matter of fact, because I am sure if anyone in the world cares for me in the least (personally) it's Muffin and I am not going to throw that away without an effort. I minded his criticism not because it was silly about the book so much as what it portended in our relationship together, anyone who could say anything so idiotic I despaired of a personal element, do you see? (Tho I still can't say I love the Jenny chapter yet).[34]

Kreymborg has asked to see *Nightwood*, so I am going to take it to him tomorrow. I have no idea what he will say as he likes my writing, but I am sure he won't take the book, as there are two others to pass it on. (Now discover he never read any of my work).

Charles Ford[35] back, with forty thousand words on a new book, he is also writing you for some poems to put in a number of that awful little magazine printed in Spain by one Sydney Salt (it's true, that's his name) of which Charles is the American editor. I gave him that part I gave him once before, and which I put into *Nightwood*, and took out again, you know his ways, can't say no to the idiot when he wants something, he's so exactly like a terrible child. I am crazy to see John's letters. When will I? Ever? . . .

Dec. 12, 1935

. . . I was reading the gospel according to St. John today, and I was struck with the saying of Jesus "I have no witness" (tho he was surrounded), it's always so with anyone who knows something that others do not; for this they disbelieve in very truth, and for this they stone and put to death; nor can one blame them, because what they do not know they fear, and what they fear they call evil, so have they been taught.

Perhaps there is no good and evil after all, only a lack of knowledge; because of this God (or whatever it is we call God, can forgive, because he sees far beyond us, as the artist sees beyond the commoner).

Really the world is (to my sight) a place filled with terrible and awful people. Then they say my writing is strange and mad. Why, great heaven, any life truly written in fact the least life, is simply appalling. Literature, and the child's lie told at the mother's knee is the only standard and decent life, as it is called, no man's such in full truth and laid bare. I begin to feel like Rimbaud, I am about to the point where I don't even care to try to write about it anymore.

Dec. 14

Just got your letter raving because you did not get mine then you got mine.

Darling, you pile up on top of me like a life work! (That by the by, is why you are not so successful with Peter. You make love so *difficult*. Fundamentally, man likes to make love, eat a sandwich and turn to the wall). I do not know where to begin to answer all your questions, and you know I never write letters anymore, and here I write you pages and pages, and then you threaten me with "well you wait!" when one comes through a little late. Really, you talk of our energy, you mean *your* energy. I have not half as much, and am getting less and less I fear. . . .

I like the way your back goes right straight up, in self defense, about Sonia, *when nobody has attacked you*! And now let's get this straight once and for all. I am *not* selfish in not wishing Sonia and others (for it's not only Sonia, it's almost anyone else, in fact anyone but my best friends and *any* stranger who might be instrumental in publishing it) to see my book. Of course I think of the book as "myself" which is exactly what it is UNTIL IT IS PUBLISHED. Then Sonia and the world can see it, have it all over the place and be damned. Its condition is all that I am arguing about, it is naked now, even when it is dressed (printed) the world and his mother can have it and light fires with it for all me, so it's not trying to keep "beauty away from those who love it." WILL you get this into your head? I tried to make you see my point while you were here, and you simply went on being yourself (as you often accuse me of being) WITHOUT LISTENING TO ME!! Damn! There.

Perhaps I should have been nicer to Sonia, purely for your sake (I can't for my own) but I found I couldn't even for you. (Probably because, like a fool, I slapped down three stiff drinks to try to overcome my side of the equation, for which I am very sorry, I'm always sorry) and I was frightened to death that she would want to see me again. . . .

Stendahl I have read very little of. His philosophy of love (which is utterly French, all scroll work, and let the lady suffer sort of thing. I may be wrong again, as it's years since I read him) and his first evil person in literature that you talk of, that I liked. Read Strachey on him, but all this long ago. Now if you keep on being in my life I'll have to read everything over again, and bull dog that you are, live my life over again! If you had got hands on Proust he would never have written his great work, he would have written letters of the remembrance of things past.

Speaking of writings, have you read the *Hydrotaphia* lately? Also can you tell me the best translation of Virgil? Read Stendahl in English if you can't stand reading in French. Greedy girl, reading in French you have to give some of your emotions to the French race, reading in English you can have them all.

I love Hoare's "You can't tell from my face; but I can tell from my bowels." Wonderful. Why there the man gives himself to you right on a platter. Love begins and ends in the stomach anyway, I think there the heart is.

By the by, before I forget it. Dr. Carrel[36] gave a lecture last night and I missed it. This I feel to be the greatest loss I've suffered in months. I thought someone would give me the date or place or expected it to be written on the wall (I never read the newspapers or that is about once a week) and it happened and I was not there. I shall go mad if I don't find someone who heard him. Nothing in the papers today but about an inch, my god what a world. But on the radio they said he raised a furor because he spoke of putting men to sleep for years (what can that be) and about memory of past time and future sight in people. Other doctors roared "nonsense" they would. I could really strangle myself for missing it. That serves me right for never reading the papers. You'll say it serves me right for never going out into the world. I can't do everything. And more and more I feel that I have not time for anything, tho I have all my time. Crowding in of past material and what I could and should do with it gives me this hurried and at the same time the impotent feeling.

"Lawrence got a wicked look later in life," you say. Do you remember John and the wickedness in his eyes sometimes very late at night, when he had been drinking far too much? I'll never forget it. He and Lawrence knew that they had been robbed of something, and all their lives they were trying to make an alibi, the wicked look in the eye was there when they could not keep their guilt from showing, they themselves were the thieves. . . . Can Peter Hoare help it that he sits on himself as if he were a door knob instead of an egg? I'll know more about him if I ever see him for ten days, instead of ten minutes. I remember all of us sitting in that strange gloomy dining hall at Hayford,[37] and Peter holding his head down and pushing his fork into something (not knife and fork, I remember that) hanging in moved silence while we talked about John, you adoring, and me, at the time, pretty skeptical, and my side of the fence he wanted, and yours he believed, and his own most uncomfortable. He's a nice boy, or I am mistaken, but I wonder if an American will ever know what a Scotsman is about? But one thing seems to me sure. No matter now what he does to keep you off he is sunk. If you stay or go. Being as he is he made his initial complete surrender when he had the *first thing to do with you.* If he tried to love someone else he would think he owed you something, and if you stick to him he will think you owe him something. God, I am not making it plain. I mean that given his nature (if I know it at all, and probably I don't) his very resistance (but with you all the time, not really refusing to see you) is a marriage. He'd feel like a scoundrel if now he succumbed to some other woman. You are around his neck now, (as they hang the dead bird about the killer dog's neck) and though he has not committed you, that very fact will hang heavier and tighter the more he tries to run away. It's probably why he wants you to go to someone else—or you say he does—to get you off, to see you, to contemplate you as an act he might commit with freedom, I said you make love so difficult, and so you have. On the other hand I don't suppose he would have noticed you at all, or would have forgotten (if you had not clung), because he is the kind of man who has to be forced (apparently) into attention, and then when he *is,* and it's *you,* it's so damned close. You treat people as if they had astigmatism!!!

. . . Now Emily! I did not mean that I was terrified of the evil in Thelma when I said I had a right to be terrified of her, that did not terrify me for a long time, because I thought she was not evil. I am still of the opinion (would take too long to go into it if my book does not show what I mean). I was terrified of losing her, that's what I mean.

I have not seen Scudder[38] for months. He does not want to be bothered with me because I can't stay up late, or anyway, won't, and his job, night clubs, require it, also he likes to be seen with pretty new clothes, poor darling, he is so feeble. I love him very much. My portrait I have been doing of him for months and months, is now coming, but it has been done several times and I always spoil it, because he won't pose for me, even for a minute, and if ever you had a brush and paint in hand and knew how the slightest mark, a dot of it even, in the wrong place, raises hell with the whole work, you'd know what a thing it is. I HATE

Van Gogh. I saw the great exhibition here. Didn't I tell you? Only liked one small canvas of two birds' nests. I can't like rough painting somehow. Paint slapped on by the inch. No smooth, smooth, gently, quietly making its way. I'll get you the man (and woman my darling!) looking through the window picture from the museum next time I go up. I have been going up a lot, just browsing as old ladies say, putting my eye on the lovely paintings, and rushing home as if I could bring it to my canvas (board) which I can't. I really could have done some wonderful paintings had I started early, given all my life to it.

. . . What a thing a female is to be sure. I spent the whole morning from eight o'clock to two thirty *cleaning up this* room. Why, because Muffin is coming! God, do I spend any morning from eight to two thirty working on my book? I do not. Funny, I used to in Paris, I worked on, let us call it the *Anatomy of Night*, if you really like it (Muffin does not, I've forgotten why now) every blessed morning from eight or so on, and at Hayford too you remember? Well then, what's the matter with me now? I wish I knew. I suppose it's possible that I have only two books in me, my life as a child, *Ryder*, and my life with Thelma *Anatomy of Night*—I can not imagine spending years writing fiction, things made up entirely out of thin air, and without a foundation in some emotion, as Muffin does (it's what's the matter with most of them I believe, but then, think of all the writers who have written forty odd books). Perhaps Muffin is right when he says my book was born, not written. A good book from a woman seems to be pretty much like childbed, which makes me sick to think of, men can scatter books all over the place like their seed.

Only thing in paper about Carrel I find: "The postponement of the death of too large a number of individuals would be a far greater calamity than death itself. Death is neither a calamity nor a blessing. It is a necessity, an indispensable condition of life. It is part of our self. It is probably the price that we have to pay for our agility, the compactness of our body, the beauty of our consciousness."

I have heard nothing from [Peggy]. I hope to heaven she does not lose Garman,[39] as you suggest might happen, she would die, because she has always had a notion that she was "too old for love" and as age catches up with that idea it will be more and more awful. I always thought I was my grandmother,[40] and now I am almost right, but fancy being right forty odd years ahead of time. But I never did have the idea that no one would love me, that's one form of inferiority complex I never got. I was always blissfully sure that anything I wanted I would have, and I was right, but I find now that I keep my gaze more at home. . . .

I don't suppose I've answered half your questions, no one could darling—it would take a secretary and four runners, a day and a night coach, and a well of ink, not to mention a colossal brain—you are the HUNGRIEST woman, I've ever known. Marvelous, but mad. Glad Hoare liked something of *Anatomy of Night* (I wonder if I like that title?) I could have killed Kreymborg, who said that he hoped I would come over again soon "You're a good show!" How would you like that? Shit, piss and corruption did I say!

Jealousy and death will have to wait. I have not thought about it for you yet, I am exhausted from my last week, Marian and Mary.

I'll have seen Muffin when I next write. Can a person live in London on 100 dollars a month? I have heard it's very expensive. I don't know what to do, my money is slowly going away from me, and I don't want a job, and I have no idea what will become of me, and would I write another book to make up for Peggy's help? You see what a spot I really am in.

Love,
Djuna

---

7 Oakley St., Jan. 3rd, 1936

Dear Djuna;

I just received your short letter . . . I don't know what has happened since you don't give any details—naturally—but you may be sure I shall see what Peggy can do. I didn't mean to give you the idea that she said directly, "What does Djuna want me to do for her—I will do it"— but just wrote you confidentially that I thought she was willing to do something for you after Eustace's[41] money stopped. I mean I think she would be willing to give you the same, probably. I'll handle this with delicacy—if I can—now that you really want to come over. . . .

I got your other letter—which hurt me a good deal—will not go into it now. I do not think you will find that I pile up on people for very long periods. I gave Peter 9 months of total freedom from me, during which time I hardly wrote him. He didn't care for it much. I've given him other periods. (I do not "press upon" him now as at first—nor have I for 2 years—I appear casual & have done so for a long time. I have not even told him I loved him for about 2 years). It is my nature to be very intense while I am in that state, and to withdraw at other times. No doubt it is wearing while it lasts. You will begin to understand why several friends are a necessity to me—to take the strain. I was in one of the most terrible periods of my life while I was writing you those letters, a fact which did not come home to you, overwhelmed as you were by the size of the correspondence. I was pretty sick. I may be more sick, but if so I will not put it on you. I remember saying several times in those miserable letters that I hated putting it on you. I wonder why it was so necessary for you, then, to rub it in. However, I know your life, and it's not a happy one, and you have much to worry you, and no doubt my energy was just too much for you at that time. I can't answer the letter, which was very sweet of you to write. I'm so fearfully sorry about Mary Blair—it is terrible—I know how that must have absorbed you—and Marian—glad that's all right at any rate. . . . Much love to you, dear Djuna—I wish I knew *what* happened—but see from your letter that it must have been something pretty appalling.

Yours—Emily

I think there is much more hope for Muffin than for Muir—(a) because M. is *not* involved with Annie emotionally (perhaps also a bad sign)—and (b) because you have really been able to get him in your hands—*influence him*—something no one has been able to do with Muir.

January 10, 1936

Emily dear:

Just got your short note, and knew before I opened it, that you were hurt, because it was so thin. I have worried ever since I said "piling up like a life work" because knowing how things that can be *said* can *not* be written . . . I am not only punished now, but very sorry, for your letters, in the greater part, bring me one of the few joys I have, and now I have cramped you and stopped you. Well, I was always like that, I am always putting my foot in it, as if my generations had me by the neck and were rubbing my nose, like a misbehaving cat, in my own doings, it's one of my troubles. I know so damned well how super-sensitive you are, and yet I go and say such a stupid thing. I have just sent you a cable, I can't bear to hurt you in this respect, particularly now when you are so unhappy and distressed but it seems to be man's fate to throw the javelin into the friend's back when bent in trouble.

I have been having a bloody time, what with one thing and another. Now Marian's baby is dying, for God's sweet sake! An internal hernia, the guts ripped and flowing up into the lungs, so that it chokes, it's in the hospital awaiting the greatest operation that can be made on a human being, and it poor child, only five weeks old. I got a hurry call from Louis, and dashed up, I was so terribly touched for the reason of his call, he said that Marian, who could not believe and who could not pray, (having read Carrel, which I gave her as a lying in bed present) wanted to trust in anything, and that she thought from what I had said, Muffin (she's never met him) sounded like a simple and holy man (he prayed for her when she was being cut up) and would I ask him to pray for her son Michael. I was not feeling at all well when I got the phone, but I dashed up to Muffin's number (has no phone) and, praying I'd meet him without her, ran into him in the entrance to the ghastly place that they now call home, a sort of mad man's arcade, chiropodists, movies, coffeehouse, piano tuners and plaster cast maker's emporium. I told him, and then went straight up to the hospital. That night when I got home I had a terrible heart attack, and thought it was all over with me, and alone. I kept fainting and suffering terrible pains in the chest and neck—and loss of breath and general horror. In the morning Muffin called and I told him, and he said I simply had to go to a doctor. I went, and was tested for everything, including a blood test. He has not made the full diagnosis yet, but he says my heart, lungs, and liver and stomach, as far as he can see at the moment, are organically O.K. but that I have inflammation of the muscles (due, he thinks to lack of exercise and my "unhealthy" life) and the rest is from *cigarettes*, neither more nor less!! Was I mad. I told him I simply had to have a fatal illness, as that was, paradoxically enough, now my only hope. He asked why, I told him, "that I may be so doomed that I will write my last and best book." I'll know the worst Thursday. My blood count is way down below hell and gone, it should be 115, and is 85! Muffin groaned "God, what will you be like when it's normal!"

I wrote to you again . . . of [Muffin's] intention of coming to England if I did. That he wanted the first two months of his sabbatical year alone, well, now he's changed that, and wants me to go way west with him in February or March (depending whether his book is out in one month or the other). And your icy, tho damned sweet letter, considering how you must have resented me at the time, about how Peggy would take it all has given me that awful feeling again, that I don't want anything from anybody, there is no use in pretending that gift money is as good as that which one earns or that which one *does not have*—it just isn't, there is a feeling about it all that I can't bear, so drop it please, and tell Peggy to also, tell her I've changed my mind. I'll go with Muffin as far west as we can scrape and when the end comes, I'll find something somehow, or let it ride. I'd really rather be a bum in the park, or die as I may, or take it as I must, than feel this work and charity over me. It is unendurable. . . .

Please, Emily darling, forgive me, *and do write me whatever is going on in your head and heart.* There's nobody I know but you who cares, really, about the same things I do, and if I can't stand a little exhaustion it's just too bad. What am I in the world for if not to be worn out by its manifestations? My protest, (tho only meant in joke,) was a sign of man's fundamental trouble, laziness and discomfort in the face of excessive emotion. And that's just what's wrong with this damned world. . . .

Had dinner with Charles Ford a few nights ago, he has gone completely proselyte on Marx, says that because my writing has no *universal* scope or interest in the contemporary scene and contemporary social condition is the reason that I am not read or wanted. That I must love Marx as Shakespeare once loved Christ, that is the new religion. I said, "If Christ and Marx stood together here tonight in this room, which would you follow?" He said, "Christ." "Exactly" I answered. "So why should I take your second hand God Marx?"

He went on to say that the Christian religion was dead, and that man must have an ideal to live by, and there was none unless it was Marx. I asked him if he had the idea that they were comparable, he said he did, then I answered you have got the thing arse end up. The Christian religion was of value because it was love of man *and a myth*, unreachable God in heaven made it what it has been to man for centuries, Marx is all very lovely, but it is only a dream bent on worldly hope, and immediate need, if it came to pass, (as it well may) that will be a biological change but not a spiritual, for the spirit grows, not only on ten dollars a day, but on the inconceivable, conceived by the artist at his highest point, and is still there to be apprehended above his greatest effort and feeling. Then he asked me why I wanted to write about the Baroness. "What great writer ever interested himself in pauper and *detraque*?" He inquired. I said I did not care what had or had not, but that she was not only the very bottom of his Marxian problem, (financial damnation) but *something* else beside. I asked him why he thought the bums in the park were bums in the park. He answered "for economic reasons only." Then I threw my hands up and said, "that's the answer to you, my poor adolescent, if you think that the bums in the park are there *only because of lack of money* you have muffed the whole great skeleton of the past, and have shelved the problem of man's psychology. Money is a very great part of man's environmental tragedy, but it *is not all*, and that all is what the artist must strive to find; nearly all of you rest on too easy a tabulation; just, as I believe, Freud, Jung and the rest are of little importance, because they now have a *canned and labeled precept* for every action, having, as it were commercialized the findings of the intuitive artists, like Dostoevsky—and the minute you succumb to that, it is only a thank you ma'am on the road to knowledge. Now I talked to Muffin about it, and God's little groat, he believes the one thing at least, that I should take my times, and the problem of my times in this the country of my birth, and write a socio-logical novel not as I wrote *Nightwood*, which is, he feels too personal, romantic and subjective. I should take an American family and write up their fall and destruction through the economic and social collapse of the structure. Oh, what am I to do! To begin with, as I said, when Charles said that what we needed was Marx and a "clean slate," I have no love for a "clean slate" it's exactly what's wrong with this damned country, we began with too clean a slate, we even killed off the few writings on that slate, which were the Indians, and what a pretty mess we have made of it. It's precisely the clean slate that frightens me about this country. Charles said "all right, what *are* your ideals then, you believe in good and evil, you *like* suffering and its outer side, riches, you like black and white, you are in other words a GANGSTER!" I answered that I was afraid that I *did* like good and evil, that I was, admittedly, a complete egoist, I was only interested in beauty, art and religion, that the purely happy and contented state of the native, say of Tahiti (before we got in there) of Bali (before we got in there) was, as Melville found, too damned heavenly and perfect for endurance; we have eaten of the apple, these peoples have music, dance (I never saw anything more beautiful than the Balinese dancers at the Paris exposition) and drawing, common to all heathen people, but they did not have *books* they have folk tale, but that, tho beautiful is not Shake-speare, they have music, (and tho I am most prone to it) they have no Bach, they have primitive drawings (which I love, in most cases,) but they are not Giotto or Veronese, or Carpaccio. Yams fall into their mouth, but perfection does not fall into their art complete and total, as it does from these masters, possibly (think of it) because of the very writing on the slate of good and evil. We condemn God, saying why has he planted evil in the world, if he is all powerful and all perfection, but what do we know of his design? It is His, and for that we should be a little reverent and a little more willing to take his terms, on which alone perhaps, we can learn our own.

Muffin, my dear, is far odder than you and I thought (as the bum in the park is far more than Charles thinks!). He has terrible pits of melancholy into which I seem to be able to throw him more completely than anyone else, himself not excepted. He also has moods of recklessness (in a modified form, that usually ends with the heat in his eyes, checked by the matrimonial gate). I think he loves me nearly to the point of being in love now, it only comes out in stress, otherwise, as I told him, his love makes me feel abandoned, left out. His terms have been, so far, pretty much his own, now slowly they begin to be mine, and as always (why is it always?) through withdrawal of myself and my emotions. When he thinks he is going to lose me (and he is about as sure of me, because of my past and my honesty in telling it) the fisherman of the trout that has slipped up-stream, he gets either frantic or melancholy, "either take her, or leave her" sort of feeling, which is based on a wish, an inertia that is appalling. I at one time did not find in him any inferiority complex, as it's called, but *there is one*, a terrific one in a way, not the usual plain seeable one, but it is there nevertheless, a proud defaming of himself that I have to overcome, over and over, and replace, only to see it melt, like snow in the sun, for what one person places in another, is like what the narcotic places in the body by needle, the body slowly overcomes it, and lives again, in its own terms. It is the great battle between one and two, and so only can a life lived together do any permanent good (or harm) because so truly the picture is everlasting, but I am afraid only everlasting because of propinquity, it is because of this personal bodily ability to overcome the injected, that we can ever "get over" a great love, as I have "gotten over" Thelma. She stayed with me last night, Muffin had been with me in the afternoon, I lay in bed looking across at her lying in the other, and I had the strangest feelings. Muffin seemed, for the first time, to be *nobody and my lover*, (the only reality, and the untouchable and now unclaimable) seemed to be her, sleeping in that other bed. Not that I could do anything about her anymore, (or her about me) but she was that terrible past reality, over which any new life can only come, as a person marching up and over the high mound of a grave. I don't quite know how to explain it. But I went over in my mind my feelings for him, and just the fact of her sleeping body across the room seemed to kill him like a powerful disinfectant. If he knew this he would die and wither. Pray God I don't tell him, I am such a *damned fool* at spouting everything, like Peggy, a beastly rotten disease; you are so much cleverer in this I believe, so much more mature, or at least, in your childishness (which is a great part) mature for *periods*, whereas the child and the mature in Peggy and me, are mixed up inevitably, like the chocolate and vanilla in a marble cake, so that we are in a constant whirlpool.

Muffin feels that he has ruined *her* life, as the casket maker thinks the corpse is his reason. Only temporarily can I make him see that she has ruined *his*.

I have been writing again, a little, and very good, I think, but it's most discouraging in a way, because it is so not what people want. I keep getting told that I don't write, with my "great talent" what anybody now wants. . . .

Emily, dear, from your short note, I take it that you are all engrossed in misery again with Barker? Is it so? I really envy you in a way. I'll *never be engrossed in misery again*. . . . I have *had* my great love, there will never be another. . . .

By the by, Muffin thinks Carrel made a great mistake in admiring Mussolini. Thelma tells me a strange portrait story of Carrel, one of her friends (a nurse in the war) knew him. He discovered some sort of disinfectant that would not heal a wound quickly, for he does not believe in this, but that it should be slow, as the tree is slow in healing, but the French government would not listen to him, the Rockefeller Institute got wind of it, and that's why he is here, and in the meantime a fellow chemist found a means by which Carrel's disinfectant could be kept indefinitely, up to this time Carrel had not been able to find how to perfect it to this point, it was a great medical aid in the war, the constituent claimed the *whole discovery*, and it is now called by his, not Carrel's name, which made Carrel (and I don't wonder) pretty bitter. This woman says he's a pompous little fellow, clinical to such a degree that he does not think of the human body at all, but of its cure, so that he would drag a dying man into the open, ruthlessly, and apply a new remedy to his groaning body without thought to that body's pain, it sounds likely, look at his picture. Still, I don't care, he's a great man, and once again, (as I have a million times), I have to swallow my idiotic idea that a great man has to be a great person.

I'll wait your next letter, pray for me, god knows where I am going, but west it seems to be with Muffin, in February, March, what will we really be like, taken out of our habits and thrown together?

Love,
D.

---

111 Waverly Place
Feb. 13, 1936

Emily darling!

Your letter came like a break in a long winter of ice and death. I am so happy that Eliot likes *Anatomy of Night* (Is this really its name?) I can't believe it. I am so happy that neither of us had hope, it makes it so much stronger and more exciting. Still I do not dare hope that it will get into print; people can love one's book and still it stays in manuscript. I'd like to think otherwise, but so long I have been hopeless, and so long my nature (according to Muffin) pessimistic that I do not believe it. Day by day I have been waiting for that cable from you, and as it has not yet come, I am sure that Faber and Faber have turned the book down. I have been deathly sick, days in bed on the flat of my back, too weak, literally, to answer the ringing phone, too lifeless to move over in bed, when I tried to get up, my legs would not hold me, I fell down by the side of the bed, I don't know what it can be, low blood pressure yes, but still, that is a bit too low for words. They say low pressure is worse than high. I am a little better now.

Thelma, when she heard that Eliot liked it, hung up on me on the phone, I've only seen her once since then, and she was frozen, and awful, as she used to be when she had done something bloody.

She gave me a book to read *The Wolf at the Door* by a Frenchman, writing under a pen name of Francis, she loves it, and it makes me sick, it's so lyric and sentimental. Talent, but all gone to the sugar bowl, I can't get through with it, and I keep wondering why is it I hate all the books that Thelma likes, wondering if I put this taste in her mouth, the lover getting back his errors as the retriever brings back the forgotten bone.

February 17

Muffin finally came down here. I managed to act as icy as a burg for two hours, he getting more and more uncomfortable, I had such a damned good platform for fury I hated to lose it, but lose it I did; but before doing so I said the most *awful* things, things that *no man can stand* without hating you the rest of your life.

Yes, that sweet Peggy did write me, just a word or two, and said that she would help me for a year (Muffin's sabbatical now gone). I have not answered, I don't know what to say, it's all over with him, that's certain, that is all over but that gentle affection of which he is composed, I don't feel anymore as I did, I can't, it's no fault of mine. I held on for two years on nothing (you on less, for Peter, but then, as I've said you are a martyr, and I am a tired, wise old lady with my "great love" past, yours still to come, or in the process) had I been as crazy about him in the last six weeks as I *was*, his behavior would have had me hanging from the neck to some beam, one can only like that man as a side thought, there's nothing else to be had of him, because that is all he has to give.

No, really, what will I do with that last chapter? It can't come out altogether, it's too good, but where on earth shall I put it if not at the end? As for the first chapter being clarified, god knows what Eliot means, anything, according to who reads. I've just dropped a heavy lead lamp base on my great toe, now I can't walk, had an engagement for a dinner party with Fitzi, can't go I guess, which does not break my heart as far as the party goes. What has happened to you and Barker?

I have applied for the Works Progress Administration for one of their re-write jobs, twenty two dollars a week, six hours work a day, and have to report every morning. I'll probably start work next week. I have to do something now, as my money is too low to allow me to eat, unless I go home, and I *can't stand that*, also to pay my doctor's bill, and have my damned dentistry (me and Muffin going to teeth!) attended to. So I'll work for the month of March and April, and then perhaps I'll get over to see you and Peggy. It would really be heaven. If you could see that Works Progress outfit you'd die. A great loft full of aimless looking bums, nobody knowing what to do, all handing in inadequate notes (the idea is to put the unemployed writer to work on a baedecker of New York) notes which I'll have to put into decent English apparently, all giving one the most extraordinary feeling of being in the park with the outcast, only not so good as that, because there they are *what* they are (which is always better than when they make an effort to be something again, or for the first time). Like being in Russia, without the fun of being a Russian. Proves one thing definitely, when you treat everyone alike, pay them the same dole, remove the possibility of fraud, cheating and gain, or in other words, hope, they are reduced to their lowest common instincts, inertia and carelessness. Thank you, I'll take a king.

Muffin should be satisfied, I'm certainly learning what my country is like, even *without* going out west.

How terribly true my last words in my book are, now "nothing but wrath and weeping;" in art one stops short of it by the dramatic curve which cuts the cord at the right moment, as for instance, when Muffin said he has taken her back, I should have, had I been a play, shown him the door forever. But in life we dangle on, lose our tragedy in wrath and weeping, wrath for what has happened, weeping for the loss of it.

I will write to Peggy now.

I should have written you days ago, it's a great effort for me to write at all, I am always so tired. Poor Marian becoming a case for the mad house. Louis sick with nerves and a reoccurrence of his stomach ulcers. For some Dostoevskian reason she finds it difficult to be kind to him now, really what a selfish lot we all are at best.

If Muffin thought *Anatomy of Night* a "dark seal on a very sad book," wonder what he'd think of my *next* if I were to write it! He says I am the most "touchy" creature he ever met, not to mention my ability at "throwing everything into a deep black pit." He's as jumpy as the devil now whenever I open my mouth. Well, I suppose I'll be a sharp old lady with two canes, a thousand black cats and the children will draw a witches circle about me, I can't say about my hut, as I shan't have one.

Muffin's like a worm-eaten old tree, the little white fat worms of A. eating (with sharp black eyes) from the inside out.

I am tired of being so old, and no hope, for time only makes it older. I am at a point where, really, I should have nothing to do with anyone. Every man reaches a ledge, sooner or later, that is only large enough for his own body, I have, but I don't keep to that proportion. As we grow older, narrower and narrower grows that ledge, and finer and finer is the hair's breadth between oneself and the fall that is the companion.

Muffin said last night that the trouble with my book was that it was *all* epigrams, no breathing space, he said one can get a fever by breathing fast enough, and this is what my book does, he went on to say that Eliot, being a poet would like epigrams, the perfect carved sentence, that my book was like the cathedral of Chartres—all intricate & perfectly meaning in every sentence, & added 2 statues are enough to look at at a time, no one can look at hundreds—I grinned, "Chartres will do me well," said what an (unintended) compliment.

Feb. 21—

Darling—I should have mailed this long ago—but never knowing what a day will bring up, keep putting it off—no cable from you. I guess your Peter was right—I am on needles & pins & no word.

Love—write soon—I only want one thing now, England, Paris or any place not New York.

Djuna

NOTES

1. Coleman's concern was not unfounded. Several editors had already told Barnes that Dr. O'Connor's monologues dominated the novel and needed to be cut. Coleman actually submitted two versions of *Nightwood* to T.S. Eliot at Faber & Faber, and Eliot, together with F.V. Morley, eventually published the shorter, which reduced the role of the doctor.

2. Scottish poet and critic Edwin Muir (1887–1959), whose eight books were published between 1925 and 1952, read manuscripts for Faber & Faber. With his novelist wife, Willa (Anderson), Muir translated the works of Franz Kafka from German into English. Muir would meet Barnes at a party a year later, and the two writers would admire each other enormously until Muir's death, after which Barnes and Willa Muir became good friends.

3. Art patroness and collector Peggy Guggenheim (1898–1979), daughter of millionaire Benjamin Guggenheim, who died on the *Titanic*. She sent Barnes $150 a month for forty-five years after the publication of *Nightwood,* in spite of Barnes' surly attitude and alcoholism.

4. John Farrar Holms (1897–1934), a decorated veteran of World War I, was famed for his vast knowledge of literature, superb physique and heavy drinking. He met Peggy Guggenheim in Saint-Tropez in 1928 and became her lover. Guggenheim subsequently left her husband, Laurence Vail, by whom she had two children. Holms could not leave his common-law wife, Dorothy, who managed to overlook his philandering with Guggenheim. Coleman loved Holms too, more intellectually than romantically. Though Barnes once described him as "God come down for the weekend," she also adored Holms and trusted his criticism as much as Coleman's. Holms died prematurely on Guggenheim's kitchen table under general anesthesia while having a broken wrist reset.

5. English poet, novelist and playwright George Granville Barker (1913–1991), whose early work was published by T.S. Eliot at Faber and Faber. Along with Dylan Thomas, Barker was probably the chief progenitor of the New Apocalypse poets.

6. Antonia White (1899–1979), Colette translator and author of several autobiographical novels, including *Frost in May* (1932).

---

7. Sonia Ginsberg Himmel, a friend and correspondent of Coleman's from 1928 to 1951.

8. The origin of this nickname for writer and painter Peter Neagoe (1881–1963) is unknown. Neagoe lived in Paris, where he met Guggenheim, Coleman and Holms in the 1920s and '30s. His 1932 edition of *Americans Abroad* included two of Barnes' short stories. For several years after the death of their mutual friend John Holms, Neagoe allowed Barnes to believe he would leave his marriage for her. He never did.

9. Barnes suffered from lifelong depression and health problems, but Coleman was probably referring here to the devastation both women felt after the 1934 death of their friend John Holms.

10. Barnes never completed a biography of her German-born friend, the Baroness Elsa von Freytag Loringhoven (1874–1927), a tragic figure well known in Greenwich Village for her eccentric outfits, thievery and outrageous behavior. After leaving her impotent first husband, Elsa was abandoned by her lover, Felix Paul Greve (aka novelist Frederick Philip Grove). She was left destitute by the suicide of her second husband, Baron Leopold von Freytag Loringhoven, in 1919. Though she died of gas asphyxiation in Paris in 1927 in what may have been a suicide, the Baroness was remembered vividly in the autobiographical works of William Carlos Williams, Stephen Watson, Harold Loeb, George Biddle, Louis Bouche and *Little Review* editor Margaret Anderson.

11. Barnes was still in possession of the Paris apartment at 9 rue Saint-Romain where she had lived with Thelma Wood.

12. Barker's 1933 *Alanna Autumnal* was a curious prose work, part fiction, part autobiography.

13. Essayist and biographer Hugh Kingsmill was befriended by John Holms in a German prison camp where they were both held during World War I.

14. Sir Alexander Samuel "Peter" Hoare (d. 1976), a Foreign Officer with whom Coleman had a long and complex relationship after their meeting at a party in Paris in 1929. His friends included poets George Barker, Dylan Thomas and David Gascoyne. He once published a paper on Rilke and enjoyed Coleman's literary company.

15. Barnes called her 1934–1935 portrait of Coleman *Madame Majeska* after the famous actress Helena Modjeska, a friend of her grandmother in London. Barnes biographer Andrew Field describes the painting as "so powerful in its radiant ugliness that it is difficult to stay with it in the same room for long."

16. Wood's infidelity, along with her drinking, doomed her relationship with Barnes.

17. Wife of the painter Louis Bouche. Barnes first met the Bouches at a party given by Norma Millay in 1920. Though she later abandoned many of her other relationships, Barnes remained friends with them until Louis's death in 1969 and Marian's in 1975.

18. Mary Blair, a friend of Barnes.

19. Saxon Barnes (1902–1991) was the brother to whom Djuna was closest. As vice president of Citibank on Fifth Avenue in New York, he was frequently able to provide support for Djuna and their ailing mother after their abandonment by their father, Wald. Saxon was impatient with Djuna's alcoholism and lack of financial initiative, but he never withdrew from her completely, as did their three other brothers.

20. As a sometime resident of Paris, Barnes was a friend of bookseller and publisher Sylvia Beach and the writers and artists who frequented her store, Shakespeare & Co. Beach (1887–1962) is best known for being the first to publish James Joyce's *Ulysses*.

21. *The Ladies' Almanack*, written by Barnes in 1928, was a satire on arts patroness Natalie Barney and her circle of friends. Barney was pleased to appear as the central character, Evangeline Musset. The risqué little book was probably not intended for wide publication; it was never copyrighted and was sold by Barnes on the streets of Paris before it was smuggled past postal authorities and sold in America.

22. Robert McAlmon (1895–1957), author of *Being Geniuses Together: 1920–1930*, considered one of the best autobiographical accounts of the "Lost Generation." He had met Barnes in New York sometime before 1920 and remained her friend and drinking companion there and in Paris and Berlin, where they partied with Fitzgerald, Joyce, Hemingway, Marsden Hartley, Charlie Chaplin and Isadora Duncan. In 1921 he married Winifred Ellerman, companion of the poet H.D. (Hilda Doolittle).

23. Author of the scandalous novel *Edna: Girl of the Streets* and the 1916 play *Lima Beans*, Kreymborg (1883–1966) was part of photographer Alfred Stieglitz's "291" group at 291 Fifth Avenue. He published a magazine called *The Glebe* from 1913–1915, which featured early works by James Joyce and Richard Aldington.

24. *American Caravan* was published from 1927 to 1936. It was an anthology of experimental writing edited by Alfred Kreymborg, Van Wyck Brooks, Lewis Mumford and Paul Rosenfeld.

25. Painter Anna Neagoe, wife of Peter "Muffin" Neagoe, usually referred to by Barnes petulantly as *she* or *her*.

26. Mary Eleanor Fitzgerald (1877–1955) met Barnes in 1918, when Fitzgerald was the tireless manager of the Provincetown Players. Prior to that time, she had, like Coleman and Guggenheim, served as Emma Goldman's secretary.

27. Coleman seems to be referring to the years around World War I, in which political turmoil was matched by upheavals in the arts, especially in Europe, with the Paris premiere of Stravinsky's *Rite of Spring* (1912) and the rise of the Expressionists in Munich. There was a growing belief in the forces of the unconscious, as evidenced by the work of Freud and Jung. Though Kafka said in 1917 that his tuberculosis was a psychosomatic symptom of his own inner turmoil, Lawrence (who would die of tuberculosis) despised Freud's theories. These were also the years in which Lawrence was hounded by authorities who regularly confiscated his work because of its sexual frankness and sent him into exile for fear that his German-born wife was a risk to Britain's security. He opposed the war and believed it hailed the end of European civilization.

28. Lloyd Ring "Deak" Coleman was an advertising executive whom Emily Holmes married in 1921. Their son's birth in 1924 and Emily's subsequent depression and institutionalization were the sources for her novel *Shutter of Snow* (1930).

29. Raffaele Bianchetti, an earlier, brief love, and correspondent of Coleman's from 1931 to 1934.

30. For some time Barnes had been receiving fairly regular support from a man identified in her letters only as Eustace, possibly Eustace Seligman, a relative of Peggy Guggenheim.

31. Coleman may be referring here to the labor strikes and police actions that were occurring all over the United States, especially in the textile industry. In early 1934 the Wagner-Connery Bill was introduced in Congress to deal with the unrest, which continued to escalate through the 1930s.

32. *Janus* was published by Faber & Faber in 1935. It was Barker's third volume of poetry.

33. A book on West African culture first printed in 1935. It was reprinted many times.

34. Barnes is referring to the fourth chapter of *Nightwood*, "The Squatter." Its main character, Jenny Petherbridge, was based on Henriette Metcalf, a writer who seduced Thelma Wood away from Barnes sometime in 1928. The title was intentionally pejorative.

35. Charles Henri Ford, founder of the short-lived *Blues: A Magazine of New Rhythms* in 1929, editor of *View* in the 1940s, and author of *The Young and Evil* (1933). He and Barnes were lovers and traveling companions before he moved on to Russian painter Pavel Tchelitchev, whom he met at Gertrude Stein's. Though Ford helped Barnes get her mind off Thelma Wood, she tired of the much younger Ford and the two parted company in Morocco in 1933.

36. Surgeon, sociologist and biologist Alexis Carrel (1873–1944), wrote a book called *Man the Unknown*, addressing questions of anthropology and human behavior, that Barnes and Coleman read and admired. He received a 1912 Nobel Prize for Medicine, honoring work that laid the foundation for transplants of blood vessels and organs. He also pioneered the Carrel-Dakin wound irrigation procedure still in use today.

37. In the summers of 1932 and 1933, Peggy Guggenheim rented Hayford Hall, a garden estate in Devon, England, and invited Holms, Coleman, Barnes and White to stay. This is where Coleman and Barnes first got to know and initially were critical of one another. It is also where much of *Nightwood* was written.

38. Scudder Middleton, another paramour, who was said by Barnes to resemble Thelma Wood and who, like Wood, was an alcoholic.

39. Doug Garman, an avant-garde publisher described by Guggenheim as a frustrated poet.

40. Barnes said her paternal grandmother was her first love and that Thelma Wood resembled her. Zadel Turner Barnes Gustafson (1841–1917) was a journalist and poet who began her career at age thirteen and hosted a literary salon in London in her forties. She witnessed "Bloody Sunday" at Trafalgar Square, was a friend of Lady Wilde (Oscar's mother) and was generally a radical reformer in her views.

JOY / *Jeff Worley*

Maybe it's always mixed,
like with Sally in 1974,

who touched me more tenderly
and convincingly

than any woman had, then spent
half an hour of pillow talk

on the Etruscans,
the Tarquin kings' iron-hand rule

in the latter half
of the 6th century.

The half pound of licorice whips
(I was 7) pulled up two teeth

the same afternoon I jerked
a snapping turtle from the canal

on a cane pole, thrilled until
I looked down to see a leech,

like a blob of cold liver,
sucking my ankle red.

Unadulterated joy? My friend
Lynn and I win the Kansas

Juniors Bowling Tournament in '65
and are handed trophies—

I'm not exaggerating—the size
of salt and pepper shakers.

He glued his plastic bowler next to
his steering wheel, a dashboard

Jesus of Bowling,
until a banana-yellow Corvette

slammed into his Mustang
and broke his trophy in two.

Bad luck? Well, joy can walk
the other side of the street, too:

The Vette belonged to
one Annette Winthrop Vickers,

who took my friend home
and asked his forgiveness

for two months. The Germans
have a word, *schadenfreude,*

for another kind of joy:
the evangelist caught

with his pants down in the choir loft,
or the child molester trapped

in the burning Tunnel of Love. . . .
To look and have one more look,

Lot's wife notwithstanding,
is also a kind of joy, the slugger

whizzing one an inch the wrong side
of the foul pole, then settling

in the box again. The next pitch
is a lollypop in his sweet zone;

he tenses his biceps, undercuts
the fat curve and like Isabella

waving Chris Columbus
over the horizon watches it

sail out of sight. . . .
It plops into the glove of

Candi McFarland, celebrating
her 10th birthday. She can't

believe it; she can't believe it!
She had her eyes closed! Joy,

a small hard sphere, turns
now in her hand, a new world

she holds up for everyone to see,
her glove hand, for weeks,

stinging gloriously.

LIES / *Jeff Worley*

> *Heigho, the tale was all a lie . . .*
> —*Housman*

I admit to the black lie, bending language
into necessary form, a glassblower breathing
molten glass into whatever shape occasion
calls for. And, uncertain or simply forgetful,
I've told the blueblack lie, the lie sheathed in
something, I tell myself, resembling innocence.
And of course the white lie we all trade in:
You were brilliant at the meeting. . . .
No, really, dear, your butt looks outstanding
in those slacks. I've told the Doberman lie:
the lie that clamps down and won't let go.
I've told the lie with the grin behind it.
I've appropriated entertaining stories
and made them my own—a friend's wild tale
of outwitting the Ponca City police,
mere borrowing I call it, knowing that's
a lie too. I've lied with cards, which is permissible.
My doctor fields my lies like routine ground balls—
all the vegetables and fruits I've been eating lately,
the four-mile jog no matter what the weather!
I have invented lovers in casual conversation
with ex-lovers—have so convincingly counterfeited
amorous evenings on nonexistent beaches
that perfect pebbles of white sand floated off my tongue
with the buoyant lie. . . .
                But how wonderfully electric
to get away with a lie, to Z it into the air like Zorro
and watch it shine in the moonlight. How, then,
I love the language even more! *Hi, boss. I woke up*
this morning with a cold/the flu/hair lice/a grouchy
disposition/Korsakov's Psychosis/ichthyosis/
a sudden fear of neckties/a bulimic psyche, and won't
be in today. . . .

If lies were helium balloons,
every H&R Block in the land would suddenly float up,
linger like a handshake, and rise toward tropopause.
The U.S. House of Representatives would zoom up
as if shot from a silo. . . . No lies, though, in the torturer's
sub-sub-basement damp with rat piss. Shackled to the rack,
who among us would stretch the truth? Burrow my eyelids
with a pneumatic drill? No thanks. What would you like
to know? And what is poetry after all, Shakespeare said,
but artful mendacity? Or perhaps it was Marlowe
who said this, who knows? I do know that sometimes
I walk shoulder to shoulder with the guilt-ridden
who feel their lies swarm around them like wrathful bees.
And some nights there's this dream I couldn't lie about
if I wanted to: An ex-lover I detest for perfectly good
reasons corners me in the men's room. She sticks the barrel
of a Magnum into my left ear. *Do you detest me?* she asks.
I blink. I clear my throat so the words can rise. I feel her
trigger finger begin to buzz. I say: *Do I detest you?*
Do I detest you? I love you I love you I love you.

SOME OBSERVATIONS WHILE
RECOVERING FROM SURGERY / *Jeff Worley*

The dogwood has exploded open
    its white buttons
        since I've been away,
and the lilac sways with pompoms.

Some purple flowers
    I wish I could name
        have been coaxed out
by a gentle morning rain.

In the near distance
    a bird I call the Barber Bird
        because of its sharp call—
snip, snip; snip, snip—is furious

with our tomcat Jaws
    for trotting across the lawn.
        She drops something
(I see through my binoculars) into

the hinged-open beak of a hatchling,
    then swoops back to the garden.

The diverticulum the surgeon snipped
    out was larger than a fist,
        she said, and shaped
like a Hallmark Valentine heart.

I never knew I had it in me.
    My father would have called
        by now from Tucson,
but his words keep failing away

from him like frizzled leaves:
    adios *pompoms, Valentine heart.*

And now I notice
all these dandelions rioting in the yard. . . .

Dad would have never allowed it.
    I remember him
            one spring at midnight
under the full Kansas moon,

a silhouette spearing up dandelions.
    From my misted window
            I thought he looked like
a man harboring a secret

loneliness too deep to ever
        be rooted out.
            My father
making his small corrections,

making his corner of the world right.

Jeff Worley has his second collection, *A Simple Human Motion*, scheduled for publication in January 2000.

KICKER / *Kathrin Perutz*

Learning to Smoke

I started smoking at six, or at least that's the age I give for when I had my first puffs, riding in the car with my mother, lighting her cigarettes, learning how not to wet the ends when I drew in the smoke.

Six, I say when people ask, though I'm reasonably sure I was younger, four or five probably, a nursery school renegade. But I've learned that most people won't buy it. They think I'm making it up, like a story from the *Examiner* or *Star* or *Enquirer*—"Baby Born Smoking"—with a photo of a diapered newborn puffing on a big cigar and a caption underneath: *Cuban infant nursed on tobacco*. They smile and say, "Really?" with an ostentatious intake of breath and the kind of bright look people get when they think they're talking to idiots.

A very few, supremely dedicated smokers have believed me and have even confessed their own delighted discovery of the weed at around that age, but generally it's regarded as either malarkey or perversion to suggest that a child might puff on a cigarette—and like it—at the same age as she first discovered the joys of playing with herself.

"Six?" shrieked the terrible French teacher at the Alliance Française, where I was taking a course in hopes of reviving my once fluent, now nearly desiccated knowledge of the language. "Sees?" *Mais non, Madame, vous voulez dire 'seize.'"*

I held up six fingers. *"Un, deux, trois . . ."*

She shrugged, defeated. It was a French class from hell that I'd signed up for the month I quit smoking, thinking it would be amusing or educational, or at least a distraction while I waited for the craving to go away. Mademoiselle Estelle d'Estaing was one of those tatterdemalion young women who come into being fully matriculated on the Boul' Mich' or rue des Ecoles, near the Sorbonne, with their ideas preformed, opinions intact; who regard Simone de Beauvoir as a retro, if not exactly a bimbo, shrink back in horror at the sight of a Coke and take pleasure in informing you on first meeting that Americans are materialistic, lacking in culture, undereducated and—with an accusatory glare—rude.

". . . cinq, six," I continued counting, ending on the extra thumb. *"J'avais six ans quand j'ai commencé de—commencé à?—fumer."*

She wouldn't help me out. In any case, whether I commenced of or at smoking, it was a lie. I wasn't six; it had happened earlier, around the time I learned to spell my first word, its pink neon flashing at the corner of Queens Boulevard and 83rd Street when we passed it coming home from nursery school. The pink shapes, on again, off again, were hypnotically beautiful, and when tiny Edward Davidson, who sat in front of me in the large station wagon, pointed to the sign and said, "B. A. R. spells BAR," I was awed. When he turned and repeated it, the letters fixed themselves like rare butterflies in my mind, and as I watched the sounds tumble from his mouth, I fell in love with him, even though he was the shortest boy in our class and I was the tallest girl.

A few days later my mother and I were riding in the Chevy and when we passed the sign I crooned out, "B. A. R. spells bar." She looked at me with a moment's incomprehension, and then she laughed. She was proud of me, being that smart. Her English was still only tolerable then, and it must have tickled her that the first spelling word of her American child was an international one, like "taxi" or "toilet," as apt in Paris or Prague as in New York.

It was around this time, the year the war ended, riding in the Chevy alone with my mother, that I began lighting her Chesterfields, making sure to keep the ends dry, holding out to her the torch of my love, handing her the burning proof of it years before I had words to declare myself.

She was beautiful, she held herself tall, she had thick auburn hair swept into a chignon and the profile of Nefertiti. Her clothes were couture, and she rustled when she walked. But I could feel she was imprisoned in a kind of silence where I couldn't reach her.

She spoke many languages but had no command of any of them. Language was her tyrant as she floundered to keep up, trying to relay her meaning despite or between words that she never actively selected. She simply allowed them to drift in, taking hold of whichever first came to mind in whatever language and then bending it to her will through intonation and gesture, as she would later shape her sculptural forms into approximations of animals.

As a little girl I felt some of her emptiness echoing through me. Her silences were reproaches, the places I couldn't fill. Bewildered, annoyed, usually resentful, she was suffocated by words that wouldn't rise to the surface, drowning in her own inarticulateness.

She was always in a sense "over there"—back in the land of her childhood, where she'd grown up with tennis courts and a French tutor, the prettiest girl in town, who wore a little fur collar in the snow and eventually, as a young woman, came to America like a banished royal, bearing her sorrow with her beauty, an Anastasia on Ellis Island, wearing a babushka.

She was a lady. As a child I never saw her cry, except for one morning when I was about three and a half or four. I'd planned to surprise her, crawling along the hallway from my bedroom to hers on all fours, quiet as a cat, avoiding the creaking floorboard and holding my breath when I came close to her door. It was ajar, and I could see her sitting at her desk with a piece of paper in her hands, doing something strange with her shoulders and her chest, making sounds I'd never heard her make. I was as terrified in that moment as I would be again a few years later—when I was sucked up into an enormous wave at Jones Beach and churned around, my mind going black until I was somehow released—and then I crept away from her door, still holding my breath. From then on I tried to make up for it, for her being alone like that, unable to speak, reading her terrible letter, her mother gassed.

The smoke warmed the car, filled it for us, riding along Queens Boulevard some time after V-E day in the 1939 Chevy, sharing the perfect happiness of a Chesterfield, from my lips to hers.

My first puffs brought me into her world, the magic and silence of Prague before the war, before my birth, before the deaths. I never thought about the ashes of my grandmother and all the others; the smoke surrounded us and held us in a nimbus.

I didn't start smoking on my own until I was close to puberty, in junior high in the wilds of central Queens, where I was one of the designated goody-goodys, one of the rich-bitch kids with IQs over 130 who were in the accelerated classes, S.P. (Special Progress), one of the Some People, usually Jewish, who were bused in from Kew Gardens and Forest Hills, who were educationally motivated, richer, younger and far more cowardly than the other students.

We had kids of sixteen still in seventh grade, stuck in remedial reading and taking courses in carpentry or electrical wiring. The girls were tough, full-breasted, and they fought like crazy over boys or imagined insults, tearing each other's hair out or bashing each other's heads on the concrete of the handball courts. Only a few students carried knives then, and if they did it was mainly for show. But the cops were called over to the school nearly every day, at morning recess and again at lunch, to break up fights or haul someone off for vandalism.

This was in the early fifties, before drugs and guns came into the schools, but even without them we had violence. We had poverty. A kid in our speedup class (not Jewish, not privileged, just smart) was one of a dozen siblings, all of whom shared a single bedroom. We who didn't have to go there were attending this school because it was scholastically exciting for all of us, who were sorted according to ability or potential instead of grades and taught by young, idealistic teachers full of fire and imagination.

We, the Smarties of 7-9 (ninth division of seventh grade) and later 9-9, read Shakespeare, wrote plays, published a newspaper from the days of *Ivanhoe* and studied either French or Spanish. My two years there were the most stimulating of my educational life—including college and graduate school—but I was a fish out of water, large and pusillanimous, still wearing braids at the time of the poodle cut, shy enough to respond with a flush if a male spoke to me—a child of another era, of prewar Mitteleuropa, where my parents had grown up in the privileged splendor of Russian novels, cultured and assimilated, polyglots at seven and on the run by '38, fleeing the Anschluss.

As their only child, I knew it was up to me to provide them with something like a family, a shadow of what they'd lost. By the time I started going to junior high, I had already accompanied them on many travels, to Europe mainly, and business trips to South America, spending most evenings alone in a hotel room in the era before television, when a child had to read or write or make up her own stories. My days were spent with adults, taken along on their pursuits, walking in silence, often not understanding the language they were speaking. I had grown up lop-sided, with too much head and too little sense—both common sense and a sense of myself.

Junior high in the slums was a shock; the first months there I cried every morning before leaving for school, and after that I started wearing makeup, bleaching my hair and carrying my own pack of cigarettes.

Quitting

That was forty years ago. Giving up, as the song says, was *awf'ly hard to do* . . . particularly since I'd come to depend on cigarettes as my juice, my gas, my inspiration for writing.

I became a writer early; I was published young. To write, I depended on cigarettes, chain-smoking my Marlboros—"coffin nails," we joked even then—four or five packs a day, eighty to a hundred little white logs to fuel my passion, churning me into a frenzy that drove me to write 2,000, 3,000, sometimes as many as 5,000 words of a morning. I'd take only two or three hours for it, my fingers dancing a mad tattoo on the Olivetti keys (and the keys of the Underwood before that), coming down from my high in time for lunch, or earlier, for "elevenses" when I lived in England after college, or for *gabelfruhstuck* in an Austrian farmhouse where I'd escaped to write, when the freshly made dumplings would arrive in my Spartan room, steaming in broth from the newly slaughtered pig or gleaming in butter, with that morning's pick of ripe plums.

I wrote in a daze, a haze, a trance of nicotine and smoke, scrambling to keep up with the flow of words that streamed out without my conscious direction. I wrote until there was no more oxygen left to breathe, when the room began to take off and black spots danced in front of my eyes, twirling into a dark snow and making me too dizzy to stand, slightly nauseated, lightheaded, gasping for breath, unable to write another word and barely able to walk.

At writers' colonies, reaching for my Marlboros at dawn, the words already popping like corks, I'd race into day on a rush of bright phrases, roaring my energy over breakfast, the high nicotine wit at the early risers' table. I'd have four cups of coffee and an ashtray filled by the time I left for my studio with a large thermos of black coffee.

And there, in my studio in the woods or up by the barn, I'd pour out the words, let them spill onto the page like pearls, gleaming. For the next few hours, smoking, in a trance, I'd let the words stream without check until a silent whistle blew in my head. Time to stop, time to breathe again. I'd look at the clock—a couple of hours gone—and read what I had done.

When I gave up smoking, I spent much time mourning my loss, in dreams as well as waking. I missed the comfort, companionship, the reassurance that life, punctuated by a reliable series of jolts to the system—a drag every every thirty-two seconds of an ordinary sixteen-hour waking day—was somehow doable, one step, one drag, one half-minute at a time.

Without cigarettes, I couldn't write. Things didn't hang together. I couldn't concentrate on anything; new projects or places or people were terrifying; the old grind and ordinary relations became boring to the point of stultification.

My lost cigarettes, my happiness. I fell into a grieving and a physical deprivation, my body not yet adjusted to the loss. I missed the taste of them, the handling of them, the bygone days, my childhood, my mother, our songs, the innocence of the American fifties when More Doctors Smoke Chesterfields Than Any Other Cigarettes and
Smoke gets in your eyes . . .
Those foolish things—
a cigarette that bears a lipstick's traces . . .
remind me of you.

Cigarettes go back to our first love, the first attachment. Smoking is sucking, our first impulse. Mammals need to suck to survive. We begin practicing in utero. Emerging from the womb (most of us still blind), we nose our way toward the warmest place on her body, the soft areola or the pulpy softness around the teats, plant ourselves there and suck. Sucking is all we know of life. Even protomammals, even the marsupials, know how to do it. A half-gestated kangaroo joey no larger than a pinky climbs up the belly and into mother's pouch, settles deep inside and sucks the fat-rich milk from her lower set of nipples. Sucking is survival, our first act, first instinct, leading to our first taste of life. Sucking is mother; sucking is love.

Freud discovered latency in the libido. Mother love in infancy becomes oedipal by adolescence. The same goes for cigarettes—they carry us back to the first pleasure we tasted, to the first act we committed on our own. No matter what addictions we move on to later, it was smoking that started us. Most dedicated smokers have started smoking regularly by their early teens.

I was thirteen when I began, my mother twelve, in her faraway snow dome beyond the great castle of Prague. It was Kafka country, circa 1920, at the onset of what would become the flapper decade—fringed dresses, a modern attitude, cigarette holders as part of fashion, emancipation in Europe from the grimness of war; a time for frivolity, costume balls, breast-baring art students, films (the great Garbo smoked, and Jean Harlow, and Dietrich in her tux), gramophone records and the thrill of Marxist "free love" for every pretty bourgeoise. My mother became a beauty, she stole her sister's boyfriends, she didn't like women, not even her mother. She referred to members of her own sex as "female" and was able to ignore all the women in a room, even a man's wife, standing next to him. I was named after the cook, she told me, and when she was dying, she sometimes called me by the name of the maid, not through confusion but to make a point. Women were servants, competitors, enemies. When she loved me most, she called me her "best admirer."

Memories trail: smoke rings over Times Square, spreading out from the wooden *o* of the Camel smoker's mouth, round as doughnuts floating down Broadway, in the forties and fifties, when I went to the theater with my parents, usually for a birthday, and then later with boys; fumbling with cigarettes, through my high school years into college, struggling with bras and lipstick, male fingers outlining my areolae, making my nipples strain against the tight purple sweater flecked with angora; hands groping their way under the soft wool like small animals seeking to feed, as I puffed into my womanhood, from the Chesterfields of home to the Marlboros of maturity.

I saw my first pack of Marlboros in the pudgy hand of a blind date, my first year of college. We'd gone to a football game (also my first), Brown vs. Columbia. At halftime I was asked to come down on the field to pose for a photo with the home team's mascot, the Brown bear. I followed instructions, thrusting my chest forward à la Lana Turner, holding the bear by a chain. Afterward my blind date laid his arm across my shoulders, the plump fingers of his right hand drooping toward the incline of my breasts and edging forward millimeter by millimeter until my throat went furry and my thighs slack. He had a tattoo on his left arm; he'd been in the navy; he smoked Marlboros. I was still "pure" in those days, hymen intact, and nothing else happened. The fingertips, exploration, the clouds of Marlboro smoke, his tongue in my ear. His name was Julius. I switched to Marlboros.

Marlboros, the world's best-selling cigarettes, first appeared on the market in 1902. Made by Philip Morris, they were intended for ladies, with a red tip to hide lipstick marks. Cigarette smoking, it was known, kept you slim.

They kept me thin, or at least prevented the bloat. Once out of college, I left America for England. The cigarettes there were perfectly disgusting, due to the bizarre English practice of curing their tobacco with saltpeter in order—so I was told—to discourage libidinous urges in the trenches and on the playing fields of Eton.

But in the byways of Soho, and of course in Mayfair, I could buy Marlboros. They were pricey, desirable. Almost everybody smoked them. Or Gauloises. Or the cigarettes of almost any other nationality. I smoked Austrian cigarettes, Dutch, French, even Spanish. I tried cigars, bought a pipe.

When I gave up smoking, it was not for any good reason. Not, for instance, to avoid death. My lungs didn't hurt, I wasn't coughing and my x-rays were gorgeous. True, I was out of breath after a flight or two en route to a walk-up apartment and I had a tendency to pant after exercising for a few minutes. But these weren't serious symptoms in and of themselves, and in any case my own doctor, whom I'd gone to since the age of fifteen, still smoked.

I stopped partly to prove I could. Proving things to oneself is undoubtedly both childish and narcissistic, but I was bored, self-preoccupied, unable to write, over fifty with wrinkles showing, and I needed an overhaul. I wondered what it would be like to be free of a lifetime habit, not to mention wrinkles. Deciding to quit and actually doing it would prove I was free—or so I deluded myself.

Once I started stopping, I knew I couldn't stop. And to make sure I'd continue quitting, I concocted the perfectly insane notion that I would write about it, fully aware that I couldn't write without smoking.

I couldn't sit down, sit still, remain at the computer or even in an armchair. In order to write *anything* I had to trick myself, jotting a word or two, sometimes a phrase, in the little black marbleized notebook I carried while walking on the street or down the aisles of the supermarket, while driving or putting on my clothes at the health club, supporting myself against the red metal locker. Writing—the physical activity—was torture. Like an overgrown toddler, I couldn't stay still long enough to put one word in front of another.

But I persevered, determined to be an observer of myself. My hope in keeping a journal was that it would permit me, by making me the subject and providing my own suspense—Will She or Won't She?—to accomplish what I set out to do. The reasons no longer mattered. The process itself took over: withdrawal and all its symptoms, the physical changes, easy tears, flatulence, strange dreams, a kind of seasickness, pitching me from wave to wave and mood to mood. There was occasional humor, too, like the time I followed a man on Fifth Avenue, inhaling his fumes like a pig nosing for truffles, until he suddenly turned and I blushed, trapped like a deer in lights, unable to explain.

At the beginning, I was caught up in the sheer physicality of it, unable, as with pain, to do anything but ride the currents of my body's needs. And then it turned out that most of my reasons for stopping came after I'd done it. It was almost as if I'd been hidden from myself and couldn't see what I was up to until the smoke began to clear.

Learning to Breathe

The type of smoking I'd been doing most of my life—more than 300 hits per day (for roughly a two-pack habit, down from my peak at 5 packs, 750-plus hits)—gave me a certain distinction, and dumped enough nicotine into my system to affect the brain like cocaine. I was, it turned out, a druggy kind of writer, like Henri Michaux or Thomas De Quincey, writing from the equivalent of a cocaine high.

This I learned through my reading, which became compulsive. Obsessed with the cigarettes I could no longer smoke, I started reading about everything to do with smoking, in history and across cultures;

medically, historically (tobacco was America's first cash crop), politically, etymologically (what is a "smoking"?), financially (especially R.J. Reynolds and Philip Morris, the Big Board sweetheart), socially, confessionally. I read *The Surgeon-General's Report on Smoking & Health of 1988*, the one titled "Nicotine Addiction," and it was there I discovered that cigarettes can (if you smoke enough of them) affect the brain more potently than cocaine; also, that withdrawal from nicotine is, for some wretched subjects, as difficult as giving up heroin. (The word "nicotine," I read somewhere else, comes from Jean Nicot, French ambassador to Portugal at the time when tobacco was imported by ship from the New World. He encouraged the cultivation of the plant in Europe.) I read *The Surgeon-General's Report of 1988* from cover to cover, the whole 639-page, in-depth survey based on the work of dozens of eminent scientists from different fields and acknowledged to be the most comprehensive study of the subject ever done: the tobacco abolitionist's Bible.

I read about addictions of all types—to liquor and coffee and chocolate, and to drugs of every type and stripe. I read about behavioral addictions too: of love slaves and money junkies, risk-runners and fitness fanatics. Books on addiction to food, of course, overran the shelves. There was a lot to read, though other people's addictions seemed excessive and unnecessary to me.

My own symptoms were more interesting. Violent mood changes, too much saliva, a need to chew anything, a lust for sweets, backache, pains of indeterminate origin. Also, I was having breaking-dependency dreams that I recounted for my hypnotist. He called it "growing pains."

I'd started going to him after my first week, when I heard myself telling my son, "I don't love you. I don't love your father. All I love are cigarettes." My son was grown, but still. The moment of fear sent me to Sandy Touchstone, appropriately named, with hair and eyebrows the color of I Can't Believe It's Not Butter. He lived and practiced in a cluttered apartment on the Upper West Side, about $100,000 short of a river view, crammed with books and the kind of interesting garbage we used to find on the street in the sixties and transform into furniture: orange-crate bookshelves, chianti-bottle lamps, peeling old chests covered with bits of Indian cloth, the glints from the tiny mirrors flitting around the room.

The place was instantly familiar. In the living room, where all activities of life appeared to be concentrated except for the eating and eliminating (those were sequestered behind room-dividing curtains), two enormous armchairs confronted each other like monarchs of equal power. On the floor between them revolved a sophisticated-looking device, something between a barometer and an electroencephalograph machine, which I took to be part of the hocus-pocus, a New Age kind of gizmo intended to measure the rate and rhythm of breathing in the hypnotized subject.

Later, I learned it's an air purifier. Touchstone is allergic to cigarettes, he explains; his parents were always smoking.

So were mine, I say. His were smoking *at* each other, he clarifies, justifying his allergy.

In any case, almost everybody's parents smoked. Mine smoked all the time. I sat in the car between them on the bump, inhaling their air, their mystery, her unspoken words, the shifts in mood between them, unaddressed reproaches, unexposed memories of the world they had come from, their childhoods, the portion of Europe that had disappeared from the earth. We lived behind veils, my mother's haute-couture wardrobe making her as glamorous as the fabled Elisabeth, Empress of Austria, the most beautiful royal of Europe. She had a dress with a wide border of large black spangles below the hips; she dazzled when she walked, auburn hair coiffed into an ornate chignon, black dress with black spangles, high heels, striding like an empress. She allowed me into her dressing room and I could watch the secrets of her beauty unfolding: the ball of cotton doused with eau de cologne mowing lanes of cleanliness on her neck. She spat onto the small block of mascara, frotted the caked brush across, touched it to the pale tips of her lashes. She put on jewels, asked my opinion, tried the emeralds, the diamonds, all of it tasteful. She straightened the seams of her stockings, she dabbed on perfume, touches of *Femme* at the ears, between her breasts. My father, when he came in, was speechless. She was always more beautiful than he could remember. He was permanently banished, like the Emperor Franz Joseph, from his empress; she distanced herself from him in many ways. They had separate bedrooms; she was an artist and a lady, a grande dame, with the demeanor of a duchess.

She smoked first thing in the morning and first thing on waking in the night. Then she'd go downstairs in her creamy silk dressing gown, her hair tousled, her eyes puffy (like an owl, she called herself, *eine Eule*; she did a series of them, owls in lithos and woodcuts), and she made espresso, the kind we had then, with the flip-over coffee pots. Earlier, in the forties, she cooked her coffee the way they did in Prague, letting it boil up three times in the pot, removing it from the fire each time until the last, when a single large bubble would form over the liquid like a dome, and she'd turn off the gas.

Coffee and cigarettes, and she never allowed herself to weigh more than 127 pounds, at five feet, six inches. At the end, she lost weight drastically. I dreamed of carrying her in my arms; she turned into a cat, a cat dying as I ran through the streets of my childhood, the closed school, the closed church at the corner, the darkening avenues.

They both smoked, always. I loved the smell, the warmth, the haze it put us under. On the front seat of the Chevy, me between them breathing their smoke, listening to them speak the admixture of languages they used with each other—German and Czech and English, French, bits of Italian, Hungarian—I felt the safety of being a part of all that, of having drifted here from another shore, a bygone world, whose reality receded as we traveled, vague and dreamy, inventing our own landscape.

In Sandy Touchstone's large chair, with only a few feet between us, I barely hear him. He mumbles, eats his words. He is primarily an eater, an inhaler. We exhalers are different, we cover the world with our own breath, we mark our territory, preserve it for ourselves.

"Eating," Sandy says, "is harder to stop than smoking. You need to eat to live."

My HMO is paying for this therapy, so I don't argue. He gets started on his routine. I can't hear what he says and don't fall into any trance. But as he mumbles on, I relax for some reason, though I know he can't put me under.

"What does smoking do for you?" he's asking.

"It lets me breathe."

"Yes. That's what they all say."

Ridiculous. I never say what they all say. I want to tell him that, but I'm too lethargic. Let it go. He asks me to breathe, breathe in through my toes, up my body, letting the breath clean out all the debris. (Later all this will be too embarrassing to repeat to anyone, but for the moment, in the huge armchair from which my legs don't quite reach the floor, I do what he says.) A few more deep breaths like that, up from the toes, cooling as they chase through the body, and I am suddenly remembering—reenacting, almost—one of my most persistent fantasies from when I was about eight or nine. It was summer. We'd rented a house near Tanglewood, in the Berkshires, a large tumbledown place with a stream on the property and a tiny path cut through a high meadow leading to my mother's studio. Sometimes I modeled for her there. Her drawings of me show a girl with pigtails, striped shirt, features unfocused.

In that house I read the books left by the owner's family: the Bobbsey Twins, Nancy Drew. But at night, in my room to the right of the stairs, I preferred telling myself stories before I fell asleep. All that summer, the story was the same.

A band of kidnappers scales the outside wall and come into my bedroom. They take me away to their gangsters' den, a cave filled with blue, smoky light.

There they make me take off my clothes. They put a lighted cigarette between my lips and make me dance for them. I dance, naked, at the center of the circle, the men looking at me with intense interest, the cigarette glued to the side of my mouth, my own little column of smoke rising in the wonderful blue of the smoky cave as I dance, dance, dance, dance.

"Yes," I heard him say. "Good." At the end of that session I was refreshed, even happy. It didn't last long, though. By the time I reached my car the overpowering need, the physical one, was back and made me shake and cry and scream out the window at people as I drove home.

But after a few weeks the intense craving was gone. I was still anxious, though, gaining weight, having palpitations, unable to sleep. "I am allergic," I told Sandy, "to the healthy life." It would be just my luck to stop smoking and a week later discover I had cancer. That kind of thing is always happening.

When I stopped smoking, life didn't improve. Yes, food tasted better, everything smelled better, but that only made me grow fat. My heroic battle was insignificant in the eyes of other people, and though I tried to perpetuate a belief in my own bravery, it faltered and finally became an embarrassment. Giving up cigarettes was my only accomplishment—of the month, the year, of the past two years. For how long, after all, can you base your self-image on your success at *not* doing something?

I gained weight. I hated my clothes. They hated me back, straining and pinching me as I walked, sometimes unwilling to let me sit down. The flesh was weak, sagging. When I went back to Sandy he suggested we "do a little work on self-image." According to him, I wasn't even fat, so why did I think I was?

Again I sat back in the ridiculously huge armchair. I closed my eyes, barely able to hear him as he asked me to breathe in the cool air through my body, picture dry leaves rustling in the wind, pull in the air, clean out all the debris inside, let the dead leaves go . . .

My mother and I are driving out to the beach on a sunny day, in the Buick convertible, the top down, the red leather seats gleaming. The wind is ruffling my hair, my new short hair. I am about thirteen, oversized, and I've just had a poodle cut finally, my pigtails cut off.

We're driving toward the small bridge over the lagoon at the basin of the bay, several miles before the obelisk and the parking lots of Jones Beach. We can smell the ocean: the salt and the sweet, fishy decomposition, and we can see the shards of silver sunlight flash across the lagoon, making the water look like wrinkled silk dotted with white sails.

She is sitting tall in the driver's seat, a scarf on her head. She's smoking; the end of her cigarette is bright red with her lipstick, and a few specks of tobacco dot her lower lip. She's wearing sunglasses, smiling slightly. She looks like a film star.

As we begin the ascent toward the bridge I see two boys with fishing gear at the side of the road. They are about fourteen or fifteen, and I quickly turn my face away. If they see only the back of my head, the bouncy curls of my poodle cut, maybe they'll think I'm pretty.

We drive by. They whistle. I am looking at my mother. "That was for me," she says, the smile still playing on her lips.*

And then I am sobbing in the big armchair, me, the mother of an adult child, facing my mousy therapist and weeping as I never did then.

My mother has been dead for twenty years. There is no gravestone. My father chose cremation for her, as he chose it for his mother, as he later chose it for himself. I never saw her dead, of a particularly virulent cancer that had lain dormant five years, then lashed out and consumed her in a month. The ashes were scattered in accordance with the laws of New York state.

When she died at seventy she was still a young woman, still beautiful except for the skin blackened by radiation, the white roots of her still luxuriant auburn hair. The thoughts she was trying to express still remained at the tip of her tongue, unuttered.

It is now seven years since I gave up smoking. Seven is a magic number. Last week it was twenty years since my mother died. In my back yard, a large bronze sculpture of hers rises from its stand, wings outspread, an owl with its head to one side, feet of clay, unwilling to fly up. It is a beautiful piece, and on the anniversary of her death I planted black-eyed Susans around it. They were her favorite flower they were in bloom when she died. We had them in large vases at the front of the room at her funeral, and her sculptures were there too.

That's what remains. No body, no grave. The monument is of her own making, her ashes scattered; hers, and her mother's before her.

Kathrin Perutz has published a number of books, including six novels.

LOVE/*Todd Pierce*

WHEN I WAS TWELVE I did not understand why my parents divorced, but looking back I can say with some assurance that my mother noticed other men. I do not mean she had an affair. Merely that she did not need my father as much as she once had. She had grown up in Australia and, a few years after her mother's death, found she missed her country a great deal. She wanted to see the mountains again, to hear English spoken with a Sydney accent, and to have her own stars spread out above her. She called her brother more often, spent evenings alone, and when my father realized how things might go, they planned to separate.

On May 10 my mother packed her bags and readied herself for the 10:35 flight, LA to Sydney direct. The last moment of tenderness I saw between my parents occurred in our living room: my mother sat next to my father, her passport tucked into her pocket, her arms looped around his neck. "Still, if you ask me now," she said, "I'll rip up my ticket and stay." My father turned away sadly, and when he turned back he was close to tears. "No," he said, "it's better we do what's right." To seal this, he took her hand and kissed it. Three hours later she disappeared down a boarding ramp. The following June, I went to live with her.

My mother had inherited a small mountain cottage in the township of Katoomba, not far from Sydney, a two-bedroom home, its exterior green and yellow, its roof nothing more than corrugated metal. In the front yard, my uncle planted flowers and a hedge; in the back my mother strung a clothesline from the verandah to a gum tree. Each Sunday I would help her hang our laundry to dry. "There are things I do miss about the States," she said. "For one, I miss the bloody electric clothes dryers. For another, I miss pizza delivery." I thought for the most part, though, she was happy there.

As for me, I liked the mountains. I liked them because they were large and open, because wallabies lived in their fields and because gum trees covered their hills. I liked them because they held my family, and because for a while I felt special there. I was the quiet American kid visiting for a year, the one who didn't know the rules to rugby but was good in English. Most of all, I liked them because they were where I first fell in love, a girl named Kelly Richardson the object of my desire.

To my surprise, my mother didn't date in Australia. At least not at first. During my childhood, she had been the type of soft, pretty, naturally flirtatious woman men often admired, but after she left my father her flirtatiousness disappeared, as did other qualities. She cut her hair; she bought darker clothes; she took an editor's job at the historical society. Her very mannerisms began to change, and I sensed she was slowly shifting back into the person she had been before she married.

For these reasons, I thought she would not marry again, that her time for romance had passed. She loved new things: the mountains and trees, the way a breeze could curve down from Echo Point, and how my grandmother's words sounded when she read them aloud. Each day she rose at sunrise and sat in our breakfast nook, sipping tea and watching fog lift out of the valley in thin, wispy clouds. Each evening she tuned in the news, watching Australian anchors rattle off stories about the queen, our prime minister, and hostages in Iran. I thought she had found a kind of peace, brought on by her home, her work, her brother. I was surprised, then, when she started to fall in love.

At first I noticed only a change in her voice, a softness that reminded me of how she once spoke to my father. She started wearing lighter colors again—whites and pinks. In the evenings, she sat next to me, her plate in her lap, watching TV, but I could tell she was not thinking about the shows, not even *Fawlty Towers,* which was her favorite. Once, in the middle of a sitcom called *Dad's Army,* she turned to me and asked seriously, "Do you ever find it hard to be the person you're supposed to be?"

"I don't know," I said. "I guess so."

"I mean, do you ever feel a little out of sorts inside?"

"Sometimes," I said.

She got up and, after clearing her plate, turned on the electric teapot. She looked out the window, where inky hues of twilight stained the sky. When *Dad's Army* finished I set my plate beside hers. By then she had placed two teacups on the counter, in saucers patterned with delicate flowers. She put a teabag in each.

"Tell me something," she said. "Do you like it here in the mountains?"

"Yes," I said. "It's pretty nice here."

"And you don't miss being in California too much?"

"Sometimes I miss it," I said. She measured a teaspoon of sugar, carefully leveling it, and as she did, I understood that she still pictured herself young. She was sometimes scared, as I was, but she would never tell me a thing like that. I understood, too, that she liked Mr. Richardson, though she had not yet confessed this to me.

Mr. Richardson was in his midthirties. Like my mother, he was recently divorced, though unlike her, he was still close to his ex-wife. He and my mother had met a number of times, as I was dating his daughter, and on the previous Sunday, my mother had asked him to stay for afternoon tea on the back verandah. Kelly and I did not hang around long—we planned to buy magazines and read them at my uncle's nursery—but before we left I heard my mother use a line I had never heard her use before: "You know," she said to Mr. Richardson, "I hate to have an afternoon cuppa all by myself." He turned to her, or perhaps I should say he turned *slowly*, taking in her tone, her demeanor, the way her hands were placed on her hips.

They stayed there that afternoon, Mr. Richardson in his white shirt and red suspenders, my mother wearing a pink summer dress purchased the previous week. When we returned, Mr. Richardson was standing on the back lawn trying to coax a wayward currawong into view by offering it bread crumbs. My mother greeted us and said, "How goes the movie page?" Kelly responded, "All the good shows come out first overseas."

From there, my mother fell in love gradually. Or at least she wanted it to appear that way. However, I immediately noticed that every other day she walked past Mr. Richardson's store, a shop near the railway station called Richardson's Antiques. Both his name (Paul) and his ex-wife's name (Annette) were stenciled on the front window, though Annette no longer figured in the business. Local high school students had taken her place, dusting the bric-a-brac and sweeping floors while Mr. Richardson worked in back or stood behind the large metal cash register, his arms draped over the top of it, his fingers laced together. He was a kind, good-natured man who joked a lot: "Okay, Sam, how do you get a Kiwi to successfully manage a small business?"

"I don't know," I said, "how?"

"Flat-out simple," he replied, "you start off by giving him a large one. Get it? A large one. And he whittles it down to something small."

In the evenings he would wait for my mother, sitting on an old oak chair he'd refinished, a banker's light on behind him as he read a novel by Tolstoy or Dickens. His eyes, magnified by reading glasses, would carefully work down each column, and then he would moisten his fingers before turning a page. When my mother arrived he looked up to find her; the doorbell jingled as she entered. He tucked his glasses into his pocket, then rose. The few times I was there, he took one of her hands and held it. I knew my mother wanted a more impassioned greeting but also knew she would satisfy herself with this elegant, somewhat formal love—which I thought might be less formal if I were not around.

"You know, Sam," he once said after my mother arrived, "it's hard to believe that a bloke like me would fall for a line like that: 'It's a shame to have a cuppa all by yourself on an afternoon like this.'"

"That's *not* what I said," my mother protested. "You're adding touches."

"From what I remember," I said, "it's pretty close."

"Sam, whose side are you on?" my mother wanted to know.

"No one's."

"See?" Mr. Richardson said. "I count on Sam to be an independent observer, no real vested interest either way."

"Men always stick together," she said. "And as for you, Mister, you're lucky to get any such chatty lines, tired or not."

"Lucky?" he said. "In the antiques business, I get them all the time. You'd be surprised at the lasses that come in here on Saturdays. Real first-rate ones. You know, models and such. Once I met the girl who reads the weather on Channel Nine. She was flat-out something."

"*Lasses*," my mother repeated. "There'd better not be any lasses. I'm putting a claim on you."

"A claim," he said. "I don't know about any such claim. Seems like I just worked meself out of a different claim."

"You're the type who likes a claim, and you know it."

At this he sighed. "Perhaps I do," he said, then kissed her cheek.

That night I walked out with them. Mr. Richardson locked the door after we exited. Outside, the world had trimmed itself and was putting on an autumn spectacle: parkway trees had shed their leaves, the stars were beginning to dust themselves across the eastern sky, in the distance, low clouds moved along the mountains. We walked down Katoomba Street, a main thoroughfare, passing restaurants, some of which displayed signs that read BYO, meaning bring your own, while others advertised Licensed. We walked past Lawson's Milk Bar and Carraway's Fish and Chips, past touristy souvenir shops, past Mr. Rollins' camera repair. When we passed my uncle's nursery, I looked to see if he was still in the cashier's shack, but he was not. Mr. Richardson and my mother turned off on a street called Waratar, after the state flower, and continued on to Cliff Drive, where they knew a small restaurant that offered a good view of the Leura Cascades. As for me, I was going to see Kelly. I had wanted to see her all day. Now that we were in Year Eight we had only one class together and did not see each other as often as we wanted.

I had met her a little over five months ago, in November, and we had gone on our first true date just before the Christmas holidays. We had taken the train to Penrith, where we saw an afternoon movie, a Disney flick about two kids who felt somewhat lost in the city. Afterward we rode the train home. The old rickety red passenger cars trudged up the mountain. Our window was open just a crack; graffiti was inked across the seat in front of us. We sat close, but I felt the space between us. I noticed the way her hands were folded in her lap, the way her shoulders were pushed slightly forward, and how her long hair had been pulled from her face and tied into a ponytail. After we'd been on the train for a while, she asked, "How come you asked me to go with you?"

"You know why," I said. "Because I like you. You just want to hear me say it again."

"But how come you like me? Most boys don't. They think I'm too forceful or something."

"I don't think you're forceful."

She considered this for a moment, then asked, "What are girls like in California?"

"Some are a lot like you," I said. Then I remembered something my dad had once said to my mom. "But not as pretty," I added.

She looked at me in a new way, her eyes a little wider, her mouth slightly open. "My father's the only one who says I'm pretty."

Though she said it truthfully, I found it hard to believe. She was the prettiest girl I'd ever met: she was tall, thin, had long, slender arms. Her hair was blond, as were her eyebrows, her eyes blue. She had a pleasant voice, one I could listen to all day, and when she wanted to she could make me laugh harder than anyone I knew. On that day, though, I did not say any of these things. I simply said, "Oh."

"Oh," she repeated, "you're just going to say, 'Oh.'"

"Oh," I said again. Then I put my hand around hers, noticing that her skin, like mine, was a little damp—from the heat, from the humidity, from our nervousness. I held it for a moment, then brought it close to me, running my thumb along the curve of her index finger. We were a good ways up the mountain. The sun was low in the sky, and shadows from outside moved through the interior of the train.

"I suppose now we're boyfriend and girlfriend," she said.

"I don't know."

"Isn't that what they do in the States? People go on a date and then they become boyfriend and girlfriend?"'

"Something like that," I said. "What do they do here?"

"From what I can tell you just go out and muck around and maybe sometime later you get married. I don't think we have rules here like you have over there."

"Which way do you prefer?" I said.

"Oh, I don't know," she said, "American or Australian. I suppose we could try one, and if that doesn't work, we could give the other a go."

"Okay," I said, and in that moment, I started to love her. I loved her because she leaned toward me, resting her back against my chest and letting me put my arm around her. I loved her because she liked me, and I had never had a girl like me in that way before. I loved her because she felt things at a much deeper level than she let on, though I realize I must have shared those same secretive ways. We rode the rest of the way like that—past Lawson, past Wentworth, past Leura. I did not say much or move, not even when my hand fell asleep, and then my arm; I was simply pleased to hold her, to be on that old passenger train on a hot December day, slowing into the station, where the stationmaster would shout, "Ka-*toom*-ba," and then we'd hear doors lumbering open. I felt, for the first time, that I was occupying the space of an adult, that I was surveying the terrain and seeing how the land lay. I knew that in the future I would live within this space, but back then I could not see its importance as clearly as I see it now. On the walk home we held hands, and she told me stories about her childhood, how she had once lived in Melbourne, then Brisbane, and now here. "I'm like you," she said. "The whole world seems a bit strange, if you ask me."

"It seems like that to me too," I said.

For a while we fell into our own happiness: after school we would go to my uncle's nursery or visit her father. We went to the milk bar, we went to the news agent, we loitered in Mountain Books, where, when she had money, Kelly bought thin collections of Sherlock Holmes stories. "He's just spot-on brilliant," she once told me. "I mean, I've never seen anyone as clever as he is." On Sunday afternoons we would often walk through town, sometimes to a historic house called Leurella, where she knew one of the groundsmen. Other times we explored the valley floor, hiking down the endless steps of the Giant Stairway. There, we would walk along dusty trails and sit next to streams and waterfalls listening to the sound of a breeze moving through trees or the cries of birds. With sticks, we would write our initials in the sand, and late in the afternoon, curled next to me on a rock, she would read me a Sherlock Holmes story while the sun fell off toward the horizon, projecting its color across clouds.

Once, on our way back, we found an old cave. Its interior led back only ten or twelve feet. On its walls we discovered aboriginal handprints painted with ochre sand, dozens of them spread over gray rock like wallpaper. Toward the back, in a place where the light was dim, we saw two painted hands, separate from the others, fixed just at our height. Kelly placed her hand over one; I placed mine over the other. The rock was cold beneath our skin. After that, we sat at the entrance and kissed for a while. We were at a stage in our intimacy between kissing and making out, a place where borders were not as defined as they once had been. For the first time I felt the sadness of leaving, a sorrow that came from the knowledge that one day I would board a jet and be transported back to California. I would have a different life there, a life without the mountains, without the valley, without her. I believed she felt this too.

We stayed there a long time. Only when twilight began to brush its charcoal hues across the horizon did we leave. We walked up the Giant Stairway—all 800-odd steps—and then continued to Martin Street, where through a window we saw our parents sitting together on the couch, her father's arm around my mother, both of them watching TV.

That night we ate dinner together—chicken, potatoes and green beans. We sat at the table my grandmother once owned, my mother and I on one side, Kelly and her father on the other. Mr. Richardson asked for seconds of everything. "There's nothing quite as lovely as a proper baked dinner," he said, handing my mother his plate. She seemed happy finally. So did he. I wondered briefly if this was the type of happiness she and my father had known when they first met but decided it was not. My mother did not love Mr. Richardson with a youthful love but with an older, more resigned affection. Yet during dinner she looked at him with such longing that I found it difficult to watch. Kelly saw this too, then met my eyes.

By midautumn, our lives had moved into a routine. My mother had her editing and her writing, and in the evenings she had her brother, she had me, she had Mr. Richardson. I had school, I had my family, I had Kelly. I liked the way this granted order to my life. Each morning I woke at seven. I showered, straightened my room and walked out to the breakfast nook, where I often found my mother gazing out our window toward a large rock formation at the edge of the valley. When she sensed my presence, she would look at me and say, "What do you feel like—tea, crumpets, a little hot cereal?" Almost always I answered, "Just crumpets," though sometimes I had hot cereal as well. After breakfast I looked over my homework, particularly the math and history, then packed my books.

At school I endured my morning classes—English, Math, Shop—and in the afternoon I saw Kelly, first at lunch, then in History. Mr. Hansen was our teacher that term, a young, brown-haired man who only the year before had graduated from the university. He was interested in England, particularly the England of Old and Middle English, and assigned us tales about King Arthur; his favorite was *Sir Gawain and the Green Knight*. On some days, he would tell us about this other England, the one poets imagined and historians half invented. To be honest, I had an easier time picturing this England than the real one that had colonized Australia. The rules there seemed better defined, more straightforward: Be loyal. Treat people with respect. Do the right thing, if for no other reason than so people won't think badly of you. I knew, though, that Kelly thought these rules simplistic. One day after class she told me, "That's the problem with men," as she cleared her things off the desk.

"What do you mean, that's the problem with men?"

"Far as I can figure," she said, "men like to tie up the world with a bunch of good-sounding laws no one can live by."

"I don't think that's true," I said.

"And women," she continued, "we would rather see things for what they are."

"I think I see things just fine," I said, but I knew in some ways she was right. I liked to think of the world as ordered, as just, as basically good. I believed good actions led to reward but knew that Kelly did not share this view.

She must have seen that she was upsetting me because she asked if I wanted to go to the milk bar. "You game for that?" she said.

"I'm game," I said, cinching my backpack closed.

When school finished, we walked to the milk bar, where we sat on bar stools. We ordered two cokes and a basket of hot chips, which we split. We stayed there for an hour, talking to Mr. Lawson, who owned the place. Afterward, we went to an old public bench that overlooked the valley, and as always we started in on our homework. She worked on English—*Animal Farm* was her present assignment—and I struggled with pre-algebra. When she tired of reading she moved beside me, and I put my arm around her. We looked off at the valley, endless gum trees and blue sky curving down to join the earth. As we prepared to leave, she asked, "Do you reckon we'll still know each other five years from now?"

"I think so," I said. "Don't you?"

"Well," she said, "I *like* thinking that. It makes me feel good."

"Then why do you think about it any other way?"

"Who can say?" she said. "I just do sometimes."

I closed my math book, marking my place. She began to gather her things: a pencil, a highlighter, two sheets of notebook paper. By then a mist was moving down from the forest, a thin veil of dew that held the colors of the evening sky. I took her hand. "If you ask me," I said, "our parents get on pretty good. I think that will keep us together."

She turned to me, her thin, girlish face trying to smile, her hair no longer restrained by a band but falling free to her shoulders, and I saw that I had said the wrong thing. She moved close, and I sensed, perhaps for the first time, that she needed me to hold her. I put my arms around her, my hands clasped behind her back. "When you go back to California," she asked, "are you going to write?"

"Of course," I said.

"I mean, you'll write me just because you like me and not for any other reason?"

"I'll write you every day," I said.

"You can't write *every* day," she said. "I'd be happy if you wrote once a week."

"I will," I said. "I'll send you pictures, too."

"I'd like that," she said. "I'd like that a lot."

We began to walk home, but by then the mist was around us, thick as a cloud. We were surrounded by fairy dust, by a delicate gauze, light that had become liquid and lifted itself into the air.

In the days that followed I saw how things changed between us. I don't mean they changed in large ways; the changes were small, almost imperceptible. We still met before History each day. We sat next to each other and occasionally shared a book, but in general she was not as attentive as she had been in previous classes, her book open to the wrong page, her pencil unsharpened, her eyes blankly staring at the blackboard. "The message of Camelot is simply," our teacher had written, "man has difficulty holding on to goodness and order."

At home, too, I felt this unease, though I knew Kelly was trying to wish it away. We would sit in my back yard, near the stone birdbath, and play checkers or read books (she again the Sherlock Holmes and I a book about young people on a camping trip), and sometimes during these bright autumn afternoons, she rolled over on our blanket and gave me such an honest expression of hope that my heart would almost break. On the verandah, my mother was reading my grandmother's memoir, slowly wading through those sections she had given up on earlier. One Saturday Mr. Richardson joined us. The two of them sat in the large wicker chairs, sharing the evening paper. My mother no longer served tea; she had grown tired of that joke.

As with many things, I suppose I was the last to know. Mr. Richardson was not the man my mother had hoped. He was a good person, honest and kind, but confused about love, as I guess we all were. More specifically, he occasionally missed the company of his ex-wife. One night after my mother had cooked lasagne for him, I heard him say, "It's hard to explain." They were in the dining room; I was in my bedroom, puzzled by what my math book called "advanced variable progressions." I heard him set his silverware against his plate and then continue: "I guess what I'm getting at is, I thought things would be different." I put my book down and looked down the hallway. I saw the glow of candlelight, the stove, the sink, but could not see either of them.

I heard my mother leave her chair; its wooden legs scraped over the wood floor. I pictured her beside him, her thin hands gently placed on his shoulders, her face tilted down to see him. "Do you still get along with her?" she asked.

"In a way," he answered, "but not really."

The house began to shrink then, its sides closing in on us; we were three people under a common roof: a man, a woman, a son down the hall, his bedroom door open more than it should be. Outside, cars moved along the street; next door, the neighbors were watching *Dad's Army*; in our house, though, there was only the sound of water dripping into the sink—that and the hushed talk of my mother and Mr. Richardson.

"Do you still love her?" my mother asked, her voice almost a whisper.

"Not like that," he said. "We were married a long time. I still love her in that I want her to do well, to be happy, but not like you're thinking."

"I know how that is," she said. "I never thought divorce could be so hard."

At that, Mr. Richardson left his chair and moved to where I could see him. He was wearing a white shirt and tie. His hands were folded together. "I shouldn't have come tonight," he said. "I'm sorry for that."

"Don't be," she said, and with a tenderness that surprised me, her arms circled his waist, her face pressed against his shoulder. He held her for a moment, the two of them close, before she said, "We are just two gay divorcés who haven't figured out what we really want." For a minute they stayed that way, their bodies swaying to imaginary music, and then he held her face with his hands, his fingers soft against her cheeks. He kissed her once, then left a few minutes later, donning his English felt hat. When he was gone I went out to see her. She stood alone, looking out our kitchen window. She was clutching a tea towel, wrapping its frayed end around her index finger and then undoing it. "Well, bugger the whole world," she said. "Bugger the whole bloody world."

I put my hand on her back. Her dress was damp from sweat, her ribs expanding with each breath. I did not know what to say, or if I should say anything at all.

"Do you hate him?" I asked finally.

She ran her hand through my hair. "You know," she said, "I'm old enough not to hate anyone. I've done enough in my own life to teach me better." She sniffed once and then smiled, though I could tell it took effort. She lifted a dish of lasagne, offering it to me. "Care for some dinner?" she said, holding it loosely as though it were already leftovers and not something she had made only that day. "I'm going to have some more." I saw how she was trying to face this situation with bravery and grace, and I admired her in a way I had not before. She was a woman with a large, sensible heart, though that heart had caused her trouble.

"Sure," I said, "I wouldn't mind some dinner. We could eat and watch TV."

"Tucker and the tube," she said, "Australiana at its best."

"We could watch the news," I said. "*Dad's Army* is already over."

"I suppose you heard," she said.

"I heard."

"Why don't you go turn on the telly? That way it's all warmed up for the news."

"All right," I said.

I continued to see Kelly after school and on Saturday afternoons. We met as we always had, though there was a desperation between us. I saw it in the way she looked at me and in the way she held my hand. When we kissed, I sensed a new longing mixed with our love, a longing we were able to convert into youthful passion. In the weeks before I left, she let me unclasp her bra and touch her breasts. Her skin was soft, and her tan lines betrayed the shape of her bathing suit—or "swimming cozzie," as she called it. We were two kids in love, fascinated with ourselves, with each other, and with the way emotion could swell inside of us.

As for my mother, she poured her efforts into work. On weekends, though, she spent entire days with me. The two of us drove up to the Hydro Majestic for lunch or caught the train down to the city, where years ago she had lived in a suburb called Burwood. She did not see Mr. Richardson for a long time, but as I understand matters, sometime after I left they became friends again, meeting every few weeks for lunch or drinks. They talked about the past, their marriages long finished, and discussed how difficult the future was to grasp. "Hold on to whatever you've got, Sam," she wrote me three years before she died, "and trust it's enough to see you through."

On the Saturday before I left, Kelly and I went again to "our" cave—though now we found evidence that other people knew about it as well: cigarette stubs in the back, a beer tin stashed in a bush. We sat near the front, an old blanket beneath us. I had expected the day to be filled with great longing, but it was not. Instead we simply enjoyed being together one last time, touching, kissing, trying to remember every detail as it happened. Gradually we took off each others' shirts, leaving only our mountain hiking shorts on, and held each other, though the previous week we had talked about doing more. As the sun moved toward the horizon, she looked at me and asked what was wrong.

"I thought it would be different today," I said. "You know, that it would feel different, because it's our last time."

She took my hand in hers, then said, "You're very emotional for a boy. It's one of the things I like about you."

"You picked a fine time to tell me," I said. "I'm leaving next week."

She curled up beside me, her head resting on my shoulder, her arm stretched across my stomach, and a good spirit moved between us, a lightness. From the bush, we heard the sounds of currawongs, magpies and bower birds, their songs soft, like twilight's anthem.

"You remember," I said, "on our first date, coming home on the train, you said we could try dating one way and if that didn't work out we could try the other?"

"Yes," she said.

"I was wondering which way have we been trying—the American or the Australian one?"

"I reckon the American way," she said. "Otherwise I wouldn't have ended up half naked beside some boy who's going to leave me next week."

"I don't want to go," I said. "You know that, right?"

"I know," she said. She stroked my chest and then my arms. "Tell me something," she said. "Tell me you love me."

"I love you," I said.

"And that you will always love me."

"I will," I said. "Will you?"

"Mm-huh," her voice quiet, almost a whisper.

I knew even then that these things might not prove true, though we wanted them to. We sat in a cave that a few years later would be closed off and protected as a historical site. The sun pulled toward the other part of the world, the part where I was from, but we did not go home. Instead we stayed down in the valley, surrounded by gum trees and mountain ash, by banksia and blackwood, by fan ferns that hung from cliffs like delicate paper ornaments. Above us, black birds flew, like shadows, across a gray horizon. We stayed there well past seven o'clock, the evening chill making us feel oddly alive, until moonlight spilled like milk down around us.

Later, as we walked up the Giant Stairway for the last time, she said, "You're really going to write me?"

"Every week."

"I thought it was every day."

"It was," I said, "but you said that was too much."

"Oh, I reckon every day might not be too much, at least at first."

"I'm a fair writer," I said.

"I'm not so good, but I'll give it a go."

That was all we said about it, perhaps because we knew how things would turn out. We'd write for a while, our letters filled with longing, but eventually the longing would lessen, the letters would be less frequent, just a few a year—at Christmas or on birthdays—until those stopped as well.

On that night, though, we simply took each other's hands and walked back to my mother's house, where lights illuminated the front windows, and where a wood stove filled the rooms with its heat. There we would talk, have tea and finally kiss more after my mother went to bed. At eleven-thirty Kelly's father arrived to pick her up. He did not come to the door or honk but simply flashed his highbeams toward our front windows. I walked her to the car, said hello to her father, then watched them drive away. The car grew smaller and smaller, its brake lights dimmer and dimmer, until its shape was finally indistinguishable from all the other things I remember about living in that quiet mountain town.

Todd Pierce has published stories in over twenty magazines, including *American Short Fiction*.

MUD / *Laura Kasischke*

This is spring's grim silk—

mud, and a love deep enough
to swim or drown or bathe
or be born in. My cat is gone, *my*

tearful sleeve, my lazy one. How long? This

is the exchangeable
merchandise of love—

wild garlic, broken glass, a hubcap in the mud. My

cat, I see, has been here. Her
French mittens in the ditch, but

she's gone on. How far? This

open field between *malignant*
and *benign. God*

is up there watching
someone crucified. Oh,

not His only son. Not mine. Not

my husband, father, me. God

is watching someone
He never noticed before
get nailed to something He'd
mistaken for a telephone pole. Tonight

I'll place a plastic cup of peas, a small
fork, a piece of cheese, and my

whole life like a shield
of fragrant vapor—weightless, shifting—
before the only one in this world

whose loss I couldn't endure.

Once, I drank a spoonful of perfume.

And the cat, the cat's a detail—crooked, impatient, sweet
and also gone

somewhere, I know and loathe it, somewhere
killed or weeping, lost
or never noticed
by a very near-sighted God. *I wanted*

to smell like violets deep inside. Once

I wore a short skirt to a dance
and kissed a boy who died
before my life began.

BUFFALO / *Laura Kasischke*

I had the baby in my arms, he was asleep.
We were waiting for Old Faithful, who was late.
The tourists smelled like flowers, or

like shafts of perfume moving
from bench to bench, from

Gift Shop to Port-o-Pot. The sun
was a fluid smear
in the sky, like white hair in water. The women
were as beautiful as the men, who were

so beautiful they never needed
to see their wives or children again.

It happened then.

Something underground. The hush of sound.
I remembered
once pretending
to have eaten a butterfly.
My mother held my arms hard
until I told her it was a lie

and then she sighed. I've

loved every minute of my life!

The day I learned to ride a bike
without training wheels, I
might as well have been riding a bike
with no wheels at all! At any time, if I'd

had to agree to bear
twenty-seven sorrows
for a single one of these joys . . .

If the agreement were that I
had to love it all so much
just, in the end, to die . . .

Still, I can taste those wings I didn't eat, the sweet
and tender lavender of them. One

tourist covered her mouth with a hand

and seemed to cry. How

could I have doubted her?
There were real tears in her eyes!
The daisies fell from her dress, and if
at that moment

she'd cracked an egg in a bowl, the bowl would have
filled with light.

If there is a God, why not
this violent froth, this
huge chiffon scarf
of pressure under water under her
white sandals in July?

The baby was asleep, still sucking, in my arms, a lazy
wand of sun moving
back and forth across his brow. I heard
a girl's laughter in the parking lot, soft
and wild, like
the last note of "Jacob's Ladder"
played by the children's handbell choir.

I turned around.

It had been watching me. Or him. Or both of us.

Good beast, I whispered to it
facetiously under my breath.

It took, in our direction, one
slow and shaggy step.

ILLINOIS / *Laura Kasischke*

We are up to our waists in the bloody
grass of it. Not yet dead or divorced.
We are driving ourselves through the tarry
artery of it. You've read this poem before.

An atom smasher, an art museum,
a Styrofoam factory, a meatpacking plant.
A lot of blood on a lot of hands.

A bloody woman at the side of the road.
A bloody child in a bloody stroller.
Blood in our bodies. Blood in vats.
Blood in our hair. Blood on our hats.

If I give you the landfill, the apple orchard's mine.
If you give me the trailer court, the car lot's yours.

Again, it is that poem. The one
in which the kids
who cannot see the future
find themselves in its accident. Today

there's a strange cloud pasted
above the freeway. A great static gray.

If we didn't know
it was pollution
we'd gasp, and say, How beautiful!

We'd say, There *is* no future! Just
a freeway cut through someone else's state

a fast car on it
without brakes

this spine connected
briefly to that brain.

But lovers do not like to think.
They do not like to work.
The strippers do not
like to swirl and stoop.
The lawyers can no longer
bear to lie. The drunken

surgeon slips with his knife.

You are a husband.
I am a wife.
I'll nag. You drive.

You are a giver, and I am a waitress.
I am a servant, and you are a slave.

We are sloppy
at our jobs

but so are they, so are they.
The weather man is always
as honest as he is vague.

GRACE / *Laura Kasischke*

Who can tell the difference between the state
of grace and the state of inebriation? Who

can tell the difference between love-drunk
and just drunk? Once

I turned around too fast
at a party with a drink in my hand
and splashed the shoes of a man, who said,

"Don't tell me. Let me guess. Your name is Grace."

Whether it's night or day
is a matter of indifference to the sun. Who cares

what year it was, what month, whether
the couple asleep on the park bench
in one another's arms
are lovers or drunks? They claimed

the *Hindenburg* was lighter than air.
Everything balanced—
the lift of the hydrogen, the weight of the ballast, a
    battleship made

out of shadow, and linen,
an emptiness like elegance
over the Atlantic, which was nothing

but a shining magazine, open. Oh, *there they go,* I
    imagined

the other people at this party
whispered to each other
as we wandered with our cocktails to the lawn. Imagine

that dirigible passing over
at this moment. Diamond rings, false teeth, swastikas—

all the little baggage
with which people travel. Imagine it as grace: that

moment just before
the moment in which the mystery
would like to speak to us

if we would like to listen, in which

pure pleasure, its
huge kind surge, could
pick us up together, speak

to us in human terms. The music
like honey. The temple
full of monkeys. To show us how much greater

is the game than any player:
How much brighter
is the porchlight
than the chalklight inside a moth.

Air pressure.
Air temperature.
The weight of the passengers.
The lift of the oxygen.
Everything balanced.
Everything gauged. But then

the fear of water again—of flight, of public restrooms, of
open spaces, bees,
bridges, traffic, grace
The *Hindenburg*

was landing
when it suddenly became

brighter than the sun at noon.
It had no weight.
In Lakehurst, New Jersey, all the dogs barked.
It was Ascension Day.
The month was May.
1937.
A light rain.

The *Hindenburg* was landing.

We all know *nothing*
is lighter than air,
but it sure felt that way.

The papery
disintegration, the star of a girl dropped
onto the world, the bird
tossed right along

with its cage into the flames.
In heaven, the burning skeleton.

For *years* he called me Grace.

Laura Kasischke is the author of three collections of poetry and two novels.

THE CHAIR/*Sharon Balentine*

THE CHAIR WAS ONE OF SIX bought in Ronda fifteen years before. An antique rush-bottomed chair of olive wood, polished by many hands over many years, repaired many times. The crosspieces between the legs were weak, but the chair was still strong and comfortable to sit in, the carved back graceful. The wood was the color of cured blond tobacco.

One night she was having a glass of wine in her study when she heard a voice call a greeting to her from the door onto the street. *Hola, Karen!* Then immediately afterward a terrible crash and the sound of something falling. She jumped up and ran up the steps from her study into the kitchen. By the time she got there, three village women stood in her doorway berating in high-pitched voices the supine man groaning on the floor amid the wreckage of her chair and the shards and earth of a large clay pot that had held a small palm. O-h-h-h, groaned the bearded man, Antonio, clutching his ribs. She had seen him drinking in the bar across the way at two. It was now ten.

She knelt down to look at him while the women shouted. Disgraceful drunk! they shrilled. Have you no shame? Karen! the man groaned. Listen to the bitches, how they talk to a man. They say I'm drunk. I'm not drunk.

Do you want a glass of water? she asked. Yes, he said. Don't move me. We must move you, she said, trying to lift him into another, unbroken chair. O-h-h-h, he moaned piteously. After some minutes, she and one of the women managed to get him to stand. They walked him slowly out to the street. I can't walk, he said. Yes, you can. Careful now. We have to get you home and into your bed. I'll find the *practicante,* Karen said. She knew her neighbor didn't want to walk him home with her, but they started off up the street. Though his house was less than five minutes away, it took them thirty, as he made much of every step, groaning, stopping, clutching his ribs. Declaring he couldn't go on, that he was going to die, that he wanted to die. You're not going to die, said Karen. Not yet. The other woman kept berating him, calling him a drunk, a disgrace to his family, a hopeless problem.

Indeed the man was a problem. He fell, on average, once a week, usually in the street somewhere, and then he tried to waylay someone to help him home. Fewer and fewer people could be bothered, and those usually foreigners like Karen. He walked with crutches now, since he had hurt all of his joints. He was, it seemed, trying to kill himself in this slow, painful way: alcohol and falling down. I just wanted to say hello, he said. Yes, she nodded. Karen asked him for his keys, opened the door to his house, and the two women helped him into his bed. The sheets were gray with dirt. The other woman wrinkled her nose in disgust. In the filthy kitchen Karen found a glass, filled it with water and put it by the bedside, along with the man's cigarettes and an ashtray.

When she had found the *practicante*, who said he would go up and check on Antonio, Karen went home and looked at the broken pieces of her chair and sighed. She hoped the carpenter could fix it. She decided she needed a glass of wine and went across the street to the little bar. The men laughed when she came in. Again? they said. She nodded. He's a drunk. You let drunks lie in the street, one said. He wasn't in the street, she answered. He was in my house. Besides, you can't let people lie in the street. The man grunted.

The next day, Juan the carpenter came and took the chair away. I'll fix it, he said, though it won't be easy. I love the chair, she said. It's one of six. Please try.

Six months later, Karen still had not seen her chair. She called the carpenter. It's very difficult, he said, the wood is rotten; it's old. It's a useless chair. You should throw this one away and buy another chair. I don't want another chair, she said. I want this chair. I told you. It's an antique, one of a set. I'll try, he said.

Two more months passed. She called Juan every week for another month. Still no chair. He promised he was working on it, said he would bring it Friday. She waited for him. He didn't show up. This happened again and again. She let it rest another two months, then began calling him again. I want the chair for Christmas, she said. Please. If you can't fix it, just bring me the pieces and I'll figure something else out, she said. He didn't bring her the chair.

She called him again. Why can't I have my chair? she said. I'm very busy, he answered. I've got rabbits, horses, pigs, and I'm doing construction work, as well as carpentry jobs. I have too much work. Listen, she said, it's all right if you don't want to fix the chair or can't, but I want the chair. Where is it? I'll come and pick it up. She knew she must not allow herself to show anger or impatience. That would ensure that he wouldn't bring the chair. Manners and forms of behavior were highly ritualized in the village. It was extremely bad form, bad luck, bad everything to show anger or impatience. Negative emotions threw everything out of balance and usually led to something terrible. Especially a foreigner must not show them toward a villager, for then the villager would sabotage something—in this case, the chair.

The chair is in my shop in the *campo*, Juan said, at the *cortijo*. Where is your *cortijo*? He rushed through complicated directions, which she didn't understand, and that was that.

This is ridiculous, she thought. Why can't he bring me the chair? I want the chair. She thought about the chair all the time. It was becoming an obsession. She looked at the bare space where it had stood against the wall and was unhappy. She brooded like this for another few months, thinking of what to do. Village ways were complex. If someone didn't want to do something or couldn't do it, he wouldn't just say so. She was afraid that this business was entering the realm of the surreal. Once that happened in the village, where things entered the realm of the surreal more often than in some places, it could well be hopeless. She began to think it possible that she would never see the chair again.

No, she thought. It's mine, and I want it. It's a special chair. One of six. There are no others like this chair. She called Juan again. She praised him for previous work he had done. She said she knew that a broken old chair seemed unimportant to him, but that she had a special feeling for this chair. Listen, he said. To be honest, this chair is a problem. I have to tell you that every time I look at the chair, Karen, I feel fear. Fear? she said. Yes. Well, I'll come and pick it up. It's just that I don't understand where your *cortijo* is. Tell me again. The next day she drove out into the hills, but she couldn't find the place. This is absurd! she fumed, angry. Clearly, she needed a better strategy.

She then found Juan's brother, who had begun coming most days to the bar across the street. She explained to him about the chair. Would you talk to him? she asked. Every day for two weeks she asked the brother if he had found out anything. No, he said, clearly getting tired of hearing about the stupid chair. Did you talk to him? Yes. Finally, he told her that his brother was going to fix the chair. He says he'll have it done after Christmas, he said. Have you actually seen it? she asked. No, he said.

She waited. Christmas and the New Year came and went. No chair. It had now been a year and a half since Antonio had broken it. She asked Juan's brother if he would drive with her out to the *cortijo* since she couldn't find it herself. Three times he said he would go with her and told her to meet him at a certain time in a certain place, but each time he stood her up.

It's in the realm of the surreal for sure, she thought. This is very bad. When something entered the realm of the surreal in the village, one had to become surreal oneself in order to deal with it. One had to go above, beyond, around, under the real. She waited for some weeks, thinking. She decided to go to the mother—always a dangerous proposition with uncertain results, for the women protected their men here like harpies. Reason did not work against this fierce mother barrier. She must tread carefully. She saw Juan's mother in the street and gently asked her about the chair. It's an old chair, the woman said. Buy a new one. Again Karen explained that it was an antique, not simply old, and that she had five others like it. The woman looked at her as if she were a maniac. What do you want with an old, broken chair? she said. She stalked off.

She saw Juan's father and asked him about the chair. I know nothing about any chair, he said, turning away.

People were beginning to think it very funny that she talked about this chair so much. The bar man, Manuel, smiled knowingly when he saw her talking to Juan's brother, but soon the brother stopped coming to the bar because he didn't want to hear about the chair anymore. You must talk only to my brother about the chair, he finally said. She looked at him, eyes wide. What have I been trying to do? He shrugged. My brother. Yes, he can be very bad.

Karen thought, I don't care if they think I'm mad. I'm going to have that chair. I'm taking this all the way, she thought, however and wherever it goes. Damn it!

All her foreign frends knew about the chair. It's ridiculous, they agreed, sympathizing. One woman said she would go with her out to the *campo* to try to find Juan's carpentry shop. Karen went up to see Juan's mother one night to get better directions. The woman glared at her suspiciously from the doorway and rattled off the route. It's very simple! she shrieked. Karen smiled and thanked her.

Twice Karen and her friend drove out to the *campo*. The first time they got lost. The second time Karen had a map drawn for her by the man who ran the burro-taxi. He had listened sympathetically to her story and said that it was a pity, yes, that Juan had no shame, that the entire family was a little suspect, certainly. This man was not from the village, however, so he could talk that way. Unprofessional, the man muttered, as he drew the map on a napkin. You understand? I think so, she said.

This time she and her friend found the *cortijo*. Karen got out of the car, leaving the other woman inside. I'll just make sure this is the place, she said. As she approached the long, low building, two large dogs ran out barking at her. She kept walking, making soothing sounds, but they didn't stop their furious yelping. Christ! she thought.

She heard a circular saw operating inside. This must be it, she thought. She walked in.

A lovely smell of wood shavings, a golden light shining on motes of wood dust in the air. Chairs, tables, half-finished door and window frames. The man operating the saw was not Juan. She waited until he finished sawing through a pine plank. He turned. She smiled. I'm looking for Juan, she said. He shook his head. Not here. I'm his brother-in-law. I'm looking for a chair of mine he's had for nearly two years. Would you know anything about it? He shook his head. You can look around, he said, turning back to his work. She looked. None of the many chairs of all kinds sitting around was her chair. None was as lovely. She felt disheartened. Where was it?

Another man came in the door out of the sunlight. She went up to him. I'm looking for a chair, she began again. The story had now become a song, assuming its own rhythms, hand motions and phrasing. Her face knew the expressions appropriate to this song and moved through each in turn. She finished, holding her hands out before her in a kind of supplication, her head tilted slightly. The man watching her nodded and said, Well, I did see Juan four or five days ago taking a chair out of here. Where? I don't know. She thanked him and walked out toward the car.

Her friend appeared on the path. I was worried about you, she said. The dogs and all. Karen explained the results of her visit, and they drove back to the village. I'm going once more to his mother, she said. There's nothing to do once I've exhausted the mother, so this is it. Do you think he took the chair away because he knew I was coming? Her friend shook her head. I don't know, she said. Could be. It's getting stranger and stranger.

A few nights later she walked up to Juan's parents' house, turning off the main road and ascending the steep steps of the smaller street. She knocked on the brown door with the brass knocker. In a moment it opened, and she again looked into the face of Juan's mother, who was obviously not pleased to see her. She told of her outing to the *cortijo*. She said that Juan had told her she could pick up the chair, and that she had looked but it was not there. She said another man had told her Juan might have taken the chair away. Had he brought it here? The older woman shook her head, no. Well, said Karen, I don't know what to do next. The woman watched her. Don't you see him? said Karen. Can't you talk to him? He lives out in the *campo* now. I hardly ever see him. Sometimes on the weekends he comes here. Karen smiled. The woman looked at her. Listen, she said, I'm going to the *campo* this weekend. I'll look for the chair. Maybe he's put it outside somewhere.

Karen nodded, thinking, outside? Why outside? She thanked the woman. It's that I like this chair, she said.

She gave Juan's mother a week, returning again one moonless winter night to walk up those gray and unwelcoming steps. She knocked. The door opened. A single dim light shone from deep within. The small, shrunken figure of the mother stood there, her wrinkled face looking up at Karen. Karen remembered this woman picking olives in a friend's *cortijo* twenty years or more ago. Even then she had been shrunken, wrinkled, thin. Her hands had worked like machines in the tree—the fastest woman olive picker in the village. Because of her nerves, the owner of the trees said. She's always been like this. Nervous. Her husband had other women that he met down on the coast. He'd even for a time had an apartment in another city where he took them. She'd raised two sons and two daughters. Karen wondered what the woman thought of her. She probably thinks nothing about me, Karen reflected. I'm foreign. Irrelevant. Incomprehensible. Yet here I am, this foreigner who won't go away.

The women looked at one another. Karen said, Did you find the chair? No, the woman answered. I looked everywhere, thinking maybe he'd gotten angry and thrown it in the woods. The woods? Yes. But it wasn't there. I don't know what he's done with it.

Karen sighed. This is awful, she said. Your son is a fine carpenter. He's done beautiful work for me. I was pleased. And now look. Look at this story. The other woman stepped outside, nodding. Yes. It's a terrible story, she said. It's just that I wanted the chair even in pieces, said Karen, raising her arms to the sky. Even in pieces! She stomped her foot. The song was beginning now to be a dance. A flamenco dance. The arms came down and swept out from her body. It's been two years, she said, swaying. I told him. Even in pieces! The arms lifted again. From the corner of her eye she saw a face at the window across the way.

The other woman raised her own arms and waved them about. You're right! she said. This is an absurd, sad story. Karen moved her head, her shoulders and hands. Well, she said. I thank you for trying, Teresa. The other woman looked down and to the side, stepping back. The two women nodded at each other formally, stylized, as in a Noh play.

Karen sat up in bed reading. Sunday evening. Still winter. *Hola,* Karen! she heard from the kitchen, then a scraping sound. She stood up, slipped on her shoes and called out, I'm here. She walked down into the kitchen, and her heart thumped. There stood Juan grinning and pointing to the chair. Here it is! Goodness! she said. She brought her hands up as in prayer, touched them to her forehead and bowed to him. She looked at the chair. It was very pale, as if it had been sitting out in the sun, and it lacked its rush bottom, but she could find someone to do that. It needs oiling, said Juan. It's very strong now. You can sit in it. He picked up the chair and banged it on the floor. Of course it won't stand being fallen on. I'll take care of it, she said. She smiled happily at him. He grinned.

How much do I owe you? Oh, Karen, he said. *Nada*. Because of your pain. Oh, she said, no, this was work. You must be paid.

She turned and went into the hallway, found her purse and extracted a bill. Back in the kitchen she handed it to him. Thank you, Juan. He smiled, pocketed the bill and left. He's just a kid, she thought. After all.

She stood there gazing at the chair, touching it. Tomorrow, she thought, I'll take it down to the coast to that wonderful old man who still does rush bottoms. Tonight I'll oil it.

That night, after oiling the chair, bringing back its rich color, she went across the street to have a glass of wine. Manuel smiled at her. I saw Juan walking up the street with a chair, he said, and I came out to see where he was taking it. When I saw him go in your doorway, I said to myself, what luck that Karen has. What luck. I had told myself that the only thing you'd see of that chair would be as a sliver to pick your teeth with, if you saw anything at all. Yes, she said, I'd given it up. I'd made my last move, the last possible one. I told myself, that chair has become a mountain goat and run away over the sierra. That chair is a ghost.

Sharon Balentine lives in a village in Andalucia. An excerpt from her recently completed novel *Pomegranate Moon* appeared in the anthology *Women in the Wild*.

THE END OF THOSE THINGS/*Philip Gould*

1.

April 1956

ABOARD THE TEN A.M. ferry from Algeciras, among the crowd of passengers, Moroccans, Spanish, French, English, Italians, Germans, others who could not so easily be identified at sight, three Americans occupied standing room on an open deck: Ben Sinclair, on assignment from the Paris bureau of the *New York Times*, and Jay Parnell Powell and Joseph Comerford, both of them simply, or not so simply, travelers traveling together, unemployed, though for a while well-enough financed. Sinclair thought Powell was about thirty-two or -three. Comerford appeared to be in his early twenties, a pale, serious-looking young man, black Irish, shy and stiff in black dress shoes, brown trousers, a black raincoat, collar up. His black Basque beret seemed worn primarily to keep his head warm in the wind. Still, in more stylish clothes and after a few days in the sun, he would be presentable enough, Sinclair thought. Powell, in contrast, was ill-favored by nature. Congenitally pudgy, he had an oversized head, reddish hair, thinning and wild, and a potato nose. It seemed unfair that he should also be cursed with bad teeth and weak eyes behind steel-rimmed glasses that had a cracked lens and a broken earpiece patched with adhesive tape. His pants, jacket and turtleneck sweater were three unmatching shades of dark green, shapeless and stained, the pants too long over brownish brogues.

Sinclair had heard Powell speaking English. Sinclair did not go out of his way to strike up conversations with fellow Americans on his travels, but he had thought from the sound of it and from their appearance that the two were Irish. What intrigued him especially was the fact that young Comerford was trying to read Joyce's *Ulysses* to himself, though Powell, between sips from a silver pocket flask, was interrupting by quoting from his copy of *Finnegan's Wake*.

The ferry plowed noisily along its thirty-mile diagonal path to the coast of Africa. Above the noise, Powell shouted, "Can't hear with the waters of . . . the hitherandthithering waters of . . . !"

"Is it Marion Tweedy's Gibraltar that brings you this far from Ireland?" Sinclair asked.

Powell roared with laughter.

"In part, in part. We're actually missionaries to the heathen," he added conspiratorially behind the back of his hand, laughed loudly again and took another swallow from his flask.

Comerford frowned. "Don't you think you should go easy with that stuff, Jay Parnell?" he said. "It isn't even noon."

Powell clapped the younger man on one shoulder. "Be not your brother's keeper, Joseph," he said amiably.

"Where in Ireland are you from?" Sinclair asked.

"Not there. New York. And Detroit," he added, jerking a thumb at his companion. "Though here, to be sure, by way of Dublin, Paris and points south." He poked his copy of *Finnegans Wake* with a stubby forefinger. "Thanks to the great black book of doubleends jined. I suppose you've heard they've torn down the Third Avenue El in Manhattan?"

"I know, and I was sorry to hear it," Sinclair said.

"Torn it down and most of the old houses it ran between, mine among them," Powell lamented. "In the trauma of moving, the book inadvertently got left behind. I returned to retrieve it. From a legal point of view, the rubble was insufficiently cordoned off by barriers and warning signs. Part of a wall fell on one leg." He took a few steps to illustrate the limp he was left with. "Weeks in hospital, twenty thousand in compensation. I think of it as poetic justice. It led me away from P. S. Nineteen, where I was teaching, and into the footsteps of the master."

Before them, as they approached, a white, compact city, a glamorous vision of the Orient, grew larger as it climbed up its limestone hill from the shore to the casbah heights at the entrance to the strait. Tangier was the Orient, the far west of it, as west as Dublin, but the Orient unmistakably, in the spring of 1956 still alive with the glittering, tawdry atmosphere of a Berber-Arab-international city, now stirred up by the prospect of being incorporated into an independent kingdom of Morocco after thirty-three years under the administration of eight European nations and the United States.

At dockside, every imaginable sort of hustler tried to carry their bags or sell them something. Sinclair, Powell and Comerford shook them off except for the last rascally-looking cabbie. Powell and Comerford, who had no hotel reservations, had decided to be guided by the accommodations booked in advance for Sinclair.

Flags flew for the Sultan. Large processions of chanting demonstrators filled the roadway, all men, wearing vertical-brown-striped, ankle-length white djellabas, yellow pointed slippers, the red tarboosh.

Veiled women in purdah, black robes to the ankles, watched or went about their business on the sidewalks. On this warm, windy day cafes were filled with tough-looking Spanish *colons* and the con men, remittance men, alcoholics, drug addicts and deviates of many nationalities who gave the city its notoriety. Still, there were family groups too, and nuns escorting uniformed schoolgirls as well as neatly dressed diplomatic types.

Their hotel, a rambling mid-Victorian pile with a view of the harbor, was Swiss run and had the faded charm of such places. Matisse had stayed and painted there; possibly John Singer Sargent before him.

Sinclair's first request was for directions to the very old American legation in the medina, where he hoped to get an informed reading of what was going on and where, and what the future might bring. After that, this first afternoon, he would wander around on his own to get the feel of the place. Before lunch he telephoned his wife in Paris.

Around donkeys carrying burdens, through crowds of robed figures straight out of the Bible or *The Arabian Nights*, his briefing over, Sinclair descended a steep labyrinth of narrow lanes of shops, looking down on turbans, hoods, skullcaps and the broad-brimmed straw hats of Riffian women squatting before rows of bright green and brilliant red peppers, and then was out of the medina and in the modern European quarter.

Tangier is a small city. Sinclair bumped into Powell and Comerford in the Place de France. They had changed into shorts and short-sleeved shirts and sandals. Sinclair joined them at a table outside the Cafe de Paris, and they watched another procession of loudly chanting men in their medieval garb marching down one of five radiating streets. Powell laughed at everything and nothing. He was drinking Pernod and water now, Comerford only lemon soda. Sinclair ordered beer to quench the thirst that followed a long walk in a new place.

They were struck by another parade, very different from the one that had just passed them.

"My God," Powell said. "Have you ever in your life seen so many queens in any one place?"

It was true, thought Sinclair, that the number of men strutting past in flamboyant blouses, gossiping and flirting on corners, slouching at cafe tables, with dyed hair, makeup, earrings and other jewelry, would be rather startling to foreigners.

"Part of the scenery," Sinclair said.

That evening there was a floor show at one of the restaurants recommended by the American consul. A fire eater performed. A robed boy juggler dashed out bearing a tray of teacups on his head, slithered to the floor, the tray still on his head, spun in a circle, got to his feet without spilling a drop, removed the tray and passed the cups, to the crowd's applause, to a party at a table near the circular dance floor. A troupe of a dozen boys from twelve to fourteen, all from the Riffian tribe specializing in this entertainment, tripped out and began to dance. Barefoot, robed to the ankles, they skipped nimbly forward and back in unison, leaped and twirled in sequence, minced to the drums, flutes, cymbals and fluttered their eyelashes and flirted with the men in the audience like chorus girls.

In the morning, Sinclair got other briefings at the legations of the UK, France and Sweden and arranged to meet Spanish officials later on. Returning to the hotel from his briefing at the Spanish legation late that afternoon, Sinclair found young Comerford sitting in the lobby and looking rather lost and distressed.

"Jay Parnell has gone off someplace by himself," he said. "He left a note not to expect him for dinner."

"Well, about eight you're welcome to join me," Sinclair said. "I'm going to another restaurant recommended by the American consul, run by some American who may have useful background information."

They took a taxi waiting outside the hotel. The entrance to the restaurant was at the end of a cul-de-sac off a main street in the European quarter, deserted at eight in the evening. There were no cafes or cinemas here, only locked and shuttered shops. They could hear their footfalls in the blind alley.

They entered a series of warmly lit rooms painted in red and decorated tastefully with Moroccan brass and pottery. A number of well-dressed European and North American couples, a few Moroccan men in Western dress, had preceded them.

Sinclair wrote a note on a calling card from his wallet and the waiter he gave it to returned shortly with the proprietor. "I'm Tyler Moon," he intoned resonantly and shook hands. "Enjoy your dinner. I'll be in the bar afterwards."

Moon put selections from "Der Drei Groschenoper" on the changer behind the bar, then served his guests ice-cold framboise, on the house. Comerford seemed astonished by the taste and effect of it. Clearly, though not too loudly, over hidden amplifiers, Lotte Lenya began singing "Surabaya Johnny."

"The party's all but over," Moon said. "Everyone is starting to pull out. I'll be gone too, as soon as I can sell this place."

"How long have you been here?" Sinclair asked.

"God, forever."

"How long is that?"

"Ten years, old boy. Ten years of fun and games and a few other things besides."

"After Tangier, where should I go?"

"Why go anywhere? Fez is claustrophobic, a tad spooky to say the least. Rabat's a bit of a bore, and anyway too soon to go there, the capital though it is. Nobody knows what they're doing. Everything's in such a state of flux you'd be weeks trying to get a handle on what the future's going to be, what the French and the Jews will do. Casablanca? Enjoy the movie but not worth the bother in real life. Marrakesh? Well, a fun place, to be sure, but an awfully long way, and if you're already here? The rest is *Beau Geste* stuff if you're into that. A dreadful lot of sand and mud castles. Everything you can find down there you can find up here, really. Cities, mountains, Berbers, all the costumes, all the colors. The rest is repetition. And only one Tangier. That will never be the same once the Tangerinos leave. The Soco Chico foreign legion and all the rest."

"The Soco Chico foreign legion," Sinclair said. "Explain, please."

"You haven't been to the Soco Chico yet? Oh, you must go. If you haven't been to the Cafe Central, the Fuentes or the Tingis you haven't been here. Open round the clock. Look for an elderly fellow named Ferdie Fyfe. He has a dog and a beard, you can't miss him. He's the doyen. Knows everyone and all the stories. Start with him."

Sinclair said, "I've never been in a place where foreign powers are about to hand over sovereignty to local rulers . . ."

"Nor have I," Moon interrupted, rolling his eyes briefly.

". . . but I should think it might seem to some people the ideal time to settle old scores. There've been attacks on Europeans. What's the mood now? The French are none too popular, I don't imagine, nor the Spanish, even though they're pulling out. And especially considering French policy next door in Algeria. What about the Americans? We've had diplomatic relations with Morocco since the eighteenth century. We've backed their independence."

"I wouldn't count on being loved. Not by your average Tanjawi. In the first place you're a Christian, I assume. Taken as such in any case. Secondly, with a few exceptions, the Europeans here—including the Jews who've been here and all over the country for centuries—and the Indians and the Americans have all the money." Moon shrugged expressively.

"Gotcha," Sinclair said, snapping shut his small notebook.

"Talk to Ferdie and whomever else he recommends. Come back here by all means. I have a few stories of my own."

"You've been very helpful," Sinclair said.

Moon arranged for a cab to be called. In the dark stretch between the light over the restaurant door and a street lamp yards away, Sinclair heard a squeaky, pinched-off exclamation of alarm from Comerford. Then Sinclair saw him too, the boy in the djellaba and wool skull cap, his blind, milky eyes looming. Sinclair recoiled from him instinctively, and then from the other boys—four of them, all about the same age, twelve to fourteen—who had pushed the blind boy into Comerford.

At the curb, no cab was yet in sight.

"You Americans, give him money, he very poor," said a sighted boy, in English.

Sinclair was angry at being accosted like this and when the cab rounded the corner he waved them all away.

"No," the kid said sharply, sucking back like an adder. "No. *You French.*" The boy stuck out a forefinger and drew it sharply across his own throat. "The Arab people, we kill the French," the boy spat.

The Soco Chico was a seedy square surrounded by dingy side-walk cafes filled with a large and motley collection of European and American male rejects. Ferdie Fyfe was easy enough to spot—an old man with a black mongrel on a leash, a cane, white beard, floppy straw hat, mismatched white suit, presiding over the terrace at the Cafe Central. A cloudy glass of Pernod and a carafe of water sat on the chipped marble-topped table before him.

"Doing the *Last Days of Pompeii* story, are you?" Fyfe barked in a British accent of some sort. "Well, you've come to the right place. Do sit down. What are you drinking? Ali!"

Sinclair shook Fyfe's hand and got an immediately creepy jolt. Most of the two middle fingers were missing. Sinclair and Comerford eased themselves onto rickety wooden chairs and ordered beer and wine from the waiter who had scurried up at Ferdie Fyfe's command.

A hunchback in a djellaba and a red fez hurried out of a side alley into the lighted square, carrying a portfolio under one arm. When he saw the newcomers he made his way in their direction. Fyfe, busy identifying the nationalities of various cafe sitters, paid no attention until the hunchback sidled up beside Sinclair's chair and had his portfolio open. Sinclair caught a glimpse of photographs, all of naked young boys, before Fyfe noticed the vendor and shook his cane at him.

"Bugger off!" Fyfe shouted. "These gentlemen aren't interested in your wares, you filthy ponce!"

The hunchback snapped shut his photo album and slunk away.

"Touting for a boy brothel, as you can deduce," Fyfe said. "Ought to know better than to bother my guests."

Comerford looked painfully distressed. Sinclair put it into words. "Now that, I think, might be stopped, don't you?" he said. "Child abuse, *slavery.*"

"Oh, they're more or less free to leave but don't, you know. Clean berth, room and board. Families might have kicked them out to make their own way. No problem getting recruits. It's a way of life among Berber males from the age of ten or so. All of them grow up bisexual. They think nothing of it."

"Who runs it?" Sinclair asked.

"Spaniards. Making a packet."

Sinclair felt the balmy evening air on his skin, thought of blue skies and brilliant sunshine, flowers, magnificent views, beaches, and knew some of the reasons why people came to Tangier and stayed and stayed. There were enough other motives, as Ferdie Fyfe explained. Living was cheap, and opportunities for making an easy profit abounded. Sexual tastes of any description could be easily and cheaply satisfied. There were female prostitutes too, from thirteen to sixty, in a couple of dozen European and Moroccan bagnios, many of them also equipped with peepholes for voyeurs. Nobody cared who you were, where you'd come from, what you might have done in the past.

Fyfe had been around since the '30s and now he was into his seventies. Flourishing his mutilated bull's-horn hand, he described various "characters," but most of them sounded to Sinclair more like deadbeats, failures, frauds or psychopaths than truly interesting people. They were interesting only by virtue of being outcasts with bad habits in a seamy corner of a picturesque Mediterranean port. Fyfe himself was amusing for an hour or so, but Sinclair suspected that he was repeating old facts and stale gossip and over time would become as tiresome as anyone else.

When Fyfe went off to relieve himself, Sinclair told Comerford, "I've heard enough." But he waited for Fyfe to return so that he could pick up the tab and thank the old man.

"My pleasure. Come back any time. I'll be here till they drag me out. For a cab I'm afraid you'll have to trot up to the Soco Grande. Not far."

On the narrow street leading away from the Soco Chico, shadowy figures passed them; a moment later the street seemed deserted.

They weren't begging this time, the boys who came out of the darkness then, out of doorways or some back alley—God knows, maybe the same boys who had accosted them outside Tyler Moon's restaurant. Which came first Sinclair didn't remember: Comerford's shout or the crashing pain that left him flat on his back. They had knocked Comerford down too with the rush of their bodies. Sinclair they'd felled with a rock the size of a cobblestone. His head felt half gone, and there was enough blood streaming in a sheet from the wound just above the hairline to make him wonder for an instant if they had severed it entirely. But if that was so it had a life of its own; it could hear Ferdie Fyfe shouting and his black dog barking.

Others from the Cafe Central had appeared with restaurant towels and ice, which someone was holding to his head. They'd gotten his wallet, though his passport and traveler's checks were in the hotel safe. Then one of the Soco Chico Legionnaires found the wallet in a gutter, only the money missing.

Comerford had a skinned knee but was otherwise only shaken up.

"Physician's not far," Ferdie Fyfe was saying. "Toledano. He's a good man. One of our chaps has gone ahead to rouse him."

Dr. Toledano pulled the last of eight stitches through the skin of Sinclair's forehead. The doctor wore a silk dressing gown over pajamas and had a long, sallow, Modigliani face. "I find no evidence of concussion," he said. "But I cannot be entirely certain this soon. The wound is deep." He turned to Comerford. "You must not allow him to sleep more than one hour at a time. Wake him every hour until . . ." He checked his watch. ". . . until seven in the morning. Talk to him a bit each time and observe him closely to make sure he is reacting normally. Then he may sleep as long as he likes. Any vomiting, severe headache, loss of memory, telephone me at once." He turned to Sinclair. "Wherever you are, have the stitches removed in two to three weeks. Take these antibiotics as directed."

Ferdie Fyfe and two of his Soco Chico friends, an Englishman, Leslie, and a Dutchman called Bas, were at the curb with a commandeered taxi.

"Shocking!" Fyfe said. "Damn lucky you weren't killed. A Canadian chap was stabbed here only a few months back. When was that?"

"February," Leslie said.

"Bloody shocking. Things are falling apart."

"I owe you a great deal," Sinclair said. "Take care of yourselves."

When Joseph Comerford woke Sinclair at four A.M., he said, "I was in a seminary. One of my grandmothers died and left me some money, and one day I just walked out and took a plane to Ireland, where my people had come from. I met Jay Parnell in a Dublin pub. He was following in the footsteps of Joyce, and it was time for him to go on to Paris, so I went along and stayed a while. I was hoping to meet a girl I could travel with, but they all had other plans. I don't know how to talk to girls. I haven't had any practice. Paris was beautiful, but I wanted to go where it was warmer. I wanted to go to towns I'd seen in pictures, with fountains and flowering trees and lion-colored walls. So Jay Parnell and I took trains and buses down through France and Spain. In Rocamadoux he climbed the two hundred and sixteen steps of the Via Sancta on his knees. In Seville it was Holy Week. He joined a group of penitents and scourged himself until he was bloody. Now he talks about going to the Sahara and becoming an anchorite. I don't want to go that far. Tangier is already too far, and I worry about where he is now, in a place like this, and what's going to become of him."

At two in the afternoon, when Sinclair finally surfaced after a long sleep, Comerford was gone from the room; he was waiting in the lobby.

"Jay Parnell never came back to the hotel," he said.

Contacted through the concierge, the police could provide only negative information. No one of Jay Parnell's description had been the victim of any reported crime.

"We're a little like Key West," said the American consul over the phone. "A lot of men come here to escape, go to ground. I wouldn't automatically assume Mr. Powell has come to any sort of physical harm."

His restaurant wasn't open during the day, but Tyler Moon was in his office.

"God, not something *else*," he said after Sinclair had first had to explain his bandaged head. "It would help if I'd seen him at least once."

Sinclair provided a physical sketch and added, "American born but very Irish in his manner. He's a rather flamboyant bachelor, a heavy drinker and smoker."

"Well," Moon said, after a heavy sigh, "I'll ask around and give you a call. Expect to hear from me late this afternoon whether I've learned anything useful or not. And by the way, watch out for mad dogs. One was shot on the beach this morning." He put one hand to his head and held it there. "Omens everywhere. We're in a teetering house of cards."

Sinclair and Comerford were sitting in the garden of the hotel, trying, not too successfully, to read, when the call came from Tyler Moon. Sinclair took it in the lobby.

"Your friend is quite safe, though no longer with us," Moon said importantly. "At eleven this morning he boarded an Italian ship bound for Marseilles, Genoa and points east. No question about it. I've seen the passenger list with my own eyes."

"Does one of those points east include Trieste?"

"I believe so, yes."

Sinclair didn't ask where Powell had been until sailing time, and Moon, if he knew—and Sinclair assumed he did—did not volunteer the answer.

Despite what Tyler Moon had said, Sinclair still felt the professional need to go on to Rabat, the capital. Comerford planned to return to Algeciras, then take a Spanish ship to Barcelona and follow the Mediterranean shoreline up the Costa Brava and into France. Sinclair hoped that after all the boy would find some American or European girls who would be nice to him. In any case, Sinclair never saw or heard from him again.

2.

In the fall of 1975, when Spain announced its intention to give the Spanish Sahara its independence, Morocco and Mauritania, the latter under pressure from its more powerful Arab brother, jointly claimed the territory. Suddenly one read of the existence of a Western Sahara independence movement, called by the acronym "Polisario," endorsed by the United Nations and backed by a militant Algeria hostile to Morocco. Morocco's King Hassan II, consummate politician and public relations specialist, organized perhaps the greatest crusade in modern times, called the "Green March." Three hundred and fifty thousand unarmed "volunteers" would walk, drive or both hundreds of miles from Morocco to El Aaiun to take peaceful possession of the territory—a stony desert, but it was rich in phosphate and its Atlantic coast lay off fishing waters. The king himself would walk with them part of the way.

In February of 1976, Spain planned to withdraw from what would henceforth be known as the Western Sahara. Elite troops of the Moroccan army led by U.S.-trained commanders moved in force into the El Aaiun area while other detachments fanned out across the northern half of the territory as far as the Algerian frontier. The Moroccan government arranged an inspection tour for the media and diplomatic representatives to observe the historic transfer of power.

This final event, Spain's second such step in two decades, seemed made to order for Ben Sinclair. Now retired from the *Times*, Sinclair, as a freelance journalist, took the long view of current affairs from Egypt to Portugal. From their home in an Italian hill town, he and his wife flew to Rabat. The U.S. embassy political officer was a friend from Paris days and briefed Sinclair on the overall situation. When he'd finished he said, "Here's an oddity for you. You may not want to use it, but it's interesting and strange.

"A middle-aged American wearing a djellaba joined the Green March. This wasn't an escapade we would have recommended, but he didn't consult us about it. Somehow he'd gotten himself to the town of Smara in the Western Sahara. From there he wandered out across the desert to a Bedouin encampment of the R'Guibat tribe. According to Spanish authorities, this fellow, whose name was Powell, approached the main tent, where he was greeted by tribal elders prepared to extend traditional hospitality. Then, without provocation, he fired point blank with a .38-caliber pistol, slightly wounding one old man in the arm. In self-defense, guards shot Powell down with rifle fire, killing him instantly."

"Good God," Sinclair said. "Were his first names Jay Parnell?"

"You rather amaze me."

"I knew him briefly in Tangier twenty years ago," Sinclair said.

"Well, there's more. Maybe a partial explanation of the whole business. From the identification and addresses in his wallet, Washington managed to locate an ex-wife, but she refused to accept his body, and there were no other known next of kin. We didn't have much choice except to have him buried in the Catholic cemetery in Casablanca.

"There's a New York police report from the early 1970s. He was teaching in a primary school in Manhattan. A pupil, a twelve-year-old boy, accused Powell of molestation. It seems not to have gone beyond the fondling and verbal phases, but Powell didn't claim he was misunderstood. He pleaded guilty, promised to get counseling and not to teach at the primary level again, did six months of community service in an old people's home. He'd been fired from his teaching job and moved to Syracuse, where he found work in a public library and reported periodically to a parole board. He broke parole to come over here.

"We buried his wallet with him. There was a scrap of paper in it. The consular officer made a copy of it," the political officer said, taking an index card from one of his desk drawers. And Sinclair read two lines from Romans VI, 21:

What fruit had ye then in those things whereof ye are now ashamed. For the end of those things is death.

Sinclair and a dozen other journalists and diplomats were flown from Rabat to El Aaiun in an American-made military cargo plane, converted for this trip to accommodate passengers ranged in bucket seats along the bare inside skin of the aircraft. The journey took four hours and was less than comfortable. As the plane banked and descended, the desert stretched endlessly in three directions east of the Atlantic, utterly treeless and as pebbly and empty as the surface of the moon.

Buses took them a mile or two into the town, which was bigger than Sinclair had expected with a number of substantial buildings in a Spanish style. *Beau Geste* was farther off.

The hotel where the foreigners were put up for the night was swarming with Moroccan military brass and the striking "Blue Men," the tall, hawk-faced Tuareg tribesmen of the Moroccan south and the Sahara beyond, in their white and sky-blue robes and black turbans, the headdress fashioned from twelve-foot lengths of cotton, folded and wrapped tightly, that provided protection against the sun and wind.

In the early morning the diplomats and journalists were driven back to the airfield, where they boarded a helicopter and soon were skimming over the desolate surface of the desert. Far off were mesas, but there were no sand dunes in sight. There were dunes farther north, where the last Moroccan oases drift into the Sahara, and farther east on the edge of the Atlantic, but here the ground was stony and unyielding.

They began descending.

"Smara," said the escort officer, and now Sinclair saw below a square, white, walled town, so small its entire perimeter was visible even from a low altitude. It was here, where the world ended, that Jay Parnell Powell had come (How? On foot? Unlikely. On the back of a camel? Probably in some rattletrap once-a-week bus) and decided to die.

They touched down just outside the town entrance. Jeeps and uniformed men were waiting, and the visitors were driven into a market square, a low-roofed, mournful, flyblown place under an overcast sky, swept with a cutting wind.

Following the advice of the escort officer in Arabic, French and English, in the dim shop of a cloth merchant the foreigners bought lengths of black cotton and were taught how to wrap them around their heads, necks and the lower halves of their faces. If they felt foolish in these turbans at first, they were soon grateful for this protection from the wind that even at that slashed their noses and hands, buffeted their heads, made their eyes water as the jeeps drove out of the town and began bouncing over the trackless wastes. They did not follow any road that Sinclair could detect. There was none, or it was all road, rough and miles wide.

Thirty minutes later something up ahead broke the monotony of emptiness and became the focal point of his vision. Tents, a half dozen of them, one larger than the others. Camels, folded, seated. This seen from a distance of the last two hundred yards.

A delegation of Blue Men awaited them, embraced the colonel and his senior officers, bowed to the rest of the group.

The visitors were ushered into the largest tent. The floor had been picked smooth and leveled and was covered with Moroccan rugs on which everyone sat cross-legged, their turban cloths pulled down below their chins. Unveiled women, intricately draped in striped, brightly colored wool laden with beaded and silver necklaces, carried in silver trays piled with silver pots of sweet mint tea that they poured into silver cups and handed to the visitors. Other women passed trays of honey cakes. The tribal chief, a tall, erect old man (of seventy-five, Sinclair was told) made a short speech in Arabic to which the colonel responded briefly in Arabic. These flowery ceremonial remarks were translated into French: We welcome our guests. We seek only friendship with our Moroccan brothers.

The reception ended, the tent flaps were held aside and Sinclair and the others were ushered out. Now Sinclair had only a few minutes left to focus his private attention on this setting, on the faces of the dozen or so tribesmen lined up for inspection. (The women had disappeared.) The members of the visiting delegation all had cameras and were free to snap pictures. Posing, these Bedouins—some young, some middle-aged, some old—smiled, *looked,* and Sinclair looked at them now through squinting, wind-watered eyes and tried to see them as Jay Parnell Powell had seen them in the last moments of his life. Alone, not surrounded by protected diplomats and journalists, not accompanied by a military escort with sophisticated arms but absolutely alone, faced not with tribesmen playing a waiting political game but with warriors sanctioned by Islam to take the lives of infidels, sanctioned by tradition, so he believed, to take their pleasure with men as well as women, to rape their captured enemies. This he thought he knew, had sought, had walked across the desert in his madness and despair to cheat them of, in death. They *looked*, they smiled, walked closer, closer, stopped and waited for him, and then he fired.

Philip Gould is the author of two previous novels, *Kitty Collins* and *The Eighth Continent*.

"I WAS PAPER TRAINED, BUT THAT WAS BECAUSE THEY THOUGHT THE PAPER WAS TOO CONSERVATIVE."

Reviews

Remembering Slavery
Ira Berlin, Marc Favreau, Steven Miller, editors
The New Press (Norton), 1998, 352 pp. + cassette, $49.95

For the past quarter century, historians of the Old South's "peculiar institution" have examined the slave experience not through the white filter of the slaveholders' perspective, which was once the accepted practice, but from the bottom up, through the experiences of the slaves themselves. The source material for this groundbreaking historiographical shift was not the famous nineteenth-century narratives of exceptional ex-slaves such as Frederick Douglass (which once served the abolitionists' cause and consequently were somewhat suspect) but written transcripts of interviews with former slaves conducted by oral historians of the Federal Writers' Project in the late 1930s. These little-known narratives had long been tucked away in the Library of Congress and were seldom accessed by the lay public.

Drawn exclusively from this unique collection, *Remembering Slavery* is a book-and-tape set of transcripts and recordings of historic interviews with former slaves who vividly recount their own experiences in bondage as well as their personal thoughts on Emancipation and the meaning of freedom. For the first time the general public is introduced to the poignant voices of the last living victims of the institution that has most shaped American history.

During the Depression, interviewers from the Federal Writers' Project spoke with hundreds of elderly ex-slaves about their lives in slavery and even managed to record a small number of them on tape. The interviewers, including such notable figures as Zora Neale Hurston and John Lomax, asked ex-slaves about everything from daily routines and ways of life to their relationships with their former masters and with other slaves.

Both taped and written interviews document almost every aspect of slave life; they reveal how slaves were born, their living arrangements, what they ate, wore and thought, their relationship with the land and their daily triumphs and frustrations. Of particular interest is the way they also illuminate the subtle dynamics behind the development of a distinct slave culture and community; we see how bondsmen created and preserved their culture in the face of oppression. We see, too, their everyday forms of resistance—survival techniques that helped them to maintain a sense of control and dignity in the face of hardship.

As expected, the narratives underscore the cruelty of American slavery and the bitterness of its victims. One woman tells how an abusive mistress crushed her head under a rocking chair, deforming her face for life. Others tell stories of serving as beasts of burden and of the excruciating ordeal of witnessing a family member or friend sold to another master. But there are also stories of happiness—of marriage and family, religious experiences, celebrations such as corn shuckings, of bonding together and looking out for one another, of outwitting masters and overseers and of escaping or helping others to escape. We hear Civil War stories from a unique perspective—experiences by slaves behind Confederate and Union lines. Finally, we hear Emancipation described—and freedom defined—by the people who endured the worst oppression in American history. (BR)

The Meme Machine
by Susan Blackmore
Oxford U.P., New York, 1999,
286 pp., $25

The word "meme" was coined by evolutionary biologist Richard Dawkins, author of the controversial theory that the gene, not the organism, is the unit of selection (*The Selfish Gene*, 1976). Dawkins argued that DNA is not the only conceivable medium in which Darwinian evolution can occur. He posited the existence of memes, nonbiological units of replication and competition that produce cultural evolution. Memes are abstract units of culture—concepts, images, instructions, stories, facts (or myths), jokes—anything that can be copied and spread. Susan Blackmore's new book, *The Meme Machine*, explores the possibility of a full-blown theory of memetics. With a blend of caution and boldness (she duly notes several fundamental problems in defining the nature of the meme but then sidesteps these obstacles to pursue larger game), she applies memetic theory to some of the most controversial issues in evolutionary psychology and consciousness, including the origin of language, sexual attitudes, altruism, and the proportionately enormous human brain.

According to Blackmore, the rise of memes on our planet is intimately connected with the evolution of the human species, with each one causally dependent on the other. Humans, she says, are the only animal that *imitates* all kinds of observed behavior, as opposed to acting by instinct, conditioned response or learning in a narrow, preset range (e.g., some bird calls). We tend to think of our imitating ability as the result of our general intelligence. Blackmore says the ex-planation is just the opposite: we were imitators first, and then the pressure of memetic selection (in combination with genetic selection) generated the increased mental power and other traits that seem to be unique to humans. Yes, being smart helps an animal stay alive and reproduce, but the human brain is so big and so costly in biological terms that it has long been a question whether it really earns its keep. But memetic selection provides an explanation for our seemingly oversized brains: more available intelligence means better meme reproduction. In the modern developed world, where genetic selection pressure on humans is pretty low, memetic selection is going stronger than ever, forcing us to invent ever more highly refined meme-spreading techniques: better computers, faxes, photocopiers, telephones, televisions, movies, CDs, etc.

The idea of an evolutionary force similar but not identical to genetic evolution is an exciting one that deserves attention regardless of whether one buys Blackmore's argument in its entirety. Some readers will be delighted, others appalled, by Blackmore's more far-reaching speculations. There is no such thing as an "inner," "true" self, she argues. That self is an illusion, just a collection of especially vigorous memes that maintain themselves in our minds by convincing us that we *are* them. If *The Merne Machine* is speculative, though, it is honorably so: Blackmore doesn't try to disguise the foundational weaknesses of her theories, though she may be inclined to take them too lightly.

The Meme Machine is pleasurable reading. It covers a lot of ground fast and skirts some controversial points, but it is engaging. Some 150 years ago the theoretical revolution that started with Darwin gave us the tools to begin thinking about life on earth without recourse to supernatural explanation. Memetic theory, a generalization and extension of the basic Darwinian idea, attempts to analyze the human condition in ways that are neither mystical nor completely reducible to biology. (JB)

For the Relief of Unbearable Urges
by Nathan Englander
Knopf, 1999, 205 pp., $22

Twenty-eight-year-old Jerusalemite Nathan Englander has produced a striking if inconsistent collection of short fiction. The stories in *For the Relief of Unbearable Urges* examine the lives of Hasidic Jews in the Old and New Worlds, following a roughly historical progression beginning in eastern Europe of the '40s and moving to America's inhospitable melting pot in the decades following, then on to contemporary Israel. Englander, a secular Jew, avoids the easy trap of exoticizing his subject, managing to provide intimate glimpses of the private and mysterious world of Hasidim that feel more compassionate than exploitative.

Englander's work does invite the easy comparisons to Malamud, Singer, Bellow and Philip Roth that have been bandied about in early reviews of his book. However, he possesses a self-assurance and a distinctive voice that prevent his work from feeling derivative. The strongest stories in the collection show a young writer of striking range and virtuosity. The opening story, "The Twenty-Seventh Man," concerning an unpublished dilettante mistakenly imprisoned and sentenced to die along with a group of subversive writers, resembles an eerie collision of Kafka and Isaac Babel as it builds to its breathtaking finish. "The Tumblers," a story of desperation and survival in the Holocaust in which hunted refugees pose as circus acrobats, is equally harrowing and resonant. "The Wig," set in America, is another exceptionally well-realized piece, focusing on a Hasidic hairdresser's struggle with vanity, covetousness and sensuality in a community that abhors these impulses.

Not all the stories are this strong. Englander sometimes seems unable to elevate a story beyond a clever premise. Despite its wry humor, "The Gilgul of Park Avenue," about a middle-aged gentile who suddenly "realizes" his past-life Jewishness, ultimately feels like second-rate Philip Roth. "Reb Kringle," which examines a disgruntled Hasidic department-store Santa, verges on sentimentality. And the title story, concerning a Hasidic husband's marital problems and his rabbi's unsettling solution, ends in easy irony, avoiding the emotional complexity the subject matter seems to demand.

Time and future publications will determine if Englander has what it takes to become the literary star he is already touted as being. The best stories of this inaugural collection suggest it's a decent bet. (JT)

White Oleander
by Janet Fitch
Little, Brown, 1999, 390 pp., $24

What is amazing about this first novel is how Fitch deftly avoids melodrama in what could so easily become a hackneyed story. The protagonist is a young girl, Astrid, whose mother is a brilliant poet with an acerbic worldview bordering on psychopathic. When Astrid's mother poisons her lover and is sentenced to life in prison, Astrid is shuffled into foster care and faces all of the perils one would expect: sexual advances from the fathers and jealous rage from the mothers, as well as abuse and the temptations of alcohol, drugs and self-mutilation. Yet somehow Fitch pushes Astrid's story into the realm of lyricism while still drawing characters that are human and humanly fascinating.

Each of Astrid's temporary homes is peopled by vivid characters, among them an ex-stripper who has been turned on to the Lord by an attractive minister, a Vietnam vet who introduces Astrid to sex, a witty and creepy caricature of a suburban housewife (her Mary Kay makeover of Astrid is one of the most startling moments of the novel) and a bevy of practical women who make their living scavenging the hills of Los Angeles for junk to sell and who teach Astrid to "glean from the wreckage what could be remade and resold." The strange crannies of foster care mesh with the California landscape as Astrid progresses from dreamy child to cautious adult. Her continual search for a substitute parent is punctuated by letters from her imprisoned mother, whose poetry and savagery Astrid learns to mistrust, even as she comes to accept her own artistic talent.

Fitch's prose carries the novel, weaving together images of poisonous flowers and hot winds, annual fires and mirrored moons until the book reads more like mythology than a hard-luck tale of a sad girl and her abusive mother. The author's skill is evident in the magical rendition of Astrid's tale alongside the all-too-contemporary and familiar moments of sexual violence. Astrid demonstrates a fairytale sensibility early on when she laments the burden her existence is to her poet-mother, observing, "She was a beautiful woman dragging a crippled foot and I was that foot. I was bricks sewn into the hem of her clothes, I was a steel dress." Moments like this that are simultaneously delicate and terrifying permeate the novel and offset the potential for maudlin indulgence. Foster care as viewed through Astrid's eyes reveals the combination of the fantastic and the modern characteristic of an American child's life at the end of the twentieth century. Like a Grimms' tale, *White Oleander* cuts to the quick, even as it captivates. (TH)

The Long Home
by William Gay
MacMurray & Beck, 1999, 257 pp., $24.95

The Long Home, William Gay's first novel, is strongly rooted in the hills and hollows of east Tennessee. Set in 1944 (with frequent flashbacks to the early 1930s, when a mysterious figure named Douglas Hardin appeared in Mormon Springs and moved in on the Hovington family, taking over their land and terrorizing them and their neighbors), the novel tells the story of a young carpenter named Nathan Winer, who is attempting to come to terms with the disappearance some years earlier of his father. Winer is befriended by William Tell Oliver, an elderly mountaineer. Oliver knows what really happened to Winer's father but for reasons of his own is reluctant to divulge the truth. When Winer goes to work for Hardin and falls in love with Amber Rose Hovington, Oliver must face the fact that he has become at least a tacit accomplice of Hardin's, helping him perpetuate evil through his own passivity.

Gay writes beautifully about the Tennessee countryside, and one of the many joys to be had from reading this novel is its texture of place and period. This often overlooked corner of America is evoked in vivid detail, as when Gay tells us of "dark bulks rising out of the mouths of hollows, trees growing through their outraged roofs. Old stone flues standing blackened and solitary like sentries frozen at their posts waiting for a relief that did not come and did not come." Stylistically, Gay owes a debt to Cormac McCarthy, but his own prose is more direct and less mannered.

Dallas Hardin is one of the more convincing villains in recent fiction, and both Nathan Winer and Amber Rose are memorable characters as well. Many of the minor characters become vivid after only two or three strokes: the Mexican bouncer, Jiminiz; the local sheriff, Bellwether; Winer's friend Buttcut Chessor; and the novel's main comic presence, the lugubrious Motormouth Hodges. The real gem of the book, however, is William Tell Oliver. At times Oliver seems puzzled as to why he has lived so long in the shadow of such evil without lifting a hand to thwart it. As he tells Bellwether, Hardin has just been "usin' up air other folks could put to good use." Oliver's epic struggle is not so much against Dallas Hardin as it is against some element of reticence in himself that he never fully seems to comprehend.

Gay is a deft craftsman who, if this novel is any indication, has a rich career ahead of him. He writes with a good ear, a fine eye and an unusually large heart. *The Long Home* is a debut that should be savored. (SY)

Vita Nova
by Louise Glück
Ecco Press, 1999, 51 pp., $22

In *Vita Nova*, Louise Glück ventures openly and gleefully into self-parody. Her trademark spareness is still there, and serves her well in self-consciously sentimental poems such as "The Winged Horse," "Evening Prayers" and "Nest." Her economy of language is, as always, praiseworthy, as is her ability to evoke discreet shadings in mood and tone. But what I like best about *Vita Nova* is that Glück, whose work has always been sharp and witty, for the first time invites us in on the joke—all the jokes, in fact. While that chumminess can be strained at times, it's a nice break from her usual dead-pan delivery. We can't help but grin when, in an absurdly melodramatic gesture, the speaker of "Vita Nova" wails, "I thought my life was over and my heart was broken./Then I moved to Cambridge."

Glück's last collection, *Meadowlands*, was a funny book too, but it lacked the ironic distance her sly wit needs to operate properly. She's not a warm writer, but I think the point some readers miss is that she's not interested in being a warm writer. The cerebral tone of Glück's work has always challenged easy ideas about womanhood and femaleness. The impenetrable tightness of the poems in *Vita Nova* successfully defies the unspoken assumption that women's poetry ought to be fluid, sensitive, invested in the emotional catharsis of both reader and writer.

Don't mistake Glück's invitation to laugh with her at the universal cruelties of fate and happenstance as an invitation to cry with her over her own private sorrows. Begging to be carried off on "my horse Abstraction," the speaker of "The Winged Horse" complains, "I am weary of my other mount/by Instinct out of Reality,/color of dust, of disappointment." Repeatedly, Glück sets us up to expect confessional narratives and, repeatedly, she denies us absolution, comprehension, understanding. Instead we are left yearning with her, unsaved, unsatisfied, and unrepentantly catty about the confessional process.

Where to locate Glück herself? In the book's final poem, Glück gives us a dream sequence about Blizzard, a dog that defies description, yet mysteriously suffers from many of Glück's own reported difficulties: "Supposing/I'm the dog, as in/my child-self, unconsolable because/completely pre-verbal? With/anorexia! O Blizzard,/be a brave dog—this is/all material; you'll wake up/in a different world,/you will eat again, you will grow up into a poet!"(MB)

Evensong
by Gail Godwin
Ballantine, 1999, 405 pp., $25

As the millennium draws to a close in High Balsam, North Carolina, Margaret Bonner, an Episcopal priest, is visited by three mysterious strangers who will enrich and change her life. First, there is Grace Munger (gracemonger?), who sweeps into town wearing her red cape, determined to lead a millennium birthday march for Jesus. Every church in the area, except Margaret's, agrees to join the fundamentalists in their march, thus reinforcing the stereotype of Episcopalians as aloof and superior. Margaret's temptation to give in to Grace's demands is strong because High Balsam, a picturesque summer retreat for the wealthy, has already been rocked by violence between the haves and the have-nots.

Margaret's second visitor is a peculiar old monk of questionable identity, wearing black Nikes beneath his habit and sporting orangish, dyed hair. A third visitor is a troubled youth, Chase Zorn, from the school at which Margaret's husband, another priest, teaches. The time of year is Advent and, given the season and the three visitors, one almost expects a baby to materialize out of all this.

In this small-town Southern setting, a Flannery O'Connor–style confrontation between Margaret Bonner and Grace Munger would hardly surprise us, with the smug Episcopalians losing the most. In fact, both sides lose: Margaret's church goes up in flames, and Grace's march is a miserable flop, proving perhaps that God snows on both the just and the unjust. The Episcopalians' measured, reasonable concept of grace does prevail throughout the novel, however. Godwin admirably refrains from oversimplification of the fundamentalists. Margaret Bonner's primary objection to Grace Munger's published "Christian Manifesto for a Wounded Town" is that it promises what it can't and shouldn't deliver: easy and instantaneous control over one's life through belief in God. Margaret preaches a more difficult vision of grace, which requires submission to the Christian paradox that one must lose one's life in order to gain it. Yet there is something very compelling in Grace's demand that Margaret recognize her as a "sister in Christ." Godwin maintains a fine tension between Margaret's well-honed integrity and her urge to embrace Grace's paradoxically worldly image of divine grace. With such a colorful, almost mythical character as Grace Munger, the reader may feel disappointed that Godwin fails to do something more dramatic with her.

The reader may also find the dialogue of *Evensong* a bit wooden at times. Not even well-educated, uppercrust Episcopalians typically speak in long paragraphs—at least not without sounding tedious. The epilogue, in which Margaret suddenly reveals that she has been speaking to her twenty-year-old daughter in the year 2020, is predictable, and entirely unnecessary to close the novel.

Godwin's *Evensong* delivers some gems of wisdom that are appealing to those of us who are still drawn to religious belief at the close of the twentieth century. For example, sin is defined as "a falling short of your totality." Marriage should make more out of both partners. On the question of belief: "I'm not sure I believe as much as *recognize*. Belief seems to me something that is willed. But there are times when I definitely recognize the presence of something beyond me working through me." (NS)

Playing for Keeps: Michael Jordan and the World He Made
by David Halberstam
Random House, 1999, 428 pp., $24.95

Every biographer of Michael Jordan—and there will be many—

must confront a monumental and seemingly impossible task: how to write a book about a supercelebrity and the overexposed basketball franchise he works for when the media has already covered every aspect of his life and team? The whole world knows the story: the beautiful, likeable Jordan becomes the most celebrated athlete in the world and "a one-man corporate conglomerate," and the Bulls win six NBA championships.

Potential biographers might take a lesson from Pulitzer Prize–winning sportswriter and historian David Halberstam's approach in this book. Halberstam shrewdly acts as if he were breaking the news of Jordan's epic career. This slightly naive, wide-eyed approach allows him to create suspense as he details the Bulls' rise to greatness and the evolution of the superstar basketball player once described as a "Jesus in Nikes." In Halberstam's hands, biography becomes page-turning mystery as he achieves the near impossible—doubt about Jordan's and the Bulls' success. Each time the team comes up against a formidable foe, he miraculously generates the fear that they could in fact lose.

Halberstam creates the same kind of anxiety in his depiction of Chicago Bulls management. Will they bring the team back together or won't they? The drama of the tug-of-war battles between players and management rivals the excitement on the court. Every story needs a villain, and Jerry Reinsdorf and Jerry Krause, cool, calculating businessmen, fit the bill. The "suits" refuse, despite sports statistics and public opinion, to admit Jordan's supremacy, believing that to

acknowledge it would detract from their own claims of masterminding the Bulls phenomenon. Unwisely, they underestimate their rival Michael Jordan, a man who becomes a shrewd operator not only in sports but also in media and business.

There are some problems with the book. Halberstam, like the rest of the world, gives in to Michaelmania. He does not seem to notice that the persona of Michael Jordan becomes indistinguishable from the person. Biography is most memorable when it reveals surprising contradictions; however, in Halberstam's account, Jordan behaves as expected both on and off the court. He is driven, hyper-competitive, the consummate winner and the classic gentleman despite his worldwide fame. But how does this pressure to be the best and the brightest bear on his personal life as a father, husband and son? Halberstam does not say. He does, however, interweave the stories of other players in the Jordan drama, and these stories are ultimately more interesting, complex, and suprising than our superhero's. We learn that Jordan's publicly flamboyant, scene-stealing teammate Dennis Rodman is by all accounts shy, childlike and sensitive. The Bulls' tough-as-nails, seemingly fearless coach Phil Jackson, the son of a fundamentalist preacher, practices Buddhist meditation and espouses Native American philosophies. Scotty Pippen is perhaps the most enigmatic and tempestuous team member, struggling to find himself as a person and player in Jordan's far-reaching shadow.

Playing for Keeps is a book to tell your friends about or buy for a relative. In the end, despite its too-loving portrayal of Jordan, Halberstam's work is entertaining, informative and as captivating as his subject is talented. (KS)

Hannibal
by Thomas Harris
New York: Delacorte, 1999, 484 pp., $27.95

A memory palace is a mental device that relies on imagined mnemonic architecture, each room in the structure containing particular objects placed to assist one's memory. In *Hannibal*, Thomas Harris' long-awaited sequel to *The Silence of the Lambs*, serial killer Hannibal Lecter escapes to his memory palace during moments of meditation or great stress.

Since his last novel, Harris' readers have eagerly awaited the chance to turn the magnifying glass on Lecter himself. But the answer to what makes the mastermind criminal tick, spelled out for readers in this novel, is disappointingly unsophisticated. The memory palace is a perfect metaphor for the novel as a whole, since a view of the inside of Lecter's mind is exactly what readers have been anticipating. Unfortunately, Harris' description of Lecter's memory palace is cursory at best and glosses over the majority of his interior life. Who would have expected the mind of Hannibal Lecter to be such a dry residence?

The only place where Harris does anything unpredictable is in some of his narrative and point-of-view shifts. Unfortunately, the oddly out-of-place techniques fail to add anything but puzzlement over why Harris employs them.

Harris focuses mainly upon Lecter's memories of Myscha, his late sister, and Clarice Starling, the young FBI agent first encountered in *The Silence of the Lambs*. The positive aspects of Starling's strong character, developed in the previous novel, are systematically dismantled in *Hannibal* until she becomes little more than a character led around by the nose. Even the purely technical details of the FBI investigative techniques, such as forensics and behavioral sciences, are painfully absent in this novel.

What Harris does give readers is a single simple answer to Lecter's character; the root of his evil is boiled down to one past incident. Even worse, any complexity that might have been associated with this answer is drowned out by the repetition of the answer itself throughout the story. The result is that neither Lecter's memory palace nor *Hannibal* itself is the masterwork of horror readers were waiting for. (HN)

Helen Keller: A Life
by Dorothy Herrmann
Knopf, 1998, 398 pp., $18

The question at the heart of Dorothy Herrmann's biography of a much-loved American woman is this: What happened after *The Miracle Worker*? The answer is both simple and complex: Helen Keller grew up. Herrmann's biography tackles the difficult task of tearing away the veneer of legend to find the real person underneath. Photographs of Keller demurely smelling a rose or playing chess with her lifelong companion and teacher, Annie Sullivan, are a stark contrast to the passionate and tough-minded woman Keller became after she was taught to communicate with the outside world.

Most readers are aware of the facts of Keller's early years: at the age of nineteen months she contracted an illness (Herrmann speculates that Keller most likely suffered from scarlet fever or meningitis) that left her both deaf and blind. Unable to communicate with her family, the young Helen grew increasingly frustrated and unruly until in 1887 her parents sought the help of Annie Sullivan, who taught Helen to speak using the manual alphabet. What many readers may not know is that Sullivan came to the Kellers' home as an impoverished young woman with no other job prospects, not as a saint who had dedicated her life to helping the disabled. Herrmann suggests that Annie's early relationship with Helen was a process of discovering her own power over Helen: rather than using physical force, she could instead refuse to spell into Helen's hand, plunging her once more into darkness and isolation, until the child behaved as Annie wanted.

The two women thus entered into a relationship marked by power struggles and mutual dependency. Without Annie, Helen was cut off from the world at large; without Helen, Annie was merely another woman at a time when women had no voice. As Helen grew into adolescence and early adulthood, however, there was, Herrmann suggests, a growing tension between the two women. Helen became a socialist, opposed to American entry into World War I; Annie, who feared for their livelihood (largely earned from public appearances and speaking engagements), tried at every turn to soften Helen's rhetoric by suggesting that Helen was too naive to understand international politics. The two disagreed on the issue of women's suffrage as well: "She was never a standard-bearer. The more we talked, the less we thought alike, except in our desire of good and our intense longing for intelligence as a universal attribute of mankind," recalls Keller in *Teacher*, her own memoir of her years with Annie Sullivan.

Perhaps the most astonishing assertion in this examination of Keller's life is that Annie Sullivan did not sacrifice her life for the sake of her brilliant student's career; rather, Sullivan benefited from her relationship with Keller in ways no one has yet acknowledged. Sullivan also suffered tremendously. Ironically, some of the most moving and disturbing passages of the book are about Sullivan's life: her nightmarish childhood and her disastrous marriage to John Macy, a well-known literary figure who became a close friend and confidant to Helen. Sullivan never fully recovered from Macy's desertion of their marriage (due in part to the symbiotic relationship between Annie and her student), but it's at this point in Helen's life that we see her strength and independence most clearly. Keller lived for thirty-two years after Sullivan's death, forging relationships with new friends and caretakers, making appearances with Hollywood notables, accepting numerous awards and promoting organizations that served the deaf-blind population. In the end, the reader is left to wonder who was the stronger force in the Keller-Sullivan relationship. (PJ)

Close Range: Wyoming Stories
by Annie Proulx
Scribner, 1999, 283 pp., $25

Having established herself as a stylist and storyteller in her three novels, having won both the National Book Award and the Pulitzer Prize, what more is there for Proulx to do? In *Close Range*, she returns to the short story, adding to her repertoire a new breed of characters in an unforgiving land.

As in her previous work, landscape infuses Proulx's fiction. The eleven stories in *Close Range* depict Wyoming natives struggling against brutal conditions, not the least of them the wild Wyoming plains. Fans will recognize the tight-knit sentences and perfectly placed ironic details as Proulx trademarks: When a fire in "Job Description" causes an explosion inside an old house, Proulx tells readers, "an object flies out of the house and strikes the fire engine hood. It is a Nintendo player and not even charred." Her matter-of-fact voice is perfectly suited to her vision of the world as a place of ironies and startling hardships.

Proulx's appreciation of Wyoming is obvious in her descriptions. It is a land whose winters are cold enough to freeze solid a "somewhat vain" cowboy who splurges on fancy boots instead of coat and gloves. In "People in Hell Just Want a Glass of Water," the country is "indigo jags of mountain, grassy plain everlasting, tumbled stones like fallen cities, the flaring roll of sky."

This vastness of the land inspires loneliness in its people. The aptly titled "The Lonely Coast" tells of small-town women who riotously consult the personals. In "The Bunchgrass Edge of the World," the protagonist, Ottaline, is so desperate for human contact that she uses a scanner to listen in on cell-phone conversations. Later, she engages in conversation with a rusted-out tractor.

Relationships that do evolve are tough, and tough to navigate. An ex-husband shoots out his adulterous former wife's tires; a love affair between two cowboys ends in the murder of one; a married man visits a young Indian prostitute. In "The Bunchgrass Edge of the World," seventy-one-year-old Old Red attacks his son Aladdin with, "Not too swift, are you? Not too smart . . . How you got a woman a marry you I don't know. You must a got a shotgun on her." The angry son retaliates by chasing down his father and pelting him with stones and other handy sharp objects. Old Red surrenders, but not before an indignant, "I made this ranch and I made you." For Old Red, this simple fact of blood relationship justifies his nastiness.

Perhaps what makes the book so enjoyable is Proulx's ability to craft and deliver a story. "The Half-Skinned Steer" follows the life of a retired rancher who returns to his childhood ranch only to die after a series of ironic twists. Each event is timed perfectly; the story unfolds without a hitch.

For Proulx's characters life is invariably a struggle. For Proulx the author, telling their stories seems to come a little more easily. *Close Range: Wyoming Stories* is an admirable addition to her growing body of critically acclaimed work. (KD)

A Saturday Night at the Flying Dog
by Marcia Southwick
Oberlin College Press (Field Poetry Series), 1999, 61 pp., $13.95

A Saturday Night at the Flying Dog, winner of the 1998 Field Poetry Prize, is a quantum leap into a universe not found in Southwick's first two books, *The Night Won't Save Us* and *Why the River Disappears.* The poems in this new book do not begin and end with straightforward narratives or hinge on the turn of a brilliant image. They do not gather their energy solely from the author and her inner reflections. These poems attempt to confront and immerse us in the contradictions of a society sinking from the weight of rampant materialism and consumerism.

Southwick succeeds admirably in describing the chaos and emptiness of such a life. She sees the absurdity in the pursuit of "things" for fulfillment and salvation. What will save us, she believes, is to step back and strip our lives down to the essentials. In the opening poem, "Augery," for example, Southwick sees the future as cast "in a teacup, a pair of Nikes, and dust on a windowsill/. . . in a tire's skid marks,/on the blade of a barber's shears." The poem is telling us that we will lose any real chance for a meaningful life if it is based on shopping for "satellite dishes,/burglar alarms and new siding." In late-twentieth-century capitalist America, the consumer becomes the consumed. We are slaves to our dreams of things that in the end can't offer us anything better than a planned-obsolescent salvation—no matter how much we believe in them. All our striving for the material fails to outstrip death. "God plays hardball," writes Southwick.

Dark though they often are, these poems are also humorous. Southwick declares, "I want my poems to be less Marcia-centric, so I'll write/about Star Trek's Seska, the undercover Cardassian spy." But as an alien spy she takes on the disguise of Barbie, (herself inhuman, in a plastic body alien to women). Though the reader will laugh, these poems are harsh commentaries on how we have trivialized our ambitions and lost sight of anything more important than perfecting a golf stroke or winning a sweepstakes.

What can we do to reassert ourselves? In the poem "In the Winter of Our Discontent & Other Seasons," Southwick advises the reader ". . . go outside and breathe in the greenery. It's a nice evening/with ground squirrels & blueberries/. . . It's a perfect night for tadpoles to nestle in the mud. Or/for getting sucked through a wormhole in the Gamma Quadrant." Underlying this and many of the other poems is a Thoreauvian love of nature and simplicity, a desire to find out what's behind the empty, ephemeral deluge of *things*. What does the poet find there? That whether or not life has meaning, one can find meaning in living, though that meaning may come at a cost. In the poem "Stone Worship," Southwick writes, "I could have spent an entire lifetime laughing in despair/ but instead I worshipped a black stone." This is not a despairing book, but it is filled with warnings.

So what is the fate of poetry in a materialistic age like this one? In "A Portrait of Larry with Trogons," an elegy for her late ex-husband, the poet Larry Levis, Southwick writes, "It's also difficult to find the exact right words for poetry/when they're camouflaged against the background of speech,/newspapers, and TV. If you were to see the trogon/against a white wall, you'd be dazzled by its brilliance." It's easy to see W.C. Williams' red wheelbarrow here: let the image speak for itself, bring us back to the real world. Marcia Southwick accomplishes this in poem after poem as she leads us out of material-istic chaos and into our essential lives. (WB)

Reviews by: Brett Rogers, Jean Braith-waite, John Tait, Tina Hall, Steve Yar-brough, Marta Boswell, Nancy Sherrod, Kris Somerville, Hoa Ngo, Pam Johnston, Katie Delay and Walter Bargen

"ARE YOU THE SON OF A BITCH WHO REVIEWED ME IN THE SUNDAY TIMES?"

Did You Know...

...that The Blue Moon Review was the first
electronic quarterly online to focus exclusively
on literary work? (First issue release: June, 1994)

...that BMR's contributors include winners of
Best American Short Stories Awards,
Guggenheim Awards, and Fellowships from
the Ingram Merrill Foundation, and the Fine Arts
Work Center in Provincetown? They also
publish in The Atlantic, The Paris Review,
The New Yorker, TriQuarterly, The New England
Review, Yale Review, Iowa Review, and
many other journals....

...that more than 5,000 individual readers visit
BMR each month?

Only Online. Proud of it.

The Blue Moon Review

 www.TheBlueMoon.com